The Meaning of Experience in the Prose of Jorge Luis Borges

American University Studies

Series II
Romance Languages and Literature

Vol. 71

PETER LANG
New York · Bern · Frankfurt am Main · Paris

Ion T. Agheana

The Meaning of Experience in the Prose of Jorge Luis Borges

PETER LANG
New York · Bern · Frankfurt am Main · Paris

Library of Congress Cataloging-in-Publication Data

Agheana, Ion Tudro.
  The meaning of experience in the prose of Jorge Luis Borges.

  (American university studies. Series II, Romance languages and literature ; vol. 71)
    1. Borges, Jorge Luis, 1899–   —Criticism and interpretation. I. Title. II. Series.
PQ7797.B635A54   1988   868   87-21504
  ISBN 0-8204-0595-7
  ISSN: 0740-9257

CIP-Titelaufnahme der Deutschen Bibliothek

Agheana, Ion T.:
The meaning of experience in the prose of Jorge
Luis Borges / Ion T. Agheana. – New York;
Bern; Frankfurt am Main; Paris: Lang, 1988.
  (American University Studies: Ser. 2,
  Romance Languages and Literature; Vol. 71)
  ISBN 0-8204-0595-7

NE: American University Studies / 02

© Peter Lang Publishing, Inc., New York 1988

Printed by Weihert-Druck GmbH, Darmstadt, West Germany

Contents

Part I
The Meaning of Experience

The Point of View...................................... 3
The Meaning of Experience 13
Essential Individuality................................. 29
The I in the Present................................... 41
The Anachronic Present 51
Waiting for the Present............................... 61
La hora sin sombra.................................... 73
Forms of Passion...................................... 83

Part II
The Literary Experience

The Point of View..................................... 97
Cervantes 101
Shakespeare... 115
Quevedo... 127
Shaw 139
Whitman... 155
Valéry as a Symbol.................................... 165
Literary Echoes 177
Language and Dialect 187

Part III
Chromatic Experience

The Point of View..................................... 199
Painting—The Medium 203

vi   *Contents*

Chromatic Perception 207
Black and White 217
The Yellow Rose 229
Chromatic Reticence................................ 237

Part I

The Meaning of Experience

Part I

The Meaning of Experience

The Point of View

The dénouement of the story "Los teólogos," Borges tells us, can only be described in metaphors, for it takes place in heaven, where there is no time.[1] The end of the story, like the story itself, speaks of experience, of an experience diversified by metaphors. The atemporality of heaven, however, is not really the element that leads to metaphorical expression. The nature of the experience is. In heaven, it turns out, Aurelianus, one of the protagonists, discovers that he and his rival, John of Pannonia, are one and the same person. The orthodox and the heretic, the accuser and the accused, are fused into one entity, or God perceives them as such. Any confusion in the divine mind must be discounted. God simply ignores religious differences (II, 37). In the expression of this kind of experience, of necessity speculative, for it remains outside of the realm of lived human experience, the presence of the metaphor is essential. In the expression of earthly, human experiences, the metaphor, while very important, is more of a complementary presence. Metaphor, Borges asserts in "Las *kenningar*," may not be a fundamental means of expression, but a rather late literary discovery (I, 350). Thus in a single statement Borges raises the fundamental questions of religion, philosophy, and literature, albeit without doctrinairism. However understandable it may be, attributing a doctrine to vital experience rather than to intellectually acquired knowledge remains an error (I, 198). Experience and time, or rather, experience in time is what affects man, and man attempts to enlarge his understanding of it through the plasticity of the metaphor. If time is always perceived by someone, as Borges states (II, 295), then the

3

metaphor is something which abstracts man from experience, from the immediacy of his presence in time. The metaphor does not negate human experience, it only expands its interpretative possibilities.

The "someone" who perceives experience in time, actually or metaphorically, is an individual, a Cartesian individual who perceives because he is, and here is where criticism, with rare exceptions, has accredited a point of view which by now is habit: that Borges categorically denies the individual, that he negates the reality of human experience. In short, Borges is said to be retrieving man from recognizable humanity.[2] Indeed Borges himself makes statements which at first seem to be of unimpeachable clarity: "Los individuos y las cosas existen en cuanto participan de la especie que los incluye, que es su realidad permanente" (I, 319). The judgment presents itself as a truism: "todo ello nos mueve a admitir la primacía de la especie y la casi perfecta nulidad de los individuos" (I, 319–20).

An attentive reader, however, can certainly find in Borges' assertion a foothold for an opposing point of view, even if one were to construe such an assertion as a Borgesian conviction. The first statement, carefully read, does not imply that individuals do not exist, only that they have two kinds of existence, an individual one and a generic one. In "El ruiseñor de Keats," Borges elaborates: "Es decir, el individuo es de algún modo la especie, y el ruiseñor de Keats es también el ruiseñor de Ruth" (II, 235). Paradoxically, the generic reality is only an abstraction. The second one, made from the standpoint of a generic "we," while accrediting the primacy of the species, speaks not of the perfect nullity of the individual, but of his "almost" perfect nullity, which is not the same thing. There is, one may say, a difference of degree but not of genre. Borges does not project an entirely metaphorical view of the individual and his reality.

To say that Borges negates individuality, that he systematically reduces man to anonymity, is to make out of Borges a more modern man than he actually is, to make him more consonant with the apocalyptic possibilities of the atomic age than with the professed realities and intentions of his craft. Borges, in the imaginings which constitute his works, is not ahead of his time. He is, if one may compare him to two figures from the past of Florentine glory, more of a Michelangelo than a Leonardo da Vinci. Borges, of course, is not innocent of the ambiguity surrounding him. He indulges in seemingly endless philosophical speculations, he postulates metaphysical issues from esthetic points of view and vice versa, he delights in blurring formal distinctions between genres and within genres, but he can honestly claim, as he does in "Sobre los clásicos," that he is not an iconoclast: "No tengo vocación de iconoclasta" (II, 302).

The remark, pointedly, aims at literature. Criticizing Mir Bahhadur Ali's novel, *The Approach to Al-Mu'tasim*, and its various "retouched" editions, Borges writes: "En la versión de 1932, las notas sobrenaturales ralean: 'el hombre llamado Almotásim' tiene su algo de símbolo, pero no carece de rasgos idiosincráticos, personales. Desgraciadamente, esa buena conducta literaria no perduró" (I, 396–97). Does Borges, in his own literary praxis, depart from the good literary conduct of giving his characters recognizable individuality? The evidence suggests that he does not. Philosophy and esthetics are not interchangeable in Borges' work. Borges himself, as it has been noted, in "Nathaniel Hawthorne," the most ambitious—and the longest—of his essays on literature, states unequivocally that reason should not interfere with the arts (II, 191). Art, simply, cannot deal in generalities: "El arte, siempre, opta por lo individual, lo concreto; el arte no es platónico" (I, 108). The *irrealidades visibles* that Borges writes about in "Avatares de la tortuga" (I, 204) constitute *lo concreto* of art. The transition from the allegory to the novel is, in Borges' own words, the passage from "especies a individuos, de realismo a nominalismo" (II, 270). Before the 14th century, Borges elucidates, realism and nominalism had different meanings: "para el realismo lo primordial eran los universales (Platón diría las ideas, las formas; nosotros, los conceptos abstractos), y para el nominalismo, los individuos" (II, 269).

Does Borges really negate the individual? Shakespeare may have multiplied himself in a seemingly endless fashion in his dramas, but he was, for better or worse, Shakespeare. Borges writes: "La identidad fundamental de existir, soñar y representar le inspiró pasajes famosos" (II, 342). Elsewhere Borges states that he unfortunately is Borges (II, 300). Neither author transcends his human condition. Even when Shakespeare retires from the stage and from playwriting, he cannot escape being an individuality: "Tenía que ser alguien; fue un empresario retirado que ha hecho fortuna y a quien le interesan los préstamos, los litigios y la pequeña usura" (II, 342). The Borgesian protagonist, far from being a spectral presence, devoid of identity, is a will in action, a personality which affirms itself. He is driven. Personal identity is the only tangible evidence of existence. Identity is shaped by experience.

What has contributed to the belief that the Borgesian protagonist is a disintegrating individuality is the fact that he is selective about the experience he seeks. He does not seek experience in general, evidence that he is alive, but experience that leads to self-knowledge, proof that he is an individual. It has been said, and with good reason, that society is only marginally present in Borges' work. This is undeniably true, but it represents a preference of emphasis, not an oversight. The Borgesian man is not a social animal, or rather, sociality does not interest him. He is not looking for knowledge, but for self-knowledge. In this respect, Borges' interest is unequivocal. Tadeo Isidoro Cruz finds self-knowledge, in Borges' words, in the experience of a fundamental night: "la noche en que por fin vio su propia cara, la noche en que por fin oyó su nombre" (II, 43). No one will fail to notice that the verb *ver*, here, is internalized, spiritualized. A lengthier quotation is necessary:

> Bien entendida, esa noche agota su historia; mejor dicho, un instante de esa noche, un acto de esa noche, porque los actos son nuestro símbolo. Cualquier destino, por largo y complicado que sea, consta en realidad *de un solo momento*: el momento en que el hombre sabe para siempre quien es.
>
> II, 43–44

All the elements are here: the instant as time, the act as experience, neither one cumulative in the revelation of self-knowledge. The self-knowledge revealed is definitive. In *"El hacedor,"* the dying protagonist is searching his memory for the few events which have given meaning to his individuality, which have remained affectively anchored in time. One such event was a revenge of honor, perpetrated in his youth. At his father's urging, with the aid of a dagger, he had redeemed his manhood: "El sabor preciso de aquel momento era lo que ahora buscaba; no le importaba lo demás: las afrentas del desafio, el torpe combate, el regreso con la hoja sangrienta" (II, 310). The urgency of his father's mandate—"Que alguien sepa que eres un hombre" (II, 310)—goes beyond the strictures of honor, to the need to be someone and something.

The self-knowledge attained by the Borgesian protagonist is an essence that transcends the contingencies of ordinary life, a glimpse of the divine mystery that we carry within: "el hombre sabe para siempre quien es." The instant and the act, action in time, as essential self-knowledge. It is, in fact, an existential act.[3] Why the instant? The philosophical implications are illuminating. María Zambrano, Ortega y Gasset's illustrious disciple, explains the matter as follows:

> Tal es el instante: un tiempo en que el tiempo se ha anulado, en que se ha anulado su transcurrir, su paso, y que por tanto no podemos medir sino externamente y cuando ha transcurrido ya por su ausencia.[4]

It is not that time has ceased to exist, but that its passing is not perceived. We are in the presence of an absolute, of an absolute allowed to man. The fact that we can measure it externally constitutes evidence, however tenuous, of the existence of such an absolute. Borges himself, not just his characters, has such an experience during his celebrated nocturnal visit to a district of Buenos Aires (II, 292–93).

The ancient Greeks, we learn from María Zambrano, propitiated the essential instant by sacrificial acts. The essential instant was the moment when the deity revealed itself. With few exceptions, like the God who speaks to Shakespeare or the god of fire who embraces the old man in "Las ruinas circulares," no deity reveals itself to man in Borges' fiction. Borges' characters are modest enough to have a glimpse of the eternal essence given to them by destiny. Significantly, like the ancient Greeks, they also propitiate the revelation through sacrifice. Knowing who one is, not only in this life but forever, and living with it, requires courage, the willingness to live with the truth. Implicitly or explicitly, all Borgesian protagonists go through a ritual of sacrifice in order to descry the truth, which is part of the *truth*. Both the propitiating of the revelation and the revelation are forms of action, not contemplative attitudes. "El sacrificio", says M. Zambrano, "es el acto o la serie de actos que hacen surgir este instante en que lo divino, se hace presente." She specifies: "No es una palabra, sino ante todo una acción, en la cual la palabra juega un papel."[5] Borges states elsewhere: "Hablar no basta" (II, 109).

The willed act, Kierkegaard asserts, is the privileged moment of existence.[6] Such is the act, the essential act, through which the Borgesian protagonist attains self-knowledge and a glimpse of eternity. Borges' choice of the moment of self-knowledge is not a nihilistic one. With few exceptions, the professed noniconoclast's protagonists do not commit suicide after finding out who they are. Isidoro Cruz goes on living, and so does the black man who kills Martín Fierro in a duel: "no tenía destino sobre la tierra y había matado a un hombre' (I, 524). His goal in life had been that of avenging the death of his brother, and he had accomplished it. Yet he will go on living. So will Emma Zunz, so does virtually every Borgesian protagonist. Given the transcendental nature of self-knowledge, we understand why Borges does not focus on ordinary knowledge, that of ordinary life. Yet he does not deny its importance, only its transcendence. It is vital but nonessential experience. It is time and action without transcendental significance. It does not affect measurably an individual's identity. After Don Quijote faces the irrational brute strength of the lions, we know that he is indeed a brave man, and that all the previous and the following acts simply confirm it. And so it is with the Borgesian protagonist, except that Borges does not offer the corroborating evidence of past or future actions. He does not write novels, he does not focus on unessential continuities. Such is his literary praxis.

Borges does not take man beyond himself. Is he really a mythmaker? Does he, as Carter Wheelock believes, mentally dissolve and remake the world?[7] Borges, demonstrably, is not interested in the world in his fiction, but in man, not in society but in the individual (II, 161–62). At the age of eighty Borges made a clear statement: "I have never attempted myth. Myth was *given* me, perhaps by readers."[8] There is no need to consider every Borges utterance as a masterpiece of ambiguity. Borges simply does not take man back to his amorphous mythological beginnings. G. Bell-Villada is sensibly accurate when he states that Borges' fictive situations, however exotic their settings, are those of our world.[9] Borges does not lead man to his mythological genesis in the past, or to his mythological possibilities in the future. He does not fade man into chaos nor make him into Superman, like Nietzsche. His medium is the present, the privileged moment of self-knowledge. He does not wish to alter the destiny of man. God dead, Nietzsche's Superman commits suicide. So does Nils Runeberg, and for the same reasons, in Borges' "Tres versiones de Judas." They commit suicide because they do not have anyone to whom to offer sacrifice. Elsewhere however, Borges does not remove the mysterious presence of divinity, of hope.

It is in Borges' preoccupation with man and the issue of knowledge that a great critic, Michel Foucault, found the seminal impulse for a study that he wished to be no less than "une archéologie des sciences humaines." The Borgesian text that inspired Foucault is humorous and deceptively simple. A Chinese encyclopedia lists in alphabetic order different categories of animals. Category a) contains ordinary dogs, category b) contains dogs which belong to the emperor, category c), dogs which, seen from a great distance, look like flies (II, 223). What Foucault learns from Borges is that the logical progression a, b, c, has been rendered meaningless by the categories enunciated, and vice versa, that language breaks down, that it has lost the "communality" of space and name.[10] There is, Foucault tells us, an order, an order constituted both by the internal order of things and the language which looks at things. When the latter component becomes opaque, when the internal order of things ceases to permeate it, language breaks down. Foucault's point: "Ainsi dans toute culture entre l'usage de ce qu'on pourrait appeler les codes ordinateurs et les réflexions sur l'ordre, il y a l'expérience nue de l'ordre et de ses modes d'être."[11] When language breaks down, it means that the unadorned experience, the middle ground, is muddled. The balance of such an experience is altered by excessive reflective knowledge.

The linguistic breakdown intuited by Borges, Foucault goes on to explain, is due to two major discontinuities in the *episteme* of the Western culture: that which inaugurates the classical age, towards the middle of the 17th century, and that which at the beginning of the 19th century initiates the modern period. Clearly stated, in Foucault's view, the foundations of our modern thinking are not those of the classical age. The classical age derived its knowledge from natural history, general grammar, and the concept of wealth, all based on external observation. The modern age, in contrast, draws its knowledge from biology, philology, economy and political science, all based on internal observation.[12] It is, of course, one thing to explain communication through grammar—a formal study of speech—and quite another to explain it through linguistics, through the inner workings of language and thinking. To be sure, Foucault's study surpasses the concerns of the present study. But the fact that it was Borges who gave him the initial impulse is indeed significant. Both authors are aware of the unreliability of the epistemological ground on which experience is represented by language. Both authors, in order to understand the degenerative process of language, have returned to the original point of departure, that of unmediated human experience. Foucault translates his endeavor into a scientific study. Borges elaborates his awareness of the meaning of experience into literary fiction. The Borgesian character always imparts—positively or negatively—meaning to experience. By individualizing himself he individualizes experience. Borges says at eighty: "I think that the only justice is private justice."[13] The statement should be retrieved from any sociological connotations: Borges is not an anarchist. What Borges is saying is that ethics loses its moral force when depersonalized, that institutionalized justice, as opposed to private justice, preserves the letter and not the spirit of righteousness. One can make propaganda with this sort of thing, but not serious literature. Needless to say, Borges opts for the latter. His hero is the individual and his directed experience, the person who, in the broadest sense, does justice to himself.

Notes

[1] Jorge Luis Borges, *Prosa completa* (Barcelona: Bruguera, 1980), two vols. Also, Jorge Luis Borges, *Obras completas* (Buenos Aires: Emecé, 1974), hereafter mentioned as *Obras*.

[2] Emir Rodriguez Monegal, "Borges: the Reader as Writer," in *Prose for Borges*, ed. by Mary Kinzie (Evanston: Northwestern University Press, 1972), 96–137;

Ana María Barrenechea, *Borges. The Labyrinth Maker* (New York: New York University Press, 1965), p. 144;

Jaime Alazraki, *La prosa narrativa de Jorge Luis Borges* (Madrid: Gredos, 1974), p. 75; Sylvia Molloy, *Las letras de Borges* (Buenos Aires: Editorial Sudamericana, 1979), p. 75;

Ronald J. Christ, *The Narrow Act. Borges' Art of Illusion* (New York: New York University Press, 1969), p. 75.

Carter Wheelock, *The Mythmaker* (Austin and London: University of Texas Press, 1969), pp. 20, 54.

[3] Jean-Paul Sartre, *L'existentialisme* (Paris: Nigel, 1958), pp. 22, 55, 58; Emmanuel Mounier, *Introduction aux existentialismes* (Paris: Gallimard, 1962), p. 24. For Borges' existential strain, see Ion T. Agheana, *The Prose of Jorge Luis Borges* (New York, Berne, Frankfort on the Main, Nancy: Peter Lang, 1984), pp. 1–41.

[4] María Zambrano, *El hombre y lo divino* (México: Fondo de cultura económica, 1955), p. 40.

[5] Ibid., pp. 40–41.

[6] Cf. Mounier, p. 53.

[7] Wheelock, p. 22.

⁸ *Borges at Eighty*, ed. by Willis Barnstone (Bloomington: Indiana University Press, 1982), p. 69.

⁹ Gene Bell-Villada, *Borges and his Fiction* (Chapel Hill: The University of North Carolina Press, 1981), p. 43.

¹⁰ Michel Foucault, *Les mots et les choses* (Paris: Gallimard, 1966), pp. 92, 310.

¹¹ Ibid., p. 12.

¹² Ibid., p. 32.

¹³ *Borges at Eighty*, p. 19.

The Meaning of Experience

In the fictive prose works of Borges experience can be defined as "tiempo vivo"—live time. The term is to be found in a brief essay of metaphysical and philosophical concern, "La perpetua carrera de Aquiles y la tortuga." The essay concisely exhibits the quintessential Borges. At the heart of Zeno's paradox lies the complex issue of experience. Zeno of Elea, Parmenides' disciple, denied that anything happens in the universe (I, 187). The statement implicitly negates experience. The unlimited division of space into progressively smaller fragments postulates not only a spatial distortion, but a temporal one as well: "Realicemos también que esos precipicios eslabonados corrompen el espacio y con mayor vértigo el tiempo vivo, en su doble desesperada persecución de la inmovilidad y del éxtasis" (I, 189). The remark lends itself to two observations. While space is mentioned without any qualification, "time" is qualified by the adjective "live." Thus time is not considered only as temporality, not as a philosophical abstraction, but as experience as well. In other words, "live time" accommodates information gained both through reason and through the senses. This is the emphasis that Borges brings to the paradox.

The paradox, needless to say, has endured throughout centuries, claiming the philosophical curiosity of Aristotle, Hobbes, Mill, Bergson, Bertrand Russell, among many others. Borges self-avowedly has evinced and maintained interest in philosophy and metaphysical perplexities—as he puts it in the inchoative paragraph of "Nueva refutación del tiempo" (*Otras inquisiciones*, 1952), or in the prolog to *El oro de los tigres* (1972)—

13

and, of course, in literature. The association of philosophy and literature is therefore not fortuitous in the works of Borges. What should be pointed out from the outset, however, is that philosophy is always subordinated to literature, rather than the opposite. "La perpetua carrera de Aquiles y la tortuga" is an illustrative example. The only refutation of the paradox that appeals to Borges is that of Bertrand Russell, a refutation worthy of the original, "virtud que la estética de la inteligencia está reclamando" (I, 190). To be sure, Borges could have said *"La lógica de la inteligencia,"* and the nature of the paradox would have justified such a formulation. Instead, as the man of letters that he is, he deliberately speaks of the esthetics of intelligence. He brings philosophy into the realm of literature, validating Bertrand Russell's assertion esthetically. Such a practice is far from being sporadic or anomalous in Borges. In the same volume, another essay, "Vindicación de Bouvard et Pécuchet," Borges defends Flaubert's last, problematical, novel in similar terms:

> La justificación de *Bouvard et Pécuchet*, me atrevo a sugerir, es de orden estético y poco o nada tiene que ver con las cuatro figuras y los diecinueve modos del silogismo. Una cosa es el rigor lógico y otra la tradición ya casi instintiva de poner las palabras fundamentales en boca de simples y de locos.
>
> I, 207

The obviously polemical tone adds to Borges' point of view. What he wishes to vindicate is Flaubert's choice of estheticism over philosophy. Since the inventions of philosophy are no less fantastic than those of art (II, 174), in doing what he does, Flaubert simply observes the exigencies of his craft. When critics reproached Goethe's departure from historical reality in dealing with Egmont, he replied that he needed an Egmont consistent with his poetic vision, an Egmont consistent with the actions dictated by such a vision, not with historical reality.[1] Borges does not contradict himself when he defends Flaubert, and with him literature in general. As he pointedly remarks, a writer should not be confused with his literature

(II, 141). The distinction between an author and his work has been made more than once. In "Nota sobre Walt Whitman" Borges quotes Edmund Gosse's observation that almost everything written on Whitman is distorted by the persistent identification of Whitman, man of letters, with Whitman, the semi-divine hero of *Leaves of Grass*. Borges emphatically agrees:

> Walt Whitman, hombre, fue director del Brooklyn Eagle, y leyó sus ideas fundamentales en las páginas de Emerson, Hegel y de Volnay; Walt Whitman, personaje poético, las edujo del contacto de América, ilustrado por experiencias imaginarias en las alcobas de New Orleans y en los campos de batalla de Georgia.
>
> I, 197

Aside from the basic distinction between the two *alter egos*, Borges circumscribes the experience of Walt Whitman, the writer, and traces such an experience to his contact with America. Since the experiences in the bedrooms of New Orleans and the battlefields of Georgia are imaginary, the idea that they originated from contact with America acquires new meaning. Is Whitman's contact with reality, or with an imagined reality? Does reality validate experience, does imagined reality invalidate it? In which case are the emotions poetically educed authentic or unauthentic? And, finally, in order to elucidate the issue, should one stay with the logically defined opposites real-unreal, true-false, authentic-unauthentic?

Borges is his own Virgil. Let us follow him. Reality is not verbal (II, 169) and philosophy is not much more than a coordination of words (I, 204). Borges does not deny that there is reality, as it has often and authoritatively been asserted, but simply that what we call reality is a linguistic convention apart from the non-verbal reality, so to speak. In nature, Borges tells us, there are no planes, lines, dots—all convenient intellectual constructs—only volumes (I, 129). Again, he does not state that there are no objects in nature, only that these objects have a form that has nothing to do with the terminology devised by the human mind. It is a point of reiterated emphasis:

Berkeley negó la materia. Ello no significa, entiéndase bien, que negó
los colores, los olores, los sabores, los sonidos y los contactos; lo que
negó fue que, además de esas percepciones, que comprenden el mundo
externo, hubiera dolores que nadie siente, colores que nadie ve, formas
que nadie toca.

II, 294

Berkeley negates absolute, but not relative, reality. When Kant
speaks about the distinction between reality and appearance,
he delineates two approaches, (1) that of considering the object
in and of itself, (2) and that by which only the perception of the
object is taken into account. In other words, the latter form of
appearance is to be found in the subject to whom the object
appears.[2] Interestingly, throughout the ages, the most conspicuous intellectual effort, from Plato to Bergson and Bradley, has
gone more into attempting to define what appearance, rather
than reality, is. Ironically, reality has remained more elusive
than appearance. Writings on reality and the nature of reality
are rather sparse.

The term "reality" was first introduced in the 13th century,
allegedly by Duns Scotus, for whom *realitas* was loosely syn-
onymous with "being."[3] Scotus himself does not distinguish
clearly between "reality" and "being." The idea introduced by
Kant, that real is that which accords with the material conditions of experience, brings reality into the realm of man. But the
term experience does not lend itself to easy explanations.
Conventional use defines it as information gained through the
senses rather than through reason. Duns Scotus held an
opposite point of view. As the foremost object of the intellect is
being, which he called *realitas*, everything comes within the
scope of the intellect.[4]

Borges does not take sides on such elusive matters. Instead,
he joins a philosophical tradition that posits reality in terms of
truth, thus avoiding the logical polarity real-unreal. This is the
correspondence theory. As usual, Borges slightly alters things.
Cervantes' work is a fertile ground. Borges insists that for
Cervantes the imaginary, poetic world of the novels of chivalry
and the real, prosaic one of 17th century Spain are antithetic.

The polarity imaginary-poetic contrasts markedly with real-prosaic. Logic prevails. But in "Parábola de Cervantes y de *Quijote*" Borges deviates: "Para los dos, para el soñador y el soñado, toda esa trama fue la oposición de dos mundos: el mundo irreal de los libros de caballerías, el mundo cotidiano y común del siglo XVII" (II, 336). While wonderful and prosaic remain clearly antithetic (II, 336), "unreal" is contrasted not with "real" but with "quotidian" and "common." Or "unreal" and "common" are not opposites. The grouping common-uncommon, once removed from the realm of real-unreal, affects differently the sensitivity of the reader. Common and uncommon are attributes of experience, rather than reality as such. The objective and the subjective are forms of perceiving reality, that is to say experiential entities, not substitutes for reality.

It may seem paradoxical, but one of the aspects least altered by Borges' metaphysical speculations is that of experience, at least in fiction. In "Historia de la eternidad," an essay that seems entirely dedicated to philosophical considerations, Borges speaks about time, "un tembloroso y exigente problema" (I, 315). If one is inclined to let his fancy soar, to meander strictly into the abstract, Borges provides a corrective point: (time is) "acaso el más vital de la metafísica" (I, 315). Etymologically, "vital" relates to life. Life, human life, relates to experience. For Borges, there is no metaphysics without man. When Borges speaks about time, he speaks of human time, of experience:

> Los ingleses que por impulsión ocasional o genial del escribiente Clive o de Warren Hastings conquistaron la India, no acumularon solamente espacio, sino tiempo: es decir experiencias, experiencias de noches, días, descampados, montes, astucias, heroísmos, traiciones, dolores, destinos, muertes, pestes, fieras, dioses, veneraciones.
>
> I, 132

The listing of items bears close scrutiny. When Borges speaks of nights and days he is not interested in a phenomenological cycle, but in the experience allowed by time. It is not mountains as geological formations that warrant their mention here, but as hardy human experience. The wild beasts of India hold no scientific interest for the British soldiers; they only test their courage. Equally, the Hindu or the Buddhist deities that they encounter do not impinge upon their religious conscience, do not influence them as religions, only as culturally different forms of experience. Heroic acts, betrayals, deaths, suffering, are not analyzed ethically, death and suffering are not viewed physiologically, only as diversified forms of human experience. This is the apology of human experience, not a scientific proposition. This is the experience of man, of men of human condition, to use one of Borges' felicitous expressions (I, 142).

When Borges says, as we have quoted, that philosophy is merely a coordination of words, he means, as so many before him, that it establishes its own conventions, which, in turn, become premises. Plato admits that ultimately truth relates to itself. Aristotelian logic is not a representation of reality (whatever reality may be), but a dialectic game: "To say of what is that it is, and of what is not that it is not, is true."[5] Truth is not an absolute but a philosophical category, and Averroes, the greatest Arab philosopher, thought that what is true in philosophy may be false in religion. True and false, Hobbes believed, are attributes of speech, not of things. Leibniz distinguished between truth of reason and truth of facts, while Hegel spoke of formal and historical truth. William James simply called truth an expedient.[6] Borges often speaks of truth, but while truth retains its philosophical implications in some of his essays, in his prose fiction it is closer to validating experience, which reinstates man into his preoccupations. He thus bridges the gap between philosophy and literature. When he speaks of the experience of man, experience in the making, he makes literature. With rare exceptions, the Borgesian protagonist defines himself through experience in action.

Borges' literary world may be incomplete and rarefied, but it is not devoid of individualized human presence. The present, George H. Mead tells us in one of the surprisingly few studies dedicated to this temporal dimension, is not a mere passage, it is the emergence of an event.⁷ One could be speaking of Borges' prose fiction. That event, in Borges, is the individual will in action. Even a cursory reading of "El milagro secreto" or a vague acquaintance with "Guayaquil," for example, would confirm such a claim. But the point that really needs to be made here is that Borges does not dispense with recognizable humanity in his work, and that such a humanity projects itself in neatly defined personalities. Not that Borges is pellucidly clear. But he is not hopelessly obscure either. At first glance, nothing could be more abstract, more intellectually analyzed, more dispassionate than "Historia de la eternidad."

The essay begins with Plotinus, a quintessential philosopher, and his supreme work, *Enneads*. Before speaking of Plato and his image of time as a reflection of eternity, Borges mentions Plotinus, and the mysteries which precede the invention of eternity. Bradley, Irenaeus, Malón de Chaide, Schopenhauer, St. Augustine, Jeremiah Taylor, Swedenborg, Boethius, Martensen, Zwingly, Aristotle, Seneca, John Scotus Erigena, philosophers, theologians, writers, carry, in this seemingly eclectic parade, the ideas that have earned them human immortality. Behind the challenging ideas that Borges mentions are the people who created them. What begins by being a mere compilation of abstractions, ends as personalities who have striven to synthesize and explain the knowledge of their time. Part III of Borges' essay begins with a significant statement: "Hasta aquí, en su orden cronológico, la historia general de la eternidad" (I, 328). This is where the scientific exposition, so to speak, the ordering of philosophical thought, ends. From here on the perennial preoccupation with time is perceived as spiritual anxiety, not as mere intellectual curiosity. For the need for eternity is spiritual rather than intellectual. We are closer to the meaning of literature. Borges speaks of individuals: "Es sabido que la identidad personal reside en la memoria y que la anulación de esa facultad comporta la idiotez" (I, 329). Personal identity makes a human being, the awareness of being a human being. Masses, Borges tells his younger *alter ego* in "El otro," do not exist as such, they only have a conceptual reality. Man, individual man, needs some form of eternity, and wishes this eternity to be a compendium of human feelings, not of human thought. The meaning is clear:

> Sin una eternidad, sin un espejo delicado y secreto de lo que pasó por las almas, la historia universal es tiempo perdido, y en ella nuestra historia personal—lo cual nos afantasma incómodamente. No basta con el disco gramofónico de Berliner o con el perspicuo cinematógrafo, meras imágenes de imágenes, ídolos de ídolos.
>
> I, 329

The syntactical framing of the issue deserves closer scrutiny. The statement does not begin as an "if" clause, as a contrary-to-fact proposition, but as a reasoned and felt conclusion; without the delicate, secret reflection of what happens to the human soul, world history is—not would be—a waste of time. Borges poignantly speaks of the soul, not of the intellect, emphasizing lived experience rather than intellectual activity. The choice of the recorder of such experience is of the utmost significance here. It is not the word, spoken or printed, not an instrument which relegates human experience to the past, but a mirror, an artifact whose reflection is simultaneous with, not posterior to, an act of experience. Since the mirror does not invent the reality that it reflects, unlike the workings of the intellect, it lends a visual dimension to experience. It relates experience to images. The mirror, needless to say, is not a perfect reflector, as Kant observed.[8] In a mirror image, otherwise unfailingly faithful, the left arm of a person becomes the right one, and so on. Bergson, whom Borges quotes frequently, explains his preference for the image unambiguously: "Now the image has at least this advantage, that it keeps us in the concrete."[9] The mirror does precisely that. So may the word, but not without delay or mediation. When Borges describes his much celebrated hallucinatory night in Buenos Aires, we are made aware of the time lapse between the experience and the recording of it: "Sólo después alcancé a definir esa imaginación" (I, 332).

The verb that describes the experience itself is *sentir*—to feel—rather than *pensar*: "Me sentí muerto, me sentí percibidor abstracto del mundo" (I, 332). Exemplary honesty, that of Borges. Every word is carefully chosen, conveying precisely the meaning with which Borges infused it. There is no secret miracle, no temporal concession, so to speak, affecting Borges or his perception of reality. Time does not move backward (*remontar* has a regressive connotation) for Borges, nor does he make such a claim. *Post factum*, he suspects that he has grasped the meaning of a word, an inconceivable word, "eternity." If Borges evinces any pride, it is not about his superior humanity, graced with a supernatural occurrence, but about his genius as a man of letters, a man who has understood the inconceivable meaning of a word: eternity. From *sentir* Borges passes to *creer* in the negative, thus marking the distinction between two ways of perceiving reality. The verb *sentir* implies individuality. Time, it shall be recalled, is time perceived by someone (II, 295). Borges dislikes the *kenningar* because, with the incompleteness with which they have come to our attention, they are cold, impersonal, that is to say, depersonalized. By contrast, he is avowedly fond of the inscriptions that carts, used for the transport of merchandise in Buenos Aires, display conspicuously. These *flores corraloneras*, as Borges affectionately calls them, are genuine poetic expressions of individuality. Borges' predilection for them, his reasoned predilection, is forthright:

> Implican drama, están en la circulación de la realidad. Corresponden a frecuencias de la emoción: son como del destino, siempre. Son ademanes perdurados por la escritura, son una afirmación incesante.
>
> I, 74

Drama, reality, emotion, an incessant affirmation, these are the words of individuality in action. Elsewhere, Borges states that the issue of immortality is a dramatic one (I, 172). He speaks of the dramatic with more than casual insistence.

> El propósito de dar interés dramático a esta biografía de la eternidad, me ha obligado a ciertas deformaciones: verbigracia, a resumir en cinco o seis nombres una gestación secular.
>
> I, 332

Why, may we ask, is Borges using the term drama? Borges, whose words in any given context are virtually irreplaceable, cannot be said to use it with literary abandon. Etymologically, drama derives from the Greek *dran*: to do, to act. It is a representation of human life, accommodated to action. It represents events organized according to dramatic unity. It is human life in action. Individuals act out their destiny. The words "biography of eternity" are arresting. The essay is not a history of eternity, as postulated in the title, but a biography of eternity. Borges is not trafficking in an impersonal history of ideas, but in individual endeavors at perceiving and understanding time in one of its supposed dimensions, in biographies of eternity:

> Hombres remotos, hombres barbados y mitrados la concibieron (i.e., "la eternidad"), públicamente para confundir herejías y para vindicar la distinción de las tres personas en una.
>
> I, 328

The deformation that Borges speaks about resides in the choice of thinkers on the matter of eternity, and in the inherent fallacies and limitations of human belief and intellect. It is the experience of man that interests Borges. Commenting on Flaminio Rufo's accounts of experience in "El inmortal," Borges states:

> El primero de todos parece convenir a un hombre de guerra, pero luego se advierte que el narrador no repara en lo bélico y sí en la suerte de los hombres.
>
> II, 22–22

From the above Borges infers that the author is a man of letters rather than a warrior. Significantly, the facts confronted by the warrior—for there are two distinct people involved (II, 21)—do not lead the author to the truth; only esthetic peculiarities do (II, 21). It is Borges the writer who speaks. He is always in the shadow of the recognizable individuality of man, in whom he takes dramatic interest. There is no history of eternity, only people like Plato, Aristotle, Plotinus, St. Augustine, Bradley, etc., whose lives are linked with attempts at defining an abstraction. About Plato and Aristotle, realism and nominalism and the diachronic evolution of the two terms, Borges writes: "A través de las latitudes y de las épocas, los dos antagonistas inmortales han cambiado de dialecto y de nombre: uno es Parménides, Platón, Spinoza, Kant, Francis Bradley; el otro, Heráclito, Aristóteles, Locke, Hume, William James" (II, 269). Nobody can mistake this statement of Borges for an apology of meaningless generalization:

> Durante muchos años, yo creí que la casi infinita literatura estaba en un hombre. Este hombre fue Carlyle, fue Johannes Becher, fue Whitman, fue Rafael Cansinos-Asséns, fue De Quincey.
>
> II, 141

There is no literature without the individual authors enumerated by Borges. Equally, universal history is not the history of a single man. When Borges raises the issue, with habitual probity he does so hypothetically, as the inchoative *si*—if—attests:

> Si los destinos de Edgar Allan Poe, de los vikingos, de Judas Iscariote y de mi lector son el mismo destino—el único destino posible—, la historia universal es la de un solo hombre.
>
> I, 362

Paraphrasing Borges' judgment on literature, we can say that indeed universal history is the history of a single man; that of Alexander the Great, of Jesus, of Julius Caesar, and so on. There is no universal history without these makers of history. Is destiny a process or an end, does it refer to life or death? Only in death would destiny be an equalizer of humanity, as it was in morality plays. Borges, obviously, and without any claim to originality, envisages destiny as an end, an inalterable end which brings the hope of justice. It is to this end that he subordinates the meaning of destiny: "En tiempos que declinan (como éstos), es la promesa de que ningún oprobio, ninguna calamidad, ningún dictador podrá empobrecernos" (I, 369). Destiny as a process is diversified in countless distinct individualities. To say that any lapse of time (except eternity) contains history integrally, that all destinies are the same, is something which Borges can refute effortlessly: "Un sabor difiere de otro sabor, diez minutos de dolor físico no equivalen a diez minutos de álgebra" (I, 368). When Borges acknowledges to have written a biography of eternity, when he says that all literature is in one man and then enumerates many of his favorite authors, he remains firmly within the realm of recognizable humanity. In the discussion of esoteric subjects, from the nature of universal history to the metaphysical perplexities of paradoxes, he does not abandon man. If Borges, who otherwise admires certain aspects of Hindu thought, imputes anything to Hindu philosophy, it is that it does not have a historical framework, that it ignores the presence of man as an individuality:

> Los hindúes no tienen sentido histórico (es decir: perversamente prefieren el examen de las ideas al de los hombres y las fechas de los filósofos) pero nos consta que esa negación radical de la introspección cuenta unos ocho siglos.
>
> II, 147–48

Two words immediately claim our attention. The adverb *perversamente*, the first term, denotes distorted, biased interpretation of an idea, a corruption. The lexical explanation is even more incriminating, designating "perverse" as something which departs from what is right or good. Borges enhances the scope of critical awarenes. The other word is "negation," negation of introspection. The movement is one of concentration of individuality rather than dissipation, an inward affirmation—"in," not "ex." What exacts Borges' criticism is that the Hindu deny individuality, of which introspection is a conspicuous attribute, deny the inward movement, affirming ideologic generalities. They prefer, in Borges' precise rendition, the examination of ideas to that of the men who have produced them. They prefer ideas to the men who have produced them, the species to the individual, literature to the writers who have generated it. Such a propensity, like Platonic idealism, is dissonant with the beliefs of a man who, albeit reluctantly, acknowledges his individuality: "Yo, desgraciademente, soy Borges" (II, 300). The onomastic entity that Borges is, is not—cannot be—a flight from individuality. Biography is individual experience.

Experience is time, live time, as Borges puts it in the essay on Achilles and the turtle. It is not live space, but live time. "El espacio," say Borges, "es un incidente en el tiempo y no una forma universal de intuición como impuso Kant. Hay enteras provincias del ser que no lo requieren; las de la olfación y audición" (I, 132). In Borges' utopic version of the world, adduced as an example, a spaceless world would continue to have a history, a temporal biography, to paraphrase Borges, in which life will be as passionate and precise as ours (I, 133). It would be populated by a humanity no less abundant in wills, tenderness, and the unexpected (I, 133). To experience is to perceive, whether space is part of perception or not. To perceive, however, implies a subject, an I. Nietzsche knew that "La más eficaz de las personas gramaticales es la primera" (I, 360). Asks Borges at the end of "La doctrina de los ciclos":

> ¿Basta la mera sucesión no verificada por nadie? ¿A falta de un arcángel especial que lleve la cuenta, qué significa el hecho de que atravesamos el ciclo trece mil quinientos catorce, y no el primero de la serie o el número trescientos veintidós con el exponente dos mil?
>
> I, 363

It is the I that experiences the live time and confers meaning upon experience. Far from being obliterated, the I imposes itself and organizes experience. The ego, in Borges' work, may find itself without the auxiliary props of society, without generic trappings, but it is always there. There is no fictive narrative of Borges in which the I does not experience live time. The I is the individual will in action. Borges is now in the shadow of Schopenhauer. In the argument between Borges—narrator and the Argentinianized historian Zimmermann, in "Guayaquil," the former's words are clear: "Sus argumentos fueron lo de menos; el poder estaba en el hombre, no en la dialéctica" (II, 420). In Schopenhauerian terms, the time-frame of the will in action is the present: "Nadie ha vivido en el pasado, nadie vivará en el futuro; el presente es la forma de toda vida" (I, 368).

One may be inclined to infer that Schopenhauer denies the existence of the past and of the future. This is not the case. When Schopenhauer states that no one has lived in the past nor will anyone live in the future, he does not mean to say that the two temporal categories do not exist, but that life—lived experience—only takes place in the present. G. H. Mead speaks unequivocally: "The first condition of consciousness is life."[10] Borges himself speaks of the ungraspable present, "el inasible presente" (I, 368). Again, the syntactic framing is important. The remark is to be found in a statement about Marcus Aurelius: "Afirma que cualquier lapso—un siglo, un año, una sola noche, tal vez el inasible presente—contiene integramente la historia" (I, 368). If the notion that any lapse of time contains history in its entirety belongs to Marcus Aurelius, the breaking down of such a lapse into units, among which is the "ungraspable present," must be attributed to Borges. Borges, patently, does not deny that the present exists, only that it is ungraspable, that it is experienced, not reasoned. The present does not interest Borges as a biological condition alone, but as a literary possibility as well (I, 368). When Borges opts for dreams, for the dream which comprises simultaneously the past, the present, and the future (II, 403), he means to say that in the magic of the dream the past, the present, and the future can become presents.

Notes

[1] Johann Wolfgang von Goethe, "Conversations with Ekerman," in *Literary Criticism*, ed. by G.W. Allen and H.H. Clark (Detroit: Wayne State University Press, 1962), p. 138.

[2] Immanuel Kant, "Transcendental Ideality of Space and Time," in *Problems of Space and Time,* ed. by J.J.C. Smart (New York: The Macmillan Co., 1969), p. 115.

[3] See "Reality," in *Dictionary of Philosophy and Religion*, ed. by W.L. Reese (Atlantic Highland: Humanities Press Inc., 1980), p. 481.

[4] Ibid., p. 481.

[5] Ibid., p. 588.

[6] Ibid., p. 589.

[7] George Herbert Mead, *The Philosophy of the Present* (Chicago, London: Open Court Publishing Co., 1932), p. 23.

[8] Immanuel Kant, "Mirror Images," in *Problems of Space and Time*, p. 126.

[9] Henri Bergson, "Duration and Intuition," in *Problems of Space and Time*, p. 141.

[10] Mead, p. 69.

Essential Individuality

The two Borges who meet each other on the banks of Charles River in Cambridge—the young man and the old man—discuss literature and life. When they speak, they present themselves as totalities of their respective experiences at a given time, not as interlocutors casually engaged in an exchange of divergent ideas. The two Borges are among the most neatly delineated protagonists to be found in Borgesian prose, and the most complete. In the course of the conversation, the elder Borges makes a statement that is crucial to the distinction between the two, and to our argument: "Sólo los individuos existen, si es que existe alguien" (II, 461). Borges is seventy six years old. The volume in which the statement appears, *El libro de Arena*, uncharacteristically, does not have a prolog, but an epilog. Borges, as we can see, makes a statement of unimpeachable clarity. Is this the Borges who elsewhere speaks of the primacy of the species over the individual, and of the almost "perfect nullity" of the individual (I, 319–20)? A Borgesian boutade? Another ambiguity that both delights and confounds critics? Borges, we should remind ourselves, has been part not only of literature but of life as well, of complex personal experiences. Borges, however, unfortunately, is Borges (II, 300). Inevitably we add, experience distilled into wisdom separates the older Borges from the younger one. The latter, not quite twenty, can only talk about literature. The former, a man in his seventies, speaks not only of literature but also of life, of the vicissitudes of experience.

The younger Borges is in Geneva, studying. He reads extensively. He reads passionately, in the hope of finding himself in

29

experience and knowledge. Naively, he thinks that his intellectual and spiritual awareness is an entirely valid substitute for
the continuous, vital participation that life is. The younger
Borges, it is movingly clear to the older one, can only discuss
literature. His age justifies his search for idealism and the belief
that such an idealism is to be found literarily in the mysterious
recesses of the soul. Fashionably, he reads Dostoevsky. The
question of the older Borges, whose memory has been enter-
taining new interests or old interests in a new way, about the
meaning of Dostoevsky's works, propels the younger one into
a predictable reaction, that of propounding generalities. The
younger Borges, with the vanity of youth, emits cosmic judgments: "El maestro ruso ha penetrado más que nadie en los
laberintos del alma eslava" (II, 460). The older, wiser Borges
perspicuously judges the statement to be a mere rhetorical
exercise (II, 460). The younger Borges is a reader, an avid and
passionate reader, but not yet a critic. When asked if he
distinguished the individuality of Dostoevsky's characters, as
one can do in Joseph Conrad's work, the young Borges,
surprised by the novelty (for him) of the question, answers
negatively. He did not. It is not a frivolous inquiry. The
question is consonant with the older Borges' statement that
only individuals are real. The younger Borges, who is barely
listening, declares his intention of fulfilling himself in verse.
His book, an expression of *engagement*, will sing of the fraternity of all men (II, 461). The older Borges is troubled by this
abstract fraternity. His answer cannot be considered ambiguous:

> Me quedé pensando y le pregunté si verdaderamente se sentía her-
> mano de todos. Por ejemplo, de todos los empresarios de pompas
> fúnebres, de todos los carteros, de todos los buzos, de todos los que
> viven en la acera de los números pares, de todos los afónicos, etcétera.
>
> II, 461

The deliberately prosaic listing of eclectic classifications of our
fellow men fails to affect the younger Borges' poetic idealism.
He vows to dedicate his volume of poetry to no less than the

great mass of the oppressed and the indigent (II, 461). The older Borges' reflection expresses itself in no uncertain terms: "Tu masa de oprimidos y de parias no es más que una abstracción. Sólo los individuos existen, si es que alguien existe. *El hombre de ayer no es el hombre de hoy*, sentenció algún griego" (II, 461). The younger Borges' failure to recognize the reference to Heraclitus is indicative of his cultural limitations. The first two sentences of the statement belong to Borges the elder, to informed literary awareness mediated by experience. The last one, self avowedly, belongs to literature and philosophy. Hunger and suffering, Borges said earlier, are abstractions and can only be perceived as individual realities (II, 291).

Only now do the two begin to discuss literature in earnest. As opposed to his *alter ego*, the older Borges believes only in the metaphors which engender intimate affinities, in the metaphors already accepted by our imagination: the aging of man, dreams and life, the flowing of water and time. What begins as an opinion will later (within the temporal coordinates of the study) be crystallized in a book (II, 461), in several books, to be precise: *Discusión* (1932), *Historia de la eternidad* (1936), *Otras inquisiciones* (1952), and to a certain degree in *El hacedor* (1960). The younger Borges, unsympathetic to the vital and literary preoccupations of an older man, barely pays any attention. Life and literature, literature and life, confront each other once more in this short story, which could serve as the pivotal analysis of the life and literary times of Borges the younger and Borges the older. When they talk about Walt Whitman, one of the few authors that the two Borges have read in this temporal mutation, the older one affirms that for Whitman happiness is an unfulfilled possibility. Opting for an esthetic consideration of literature, the older Borges considers a particular poem of Whitman to be the manifestation of a desire, not the history of a fact (II, 462). The lofty, literary idealism of the younger Borges surfaces again with youthful ardor: "Usted no lo conoce. Whitman es incapaz de mentir" (II, 462). Only a young, inexperienced Borges can posit the business of literature in philosophical or ethical terms, just as earlier he had taken one of Whitman's poems to be a faithful rendition of reality, an historical fact. The older Borges cannot be more explicit:

> Medio siglo no pasa en vano. Bajo nuestra conversación de personas de miscelánea lectura y gustos diversos, comprendí que no podíamos entendernos. Eramos demasiado distintos y demasiado parecidos. No podíamos engañarnos, lo cual hace difícil el diálogo. Cada uno de los dos era el remedo caricaturesco del otro. La situación era harto anormal para durar mucho más tiempo. Aconsejar o discutir es inútil, porque su inevitable destino era ser el que soy.
>
> II, 462

Borges has always had the name of Borges, but he has not always been Borges, or rather, he has been all the Borges that the Borges who writes this story embodies. It is Heraclitus' statement applied to life and literature.

When the older Borges says that half a century does not pass in vain, he raises the crucial issue of experience. It is not only that he has read more books than the younger Borges, which, of course, he has, but that his relationship with the written word has changed over the years. When the younger Borges pontificates about Dostoevsky's definite elucidation of the labyrinthic Slavic soul, the older one thinks that the idea of the definitive text belongs only to fatigue or to religion (I, 181). The younger Borges, to the dismay of the older one, insists on literary references: "no hemos cambiado nada, pensé. Siempre las referencias librescas" (II, 463). But literary references and the emphatic eclecticism of idealism do not constitute comprehension or literary criticism. Reading literature as mere ideology is not a legitimate literary endeavor. The younger Borges does not distinguish or recognize the individuality of Dostoevsky's protagonists, nor does he intend to analyze the Russian author's work in depth. Borges, we recall, does not impute to H.G. Wells the formulation of doctrinaire statements, only the insertion of such statements into his literary works (II, 211). The younger Borges can *only* talk about literature. The older one can speak of literature and life:

Hubo otra guerra, casi entre los mismos antagonistas. Francia no tardó en capitular; Inglaterra y América libraron contra un dictador alemán, que se llamaba Hitler, la cíclica batalla de Waterloo. Buenos Aires, hacia mil novecientos cuarenta y seis, engendró otro Rosas, bastante parecido a nuestro pariente. El cincuenta y cinco, la provincia de Córdoba nos salvó, como antes Entre Ríos. Ahora, las cosas andan mal. Rusia está apoderándose del planeta; América, trabada por la superstición de la democracia, no se resuelve a ser un imperio. Cada día que pasa nuestro país es más provinciano.

II, 460

These are not literary references, not abstractions. They are the points of view of an individual, perhaps flawed and subjective in their intention, but nevertheless points of view. A witness to history subjectively looks at the world and at his own land. There is no pretense of giving his opinions literary merit. He is utterly moved by the idealistic, inexperienced, awed young man that his *alter ego* is: "Yo, que no he sido padre, sentí por ese pobre muchacho, más íntimo que un hijo de mi carne, una oleada de amor" (II, 460). The statement has a double purpose, that of projecting the old man's emotion, and that of showing that such an emotion is dramatically powerful only when specifically directed. Borges does not feel love for all the idealistic young men of the world, but for a particular one, an identifiable human being, flesh and blood of himself.

The two Borges of "Borges y yo" do not—cannot—live separately, they are not generalities as far as each one is concerned: "Yo vivo, yo me dejo vivir, para que Borges pueda tramar su literatura y esa literatura me justifica" (II, 347). The mature Borges, unlike the young one who will sit next to him on a bench in Cambridge, has learned to accommodate his idealism to the confines of his humanity, has accepted being Borges. It is the wisdom that the younger Borges is yet to acquire. Time, Borges tells us, does not pass in vain, and we change with time. Even in the abject misery and isolation of the prison cell in which he lives, Tzinacán, the Aztec priest condemned to slow death by Pedro de Alvarado, changes. Tzinacán changes, to use Borges' own words, "Urgido por la fatalidad de hacer algo, de poblar de algún modo el tiempo"

(II, 87). Beautiful words, describing both the plight and the greatness of man. Borges himself, like Tzinacán, like all of us, can describe and justify his own existence in the same terms. Such a justification can only be individual. Says Borges about Shakespeare: "La identidad fundamental de existir, soñar y representar le inspiró pasajes famosos" (II, 342). The Protean diversification of the Shakespearean theatre is the work of one individual, William Shakespeare, in his fundamental identity. Iago, in *Othello*, does not claim that he does not exist, only that he is not what he is (II, 432). Like Tzinacán, Shakespeare was inexorably someone: "Tenía que ser alguien" (II, 342). It is by now a commonplace to say that Borges dissolved Shakespeare's personality into nothingness. The title of the essay is, in fact, "Everything and Nothing." Another essay of Borges is entitled "De alguien a nadie." But from the organicity of these essays an affirmation of individuality, rather than a negation, emerges. Borges speaks about Shakespeare:

> Al principio creyó que todas las personas eran como él, pero la extrañeza de un compañero con el que había empezado a comentar esa vacuidad, le reveló su error y le dejó sentir, para siempre, que un individuo no debe diferir de la especie.
>
> II, 341

This is not one of Borges' celebrated ambiguities. In the beginning Shakespeare thought that his humanity was undifferentiated, that he was like everybody else, only to be confronted by the utter disbelief of his colleague. He stands in error. Shakespeare's wish to be like everybody else has to do with the fear of his uniqueness, of his inability to find generic solace and reassurance, not with a reality which makes him inexorably an individual. Hazlitt's judgment, as quoted by Borges, is to the point: "Shakespeare se parecía a todos los hombres, salvo en lo de parecerse a todos los hombres. Intimamente no era nada, pero era todo lo que son los demás, o lo que pueden ser" (II, 261). We are told that intimately Shakespeare was nothing, not that he was nobody. The distinction is important, for the philosophical "nothing" in questions does not invalidate the living individuality that Shakespeare was. Borges writes: "Ser una cosa es inexorablemente no ser todas las cosas; la intuición confusa de esa verdad ha inducido a los hombres a imaginar que no ser es más que ser algo y que, de alguna manera, es ser todo. Esa falacia . . ." (II, 261). Similarly, applying the statement to man, one can state that being someone is inexorably not being everybody. It would be preposterous to improve upon Borges' words.

When Borges considers Droctulft, the protagonist of "Historia del guerrero y de la cautiva," *sub specie aeternitatis,* he does not do it at the expense of his individuality. There is no deliberate attempt on his part to accredit the absolute validity of his procedure. He simply states, as far as his short story is concerned, a preference. Droctulft the individual, Borges insists, ". . . sin duda fue único e insondable (todos los individuos lo son)," (II, 39). Contrary to a widely accepted opinion, Borges does not discard the individual in favor of the species, any more than he denies the validity of human endeavors in the face of the impenetrability of the divine scheme of the world (II, 224). Man must continue to construct his own vision, even if such a vision may at best be provisional (II, 224). Borges' honesty and aesthetic decency would not allow him to think otherwise. Early on, in "La poesía gauchesca," Borges emphasized that Fierro was not simply a *gaucho*—a generic entity—but the *gaucho* Fierro, a distinct individual. "Ya veremos después," he writes, "que de todos los héroes de esa poesía, Fierro es el más individual, el que menos responde a una tradición" (I, 108). In the second prolog to *Historia universal de la infamia* (1935), the 1954 edition, Borges is equally emphatic, with the added weight of his own literary practice. Referring to "Hombre en la esquina rosada," he writes:

> En su texto, que es de entonación orillera, se notará que he intercalado algunas palabras cultas: vísceras, conversiones, etc. Lo hice, porque el compadre aspira a la finura, o (esta razón excluye la otra, pero es quizá la verdadera) porque los compadres son individuos y no hablan siempre como el Compadre, que es una figura platónica.
>
> I, 244

There is no need to underline the salient points. The *compadre* is an abstraction, a literary composite, the individual is not. Interestingly, while the terms *"compadres"* and *"individuos"* are in the plural, they do not convey the same meaning.

When Borges speaks of Hawthorne's work, he notes critically that the American author used to imagine first situations, and then the protagonists who populated them, which inevitably displaces the attention of the reader. Joseph Conrad believed that a protagonist like Schomberg was real, and such a belief permeates his works. This was also the lesson of Cervantes. Borges notes:

> Las aventuras del *Quijote* no están muy bien ideadas, los lentos y antitéticos diálogos—razonamientos, creo que los llama el autor— pecan de inverosímiles, pero no cabe duda que Cervantes conocía bien a Don Quijote y podía creer en él. Nuestra creencia en la creencia del novelista salva todas las negligencias y fallas. ¿Qué importan hechos increíbles o torpes si nos consta que el autor los ha ideado, no para sorprender nuestra buena fe, sino para definir a sus personajes?
>
> II, 182

To Borges' mind, one may sacrifice some aspects of the narrative, one can abuse the credibility of the circumstance, but should not in good literary faith diffuse the recognizable humanity of the protagonist. We recall Borges' observation that giving a character personal, idiosyncratic traits is a good literary habit (I, 397). Borges' lecture on Hawthorne was criticized for being too lengthy and erudite, not for being critically unsound. Before being included in *Obras completas*, this essay was presented in public, an event upon which Borges' reputation, along with other things, depended. Borges, we can be sure, does not make a statement of this nature tongue in cheek.

Borges, of course, claims not to be a novelist, and he, by choice, is not. But he is a writer, and as such he is eminently well qualified to comment on literature. When Borges notes Hawthorne's curious practice of making a protagonist secondary to a circumstance, he adds, not without confidence: "No soy novelista, pero sospecho que ningún novelista ha procedido así" (II, 192). The matter is not one of "simulación psicológica," as Borges put it elsewhere (I, 170). The reader simply relates to the experience of the protagonist, not to the peculiarity of his circumstance. The *kenningar*, one of the earliest manifestations of Icelandic literature, fail to appeal to us because they are skeletal constructs ("descarnada fórmula," I, 347), at best circumstantial hints. "Imposible saber", Borges writes, "con qué inflexión de voz eran dichas, desde qué caras, individuales como una música, con qué admirable decisión o modestia" (I, 347). Again Borges, with his inimitable conciseness: (the *kenningar*) "No invitan a soñar, no procuran imágenes o pasiones: no son un punto de partida, son términos" (I, 336–37). Voice inflection, faces unique like music, emphases, in short, the individuality of human beings, this is what modern man misses in the *kenningar*. The *kenningar* are verbal objects, which makes them into terminal points. Only man, with his passion, can be a point of departure.

Borges' exaltion of individuality is far from sporadic. The quotations on the subject have been deliberately chosen with disregard to chronology in order to illustrate thematic continuity. As early as in 1932, in a cogent essay, "Las versiones homéricas," Borges spoke of an imbalance between circumstance and protagonist in the *Iliad* and the *Odyssey*: "Los hechos de la *Ilíada* y la *Odisea* sobreviven con plenitud, pero han desaparecido Aquiles y Ulises, lo que Homero se representaba al nombrarlos, y lo que en realidad pensó de ellos" (I, 183). Facts cannot replace the dramatic individuality of the two heroes, their internal events. The reader is thus unable to assess the intimate humanity of Achilles and Ulysses, or the true human intention artistically rendered by Homer. Borges observes that one of Browning's books, which consists of ten versions given by ten persons implicated in a crime, although as intense and abysmal as Homer's poems, has a salutary peculiarity: "Todo el contraste deriva de los caracteres, no de los hechos" (I, 183). There is no reason to accumulate more examples. In his synoptic, if eclectic, review of literature, Borges consistently underscores individuality as the central business in literature. The *yo* of the Borgesian protagonist is the symbiotic entity of the *yo* and its circumstance, promoted by Ortega y Gasset. The markedly sociological bent of "nuestro pobre individualismo"—hence the inevitable use of generalities—cannot eclipse Borges' proud insistence on the individuality of the Argentine. The well known statement bears quotation:

> El argentino, a diferencia de los americanos del Norte y de casi todos los europeos, no se identifica con el Estado. Ello puede atribuirse a la circunstancia de que, en este país, los gobiernos pueden ser pésimos o al hecho general de que el Estado es una inconcebible abstracción; lo cierto es que el argentino es un individuo, no un ciudadano.
>
> II, 161

It is therefore understandable that the Argentine cannot tolerate Hegel's notion that the state is the reality of the moral idea, or Hollywood's incomprehensible practice of subordinating or sacrificing personal friendship to institutional justice (II, 161–62). The passion that is friendship for the Argentine is felt for an individual, not for institutions or abstractions, like the mass of the oppressed. "Su héroe popular," Borges says about the Argentine, "es el hombre solo que pelea con la partida, ya en acto (Fierro, Moreira, Hormiga Negra), ya en potencia o en el pasado (Segundo Sombra)" (II, 162). The quintessential Argentine spirit is confirmed by one night in Argentine literature: "esa desesperada noche en la que un sargento de la policía rural gritó que no iba a consentir el delito de que se matara a un valiente y se puso a pelear contra sus soldados, junto al desertor Martín Fierro" (II, 162).

Isidoro Cruz' act is significant in itself and a signal one in Argentine letters. It is its genuineness that gives it such resonance. At the level of action, and in the literature that records such action, the *gaucho* is not a generic type. Borges, we recall, squarely states that in *gaucho* poetry Fierro is the least literarily traditional, the most recognizably individual (I, 108). There is *gaucho* literature, to be sure, but not all the *gauchos* who inhabit it are cosmetic diversifications of a type. Bergson writes: "Because a feeling is generally recognized as true, it does not follow that it is a general feeling."[1] While the term "true" may lend itself to various possibilities of interpretation, it is clear that a feeling, just because it is part of a generic appellation, does not lose its individual validity. Borges' ideas echo Bergson's thought. One of Borges' surprises, upon hearing of the liberation of Paris, is "el descubrimiento de que una emoción colectiva puede no ser innoble" (II, 247). In other words, the nobility of an emotion is not distinguished by the number of people who experience it, but by its individual authenticity. In Borges' characters as in Nietzsche's Apollo, there is an unmistakable *principium individuationis*.[2]

It is in the irony of a statement that we find one of Borges' most poignant defenses of individuality. Lamenting some of the most tellingly stultified aspects of Argentine society, Borges writes at the death of one of his characters:

> Las columnas de los diarios le consagraron largas cronologías, de las que todavía son de rigor en nuestro país, donde la mujer es un ejemplar de la especie, no un individuo.
>
> II, 410

This compilation of emphasized individuality does not pretend to be the central point of Borgesian esthetics, disclaimed by Borges himself (II, 351), but that of an ever fluid preoccupation with life and literature, better said, with the life reflected in literature. The textual evidence is convincing.

Notes

[1] Henri Bergson, "The Object of Art," in *Literary Criticism*, p. 618.
[2] Friedrich Nietzsche, *The Birth of Tragedy and the Genealogy of Morals* (Garden City: Doubleday Anchor, 1956), p. 97.

The I in the Present

The present is the time frame which witnesses the emergence of an event.[1] It is not merely passage of time. The paradox of Achilles and the turtle intrigues Borges not because it corrupts time, as he puts it, but because it suggests incongruent events. We do not perceive the corruption of time, only the incongruity of events. If we accept absolutes we avoid the abyss of the paradox (I, 192), but we also avoid ourselves, individuality, the delicate mirror of the soul. Borges does not abandon his humanity and that of others. Our individuality emerges with an emergent event. Says G. H. Mead:

> Given an emergent event, its relations to antecedent processes become conditions or causes. Such a situation is the present. It marks out and in a sense selects what has made its peculiarity possible. It creates with its uniqueness a past and a future. As soon as we view it, it becomes a history and prophecy. Its own temporal diameter varies with the extent of the event.[2]

To complete Mead's thought: the present emerges not only in actuality, but in ideation as well. The subject chooses the time extension. Borges' beliefs are not dissimilar. The emergence of an event in ideation is brilliantly dealt with in the known quotation from "Kafka y sus precursores": "El hecho es que cada escritor *crea* a sus precursores. Su labor modifica nuestra concepción del pasado, como ha de modificar el futuro" (II, 228). Borges' textual evidence is reliable. The labor of a writer who creates his precursors does not modify the past, only our concept of it. The same with the future. The constructed past is not the real past. In other words, says Mead, even if one gathered all the facts about Julius Caesar, one could not organize them from his present. To understand such a matter, one would have to read not only Mead, but Borges as well. "Pierre Menard, autor del *Quijote*" is the esthetic version of a philosophical point, and equally valid. Again, the clear words of G. H. Mead: "The novelty of every future demands a novel past."[3] This is what gives to Pierre Menard's creation its peculiar meaning.

The time of experience is the present. The past and the future are both outside live experience, that is to say, contact experience. They are not, however, outside what Mead calls distance experience, the experience that unfolds itself in ideation. Time—past, present, future—and the prominent thinkers who have wrestled with it philosophically or metaphysically, engage Borges' attention in "Historia de la eternidad." From this essay, only the elements which find application or expression in Borges' fiction are of concern to us, not the postulates on the nature of time. Even a casual acquaintance with Borges' prose fiction would make clear that he prefers acts to facts, an emergent action to a completed one. Live time can only be experienced in the present, actually or potentially. The expression "en potencia o en acto," educed from Herbert Quain, appears no less than three times in Borges' prose works (I, 453; II, 162; II, 165). The fact closes the horizon of dramatic possibilities, it belongs to the past. A fact cannot be experienced. What is missing is an irretrievable link, the live time of the unfolding act: "Los hechos de la *Ilíada* y la *Odisea* sobreviven con plenitud, pero han desaparecido Aquiles y Ulises, lo que Homero se representaba al nombrarlos, y lo que en realidad pensó de ellos" (I, 183). Since we cannot recreate Homer and his work, we have to "create" them, as in the manner in which Pierre Menard "created" the *Quijote*. Facts can be rather unreliable. In one of Chesterton's *fantasmagorías*, as Borges calls them, a man gives a stranger a violent push, in order to remove him from the path of an oncoming truck. This is the act, the act that, in effect, saves the stranger's life. When it becomes a fact, when it has ceased to emerge, the edge of certainty is blurred. The fact, in this context, records the violence of the act, violence which shall later be adduced as proof of the man's insanity in order to exonerate him from another crime (I, 169–70).

Live time implies freedom, possibilities. Tzinacán, the Aztec priest imprisoned by the conquistador Pedro de Alvarado, attempts to give meaning to his life by drawing from the past. It is not a fulfilling experience: "Noches enteras malgasté en recordar el número de unas serpientes de piedra o la forma de un árbol medicinal" (II, 86). His former vocation and the natural and magical acts that it embodied are now part of the past, useless to him. He finally understands that the present is his destiny, that it is his only vital possibility, that there is freedom in it:

> Más que un descifrador o un vengador, más que un sacerdote del dios, yo era un encarcelado. Del incansable laberinto de sueños yo regresé como a mi casa a la dura prisión.
>
> II, 89

The oneiric quality of the past fails to deliver any vital justification to the present. This, of course, does not mean that Tzinacán denies the existence of his past, only that such a past cannot be a valid substitute for the present. The present, as Tzinacán beautifully expresses it, is the cause and the effect fused into one (II, 89). Flaubert does not explain the acts of Bouvard and Pécuchet. Like Spencer, of whom he was rather fond, he believes that to explain is to refer something to ever-receding generalities (I, 208). This is why Bouvard and Pécuchet live in the present, submerged in acts. This has disconcerted some critics, who have seen in Flaubert's novel a failure of sorts. Predictably, Borges is of another opinion:

> El tiempo de *Bouvard et Pécuchet* se inclina a la eternidad; por eso, los protagonistas no mueren y seguirán copiando, cerca de Caen, su anacrónico *Sottisier*, tan ignorantes de 1914 como de 1870.
>
> I, 209

Without going into the nature of eternity, it suffices to say that the live present, not the memories of the past or the ideation of the future, is what validates the experiences of Bouvard and Pécuchet. Nor is literary immortality necessary in order to explore the possibilities of the present. Funes, like Bouvard and Pécuchet, trapped in a relentless present composes his own *Sottisier*. María Justina Rubio de Jáuregui, in "La señora mayor," is a protagonist whose existence is almost entirely fused with the present. She was (like) one of the begonias that she cultivated (II, 403). María Justina is close to the mystery:

> Decir que la señora de Jáuregui pasó diez años en un caos tranquilo es acaso un error; cada instante de esos diez años puede haber sido un puro presente, sin antes ni después.
>
> II, 403

It is a matter of perception, not of denial of the past. Borges elaborates:

> No nos maravillemos demasiado de ese presente que contamos por días y por noches y por los centenares de hojas y de muchos calendarios y por ansiedades y hechos; es el que atravesamos cada mañana antes de recordarnos y cada noche antes del sueño.
>
> II, 403

In order to retrieve such an experience from uniqueness, he adds: "Todos los días somos dos veces la señora mayor" (II, 403). We are either oblivious or fearful to recognize it.

Borges opts for the present because the present is the least conventional of our temporal conventions. It would be difficult not to descry conviction in these words of Borges: "Cada momento que vivimos existe, no su imaginario conjunto" (II, 290). Borges is not unduly complicated here. The first part of the sentence defines, almost perfectly, the meaning of experience. The second part is complementary, pointing out not so much the inexistence of a whole as our inability to comprehend it. Borges imputes to Hawthorne the pantheistic belief that a man is all men (II, 181). Commenting on F. H. Bradley's arguments in *Appearance and Reality*, Borges states unequivocally: "Tales razonamientos, como se ve, niegan las partes para luego negar el todo; yo rechazo el todo para exaltar cada una de las partes" (II, 299). Borges does not deny the whole in the same way as Bradley does. He simply states that the whole, as organized and conceived by man, is imaginary. Borges' St. Augustine, speaking of the meaning of totality in a poem, states that such totality reflects, in essence, the dynamics of each verse, each syllable. He writes:

> Lo que sucede con la totalidad del poema, sucede con cada verso y con cada sílaba. Digo lo mismo, de la acción más larga de la que forma parte el poema, y del destino individual, que se compone de una serie de acciones, y de la humanidad, que es una serie de destinos individuales.
>
> I, 330

Three of the main religions of the world—Judaism, Christianity, and Islam—circumscribe the first century as the beginning of salvation, ignoring or ascribing lesser importance to the others. There is, in Borges' view, unreasonable certainty in such a point of view. Hinduism, by contrast, does not single out any beginning or any end. To be sure, Hinduism has a law of causality, but it is a law whose mechanism remains unknown to us.

> Más razonable me parece la rueda de ciertas religiones del Indostán; en esa rueda, que no tiene principio ni fin, cada vida es efecto de la anterior y engendra la siguiente, pero ninguna determina el conjunto.
>
> II, 18

We can now appreciate why Borges rejects a whole arbitrarily conceived by the human mind. To elevate a fact or a period of time to the rank of justification of the whole supposes risk and irresponsibility. Borges' Marcus Aurelius, it shall be recalled, knows that in matters of religion there is no novelty without risk (II, 31). Borges chooses the present because it authenticates experience. But Borges, we should remind ourselves, is not a philosopher, only a man fond of philosophizing. He is, above all, a writer. In the epilog to *Otras inquisiciones*, with exemplary honesty and clarity, Borges states that the purpose of the volume is that of evaluating religious and philosophical ideas

esthetically, which is consonant with his literary praxis: "A
estimar las ideas religiosas o filosóficas por su valor estético y
aún por lo que encierran de singular y de maravilloso" (II, 304).
This is the quintessential Borges. He is not reluctant to enter-
tain generalities, but prefers to consider them esthetically.
When he looks for the wondrous and the particular in such
ideas, Borges is firmly on the ground of literature. No careful
reader of Borges' fiction will fail to notice the individuality of
Borgesian protagonists, their incessant affirmation of it.

Dealing with the present is a form of avoiding the invention
of continuities, of pasts or futures. It is, undoubtedly, not
without irony that in "Historia de la eternidad" Borges speaks
of eternities, "Las varias eternidades que planearon los hombres" (I, 317). No less ironical is Borges about Leibniz, the
inventor of preestablished harmony. To invent, like Leibniz,
"la armonía preestablecida" (I, 491), is to invent a questionable
continuity. The choice of terms is unequivocal here. Had
Borges said that Leibniz "discovered" the universal harmony
in question, he would have credited Leibniz with having
recovered a truth. Instead, he uses the word "invented," thus
removing the possibility of objectivity from the German philosopher's concept. The present marks the interaction between
the self and what, for better or worse, we have to call reality.
The present constitutes the fundamental relation between the
past and the future.[4] If Borges imputes anything to classical
literature, it is that experience is inferred—but not contained—
in the narrative. The classic writer, "no escribe los primeros
contactos de la realidad, sino su elaboración final en concepto"
(I, 154). Live time is absent, and so the I. According to Mead,
experience is individual. To paraphrase the statement, experience is an individual, an individual is experience. Borges
himself puts matters as follows:

El tiempo es la sustancia de que estoy hecho. El tiempo es un río que me
arrebata, pero yo soy el río; es un tigre que me destroza, pero yo soy el
tigre; es un fuego que me consume, pero yo soy el fuego.

                                                              II, 300

The present, however, although the medium in which individuality emerges, does not offer man unlimited access to reality. "Para ver una cosa," says Borges towards the end of his productive literary career, "hay que comprenderla" (II, 489). Funes, the memorious, saw but did not—could not—understand. Some events in history retain their secret meaning: "Tácito no percibió la Crucifixión, aunque la registra su libro" (II, 280). Among Borges' early poems, there is one which states an opinion which in due time became conviction: "El tiempo está viviéndome" (*Obras*, 62).

Reality and experience are not one and the same thing. At best, experience is a fragmentary perception of reality, a partial interaction. If there is a philosophical doctrine that Borges repudiates firmly, it is that of realism, "doctrina tan apartada de nuestro ser que descreo de todas sus interpretaciones" (I, 328). Again, a cautionary note. Borges rejects a doctrine of reality, not reality as such. Materialism gained authority as a result of Newton's mechanics (mass, weight, volume), and dominated human thought for an extended period of time. Says G. H. Mead:

> It has been customary to find the reality of the perception in the experience of the individual, and there have arisen all the multiform difficulties in placing the individual experience in the reality of the world to which he belongs.[5]

It was simpler, G. H. Mead assures us, to state that the real thing lies behind subjective, phenomenal experience. Unlike Mead, a scientist, Borges contemplates the matter in inverted order. His primary interest is the individual and his experience, not the object of experience called reality. The discovery of the laws of thermodynamics and of electro-magnetism, to draw again from Mead, has partly invalidated the universality of Newtonian mechanics, as has done relativity.[6] If nothing is gained and nothing is lost, as Lavoisier's law has it, then in the endless cycle of cause and effect the past is retrievable. Borges brings to the fore Nietzsche's reasoning in order to throw doubt on the theory of the Eternal Return:

Nietzsche recurre a la energía; la segunda ley de la termodinámica declara que hay procesos energéticos que son irreversibles. El calor y la luz no son más que formas de energía. Basta proyectar una luz sobre una superficie negra para que se convierta en calor. El calor, en cambio, ya no volverá a la forma de luz. Esa comprobación, de aspecto inofensivo o insípido, anula el "laberinto circular" del Eterno Retorno.

I, 362

Having presented both sides of the proposition, Borges takes refuge in a metaphysical uncertainty which remains fecund in literary possibilities. In these possibilities, not in the demise of the universe according to the law of thermodynamics, does Borges search for meaning. The hypothetical uniformity of the world as Tlön does not concern Borges:

Yo no hago caso, yo sigo revisando en los quietos días del hotel de Adrogué una indecisa traducción quevediana (que no pienso dar a la imprenta) del *Urn Burial* de Browne.

I, 424

If we discount the passage of time, individuality is lost.[7] Borges, as we have seen, does not deny the passage of time. On the contrary, he affirms it as the essence of individuality. Strictly scientific propositions do not appeal to Borges. One cannot do literature with abstractions, with matters that address themselves only to our "entendimiento aritmético," to use Borges' own words. Live time is needed. An intellectual operation detached from individualized humanity can be misleading. G. H. Mead states:

We are subject to a psychological illusion if we assume that the rhythms of counting and the order which arises out of counting answers to a structure of passage itself.[8]

In "La doctrina de los ciclos" Borges allows Georg Cantor to destroy the foundation of Nietzsche's thesis:

La operación de contar no es otra cosa para él que la de equiparar dos series. Por ejemplo, si los primogénitos de todas las casas de Egipto fueron matados por el Angel, salvo los que habitaban en casa que tenía

en la puerta una señal roja, es evidente que tantos se salvaron como
señales rojas había, sin que esto importe enumerar cuántos fueron.

I, 356

Borges continues: "El roce del hermoso juego de Cantor con el
hermoso juego de Zarathustra es mortal para Zarathustra"
(I, 358). If the universe contains an infinite number of terms,
then such terms can be infinitely combined—which annihilates
the Eternal Return. Personal mortality displaces personal immortality. Borges accepts Nietzsche only when the latter reduces the certainty of his theory to a mere regenerative
possibility (I, 361). That is to say, when literature is possible
again. When Borges says that all writers are but one, he teases
us with a sociological formulation of literature. When, however, he mentions that "One" is a diversification of "ones,"
from De Quincey to Cansinos-Asséns, we know that he does
not do sociology of literature, but literature. Pater, occasionally
cited by Borges, writes that any theory, idea or system which
invites us to sacrifice any part of the experience for the sake of
an abstraction should have no real claim upon us.[9] In such
instances, Borges speaks with authority. Arnold Hauser considers art to be superior to philosophy, because it does not
dwell on oppositions. The opposition between the totality and
the particularity of elements is a conflictive one in philosophy;
not so in the work of art, where the opposition, although
occasionally present, does not lead to conflict with unity.[10]
Borges pointedly quotes G. B. Shaw who, in his *Guide to
Socialism*, states that the sum total of human suffering does not
really exist for it is an abstraction: "la tal suma no existe"
(II, 291). In art, the parts and the whole are not in conflict.
Hauser states: "Sólo aquí late en ellos la misma vida que en el
organismo del que son miembros." Borges, instinctively,
knows this.

Notes

[1] Mead, p. 23.
[2] Ibid., p. 23.

[3] Ibid., p. 31.

[4] Ibid., p. 37.

[5] Ibid., p. 60.

[6] Ibid., p. 150.

[7] Ibid., p. 176.

[8] Ibid., p. 22.

[9] Walter Horatio Pater, conclusion to "Studies in the History of Renaissance," in *Literary Criticism*, pp. 526–37.

[10] Arnold Hauser, *Dialéctica de lo estético*, 2nd ed. (Madrid: Ediciones Guadarrama, 1977), p. 305.

The Anachronic Present

Man's obsession with the sequential equation of cause and effect leads to a perennial misunderstanding of history. An intellectual's attitude vis-a-vis this matter determines, in Borges' view, the authenticity of his vocation. Reality, *grosso modo*, is not the present: "De ahí que el verdadero intelectual rehuya los debates contemporáneos: la realidad es siempre anacrónica" (II, 245). We understand now why Funes, the memorious, cannot be an intellectual. He simply cannot detach himself from the present. The anachronism that Borges speaks about is not really a component of reality, but of our attitude about reality. The philosophical and metaphysical dimensions of the proposition, as well as Borges' erudition on the subject, have generated ample and competent critical attention. Not so the historical implications and the esthetic possibilities and limitations of the issue, which deserve further consideration.

The observation that reality is always anachronous belongs to Bertrand Russell who, in "The Genealogy of Fascism," quoted by Borges, postulates that political and historical events are factual projections of past doctrines. Borges does not disagree with Bertrand Russell; if anything, he improves upon the latter, who evinced some timidity in expressing the matter (II, 246). It is not surprising that Borges titles one of his essays on history "El pudor de la historia." To personify history is to endow it with human attributes, to make it understandable not as an objective phenomenon but as human experience.

Borges believes that there are two histories (like the visible and the invisible arguments in Hudson's *The Purple Land*, the second part of the *Quijote*, or *The Adventures of Huckleberry Finn*), one made of contrived events, the other of events and dates. Often such dates remain secret for extended periods of time, which places in question the reality that the present is supposed to represent. Tacitus, Borges notes, did not perceive the Crucifixion, although he was a contemporary of the passion and death of Jesus Christ. The Greeks who, perhaps not without indignation, witnessed the emergence of another actor in Eschylus' plays, could not have foreseen the birth of Hamlets, Fausts, Segismundos, Macbeths, and Peer Gynts, and those yet to come.

Harold Sigurdarson had only a vague intimation of what the end of one day in 1225 would later mean when he, at the head of a Norwegian army, attempted to unseat Harold, the Saxon King of England. He did not know that a nation was to emerge. The secret dates of history reveal their true reality later, according to dynamics which Borges describes as follows: "No el día en que el rey sajón dijo sus palabras, sino aquél en que un enemigo las perpetuó marca una fecha histórica" (II, 283). The true history of the event, we are told, began not when the English monarch uttered it, but when an Irishman, of the blood of the defeated, recognized and perpetuated its greatness. It is, in fact, Snorri Sturluson, the narrator, who dates the event, so to speak, not Harold. The courage of a handful of German soldiers battling the British is recognized as such not when it is perpetrated but when Lawrence, in the *Seven Pilars of Wisdom*, perceives its meaning.

Like a gold nugget or a precious stone which, although real, remains hidden in the ground until discovered, facts become significant only when meaning is attached to them. It is this temporal discrepancy that renders the present anachronous. It is a form of hope. It is a date in which Borges has faith: "Una fecha de algo profético que aún está en el futuro: el olvido de sangres y de naciones, la solidaridad del género humano" (II, 283). Few of Borges' statements can rival this one in the beauty of its sincerity. Such a future, Borges tells us with his fondness for the paradox, already exists in Saxus Grammaticus' *Gesta Danorum*: "A los hombres de Thule (Islandia) les deleita aprender y registrar la historia de todos los pueblos y no tienen por menos glorioso publicar las excelencias ajenas que las propias" (II, 283).

The title that Borges chose for his essay and the examples listed and commented upon lead to a challenging proposition: that the true significance of an event is revealed by literature rather than by history, by esthetic rather than historical facts. History fragments human experience, literature unifies it. What ultimately redeems history is not historicity but the emotion esthetically presented (I, 136). Needless to say, the events of history do not survive as an historical reality but as an esthetic one: "En el tiempo hubo un día que apagó los últimos ojos que vieron a Cristo; la batalla de Junín y el amor de Helena murieron con la muerte de un hombre" (II, 331–32). Asks Borges ruefully: "¿Qué morirá conmigo cuando yo muera, qué forma patética y deleznable perderá el mundo?" (II, 332). Borges and his friend—his body (II, 363)—will die, but not his literature. The witness, in the essay "El testigo", will die, and with him "las últimas imágenes inmediatas de los ritos paganos" (II, 331). The words bear close scrutiny: the last immediate images will die, not the rites themselves; they would endure in tradition, in literature, in Borges' essay. The heroic, the greatness of man, survives in the same manner. The term heroic, here, should be stripped of any social or political connotation. Exhortations to etymological purity are not infrequent in Borges' work (I, 153). Heroic in Borges is the epithet which describes the best moments of the human being (II, 273), a vital justification. This is not Carlyle's exultation of heroism as a means of political leadership, but the esthetic recognition of an elemental human quality (II, 282). For Borges such an esthetic encomium of valor is to be found in the *Poema del Cid*, in the *Aeneid* ("Hijo, aprende de mi valor y firmeza; de otros el éxito," II, 282), in the Anglo Saxon ballad of Maldon, in *Chanson de Rolland*, in Victor Hugo, in Whitman, in Faulkner, in Houseman (II, 282).

Factual reality and its esthetic perception and rendition are not concomitant: "el hecho estético sólo puede ocurrir cuando lo escriben o lo leen" (II, 352). Our ordinary images of phenomena or objects are staggered. "La imagen que tenemos de la ciudad," Borges writes in "El indigno," "siempre es algo anacrónica" (II, 377). It is not only an intellectual proposition. Borges' own experience is illustrative: "Así, yo creí durante muchos años que a determinada altura de Talcahuano me esperaba la Librería Buenos Aires; una mañana comprobé que la había reemplazado un casa de antigüedades" (II, 377). This is why the present is anachronous, this is why chronology is irrelevant. There are two esthetic facts, that of the writer and that of the reader, even if both are generated by the same factitiousness. The reader's esthetic fact is not merely a reconstruction of the author's esthetic fact, but an act of creation premised on his individuality. The esthetic act has individualized human authenticity. The esthetic fact is a significant present. History books have not only the bad habit of fabricating historical dates (II, 280), but also that of appending memorable sentences to events: "Salvo en las severas páginas de la Historia, los hechos memorables prescinden de frases memorables" (II, 461). The soldiers who are about to die in combat talk about the mud on their boots and the unreasonableness of their commander, not about metaphysical issues, (II, 461). The present of history is not as reliable as the esthetic present. Borges' words are as encompassing as they are pellucidly clear: ". . . la fijación cronológica de un suceso, de cualquier suceso del orbe, es ajena a él, y exterior" (II, 298).

Borges reiterates the notion that man does not really understand time. The only aspect of time that man purports to understand is chronology. It is, alas, a self-deluding proposition. Chronology, rendered unreliable by cultural diversity (Buddhist chronology does not coincide with, say, Christian chronology), fails to provide a continuity. The present that is, is not the present that was or that will be. The present that was survives in the present that is as elevated or debased symbols (II, 335). The matter is succinctly dealt with in an essay suggestively titled "Mutaciones." The perfect present—not the grammatical tense but a hypothetical entity—would be a time without time. Borges, in his much celebrated hallucinatory night in Buenos Aires, has a fleeting metaphysical glimpse of it, and Avelino Arredondo, one of his characters, almost attains it (II, 526). Mystics of all faiths have claimed throughout the centuries to have experienced it. Ordinary people, however, have a different temporal perception of the present: "A uno le suceden las cosas y uno las va entendiendo con los años" (II, 384). When such an understanding is put into artistic form, we have an esthetic fact. Borges' night in Buenos Aires is an act; his description of it, anachronously formulated, is an esthetic fact: "Sólo después alcancé a definir esa imaginación" (I, 332). For Borges, literature is the esthetic defining of an imagining.

The best of Borges' short stories are constructed along these lines. In "El jardín de los senderos que se bifurcan" Yu Tsun, the Chinese whose misguided patriotism transforms him into a German spy, murders Stephen Albert, a British sinologist. This is the fact, a fact yet to be rendered esthetically. When it is, we have a short story. Within the story, Ts'ui Pên's labyrinth remains a fact, a strange fact, until Stephen Albert shapes it esthetically. Here is the dynamics of the metamorphosis: "¡Un laberinto de marfil!—exclamé. Un laberinto mínimo . . .—Un laberinto de símbolos—corrigió" (I, 469). Only when Albert transcends the mere facticity of the labyrinth, when he perceives the symbolic intention of Ts'ui Pên, does he elevate the matter to esthetic significance. The letter that contributes to the elucidation of the mystery can be interpreted analogously. Stephen Albert elucidates: "Antes de exhumar esa carta, yo me había preguntado de qué manera un libro puede ser infinito. No conjeturé otro procedimiento que el de un volumen cíclico, circular" (I, 470). Albert, however, is unable to reconcile the contradictory chapters of the book with logic. When he reads in the manuscript, "*Dejo a los varios porvenires (no a todos) un jardín de senderos que se bifurcan*" (I, 470), he realizes that the bifurcation in question is realized in time, not in space. The philosophical issue is dressed in esthetic clothing. It is also a lesson in literary interpretation as a creative act:

En todas las ficciones, cada vez que un hombre se enfrenta con diversas alternativas, opta por una y elimina las otras; en la del casi inexplicable Ts'ui Pên opta—simultáneamente—por otras. *Crea, así, diversos porvenires, diversos tiempos, que también proliferan y se bifurcan"*

I, 470

"Tema del traidor y del heroe" is an esthetic version of some events which took place in Ireland in 1824. It is, in fact, the esthetic version of another esthetic version authored by Ryan, grandson of Fergus Kilpatrick, conspirator and protagonist. There is also the version of Nolan, the man who discovers the truth about Kilpatrick, the man who interprets history esthetically. To be sure, the most esthetic—and also the most truthful—of all versions is that of Borges, who breaks out of the circularity perpetuated by the others. In other words, Borges' is not a mere spin-off version of Nolan's works, not the specious image of an image (I, 329), but an imagining, a voluntary dream, a story that holds within itself a coherent notion of what the craft of literature is all about. "La muerte y la brújula" is, in recognizable ways, similar to "El jardín de los senderos que se bifurcan." Some elements are ordered differently. Scharlach, rather than Lönnrot, imparts to the present of the story an esthetic reality which the latter, fatally, mistakes for his own. The mere facts are utterly misleading. Perhaps the importance of the esthetic fact is nowhere presented with more paradigmatic force than in "El milagro secreto." The story begins not with the factual reality of the present, but with another present, a dream. The dream epitomizes the anachronism of the present. Let us follow the beginning of the story. Retrieved from the rigor of logic, the dream, in this case, magnifies false continuities. In Hladik's dream, the Judaic tradition, like the Islamic one that it confronts, in its quest for righteousness, does not receive a validation for its purpose from the past. The two illustrious families are engaged in a protracted game of chess:

La partida había sido entablada hace muchos siglos; nadie era capaz de nombrar el olvidado premio, pero se murmuraba que era enorme y quizás infinito; las piezas y el tablero estaban en una torre secreta.

I, 507

The issue is framed brilliantly:

> Jaromir (en el sueño) era el primogénito de una de las familias hostiles; en los relojes resonaba la hora de la impostergable jugada; el soñador corría por las arenas de un desierto lluvioso y no lograba recordar las figuras ni las leyes del ajedrez. En este punto, se despertó.

I, 507

The parenthetical note shows that Borges carefully sets Jaromir's oneiric experience apart from the actual present. From the esthetic fact he returns to the present. Arrested by the Gestapo, condemned to death, Hladik will create for himself an esthetic present, a voluntary dream. It is the only dignity left to him. Hence the esthetic necessity. The esthetic fact, as Borges calls it, "esta inminencia de una revelación, que no se produce" (II, 133), is an unfulfilled possibility.[1] Hladik's successive esthetic acts—the hundreds of anticipatory deaths (I, 508)—remain a promise, but that is sufficient. In spite of transient moments of despair, Hladik continues his "vana tarea de imaginar" (I, 509). Let us follow Hladik's reasoning.

That which is impossible, indeed absurd, is his inability to exhaust all such possibilities. The esthetic imminence is actualized only in death. Prudently, Borges ends the story here. Technically, "El sur" reflects the same resolution of two realities: Dahlmann's death occurs in a hospital room; the esthetic revelation is an imagined eventful voyage down south. Again, Borges brings the story to an end. He does not depart from recognizable human experience. When he does, he makes the transition obvious. "El final de la historia", says Borges in "Los teólogos:, "sólo es referible en metáforas, ya que pasa en el reino de los cielos, donde no hay tiempo" (II, 37). We now know that Borges has extricated himself from the story, that whatever follows is just a personal point of view, like any reader's, that he does not confer any claim to organicity to his afterthought.

As actualized by experience, literature is distinct from history. Also, the inventions of literature are dissimilar to those of history. In Borges' understanding, literature implies a double invention: that of episodes, and that of the feelings of the protagonist (I, 127). It is in grafting upon an event the feelings or the ethical strictures of an historical figure that historians betray history. This is the nature of the anachronism that marks history. The "invention" discredits the objectivity of the event. The events of literature do not pretend to be actual reality or anything else, for that matter; they are esthetic facts. The good literary "invention" emphasizes the protagonist rather than the event. Hernández is indeed telling us the story of Martín Fierro, and the protagonist's character is to be found in the story. Let us quote:

> La fornida pelea con el negro, en el canto séptimo, no corresponde ni a la sensación de pelear ni a las momentáneas luces y sombras que rinden la memoria de un hecho, sino al paisano Martín Fierro contándola.
>
> I, 126

And again:

> Su tema—lo repito—no es la imposible presentación de todos los hechos que atravesaron la conciencia de un hombre, ni tampoco la desfigurada, mínima parte que de ellos puede rescatar el recuerdo, sino la narración del paisano, el hombre que se muestra al contar.
>
> I, 127

It is a beautiful apology of the esthetic fact. In a way, it is also the apology of the short story.

The short story accommodates Borges' intention because, such as it stands, it deals with a single event which individualizes the protagonist. Borges agrees with Nietzsche that it is impossible to fathom the complexities of the human conscience and experience. Memory, of whose retentive virtues Borges is forever diffident, is not a witness to reality, but a retrospective interpreter of it. Borges' memory of Beatriz Viterbo, in "El Aleph", is not equivalent to history: "yo mismo estoy falseando y perdiendo, bajo la trágica erosión de los años, los rasgos de Beatriz" (II, 125). Borges' story is not about Beatriz' traits but about Beatriz' character. His recourse is not to reproduce an historical facsimile of Beatriz, only an esthetic representation of her. The perfect present is only in the present, just as the perfect past can only be in the past. Funes' attempt at living only in the present—perception without reflection— is not only frustrating, it is utterly useless as well (I, 483). He cannot reason, he is incapable of esthetic facts. Esthetically, the present is an actualized past, yet a creation more than a recreation. Contemporaneity with an event does not generate any particular wisdom. Perhaps this is why, as Borges observes, Samuel Johnson did not like to owe or acknowledge any debt to his contemporaries: "Quizá obró bien; quizá nuestros contemporáneos—siempre—se parecen demasiado a nosotros, y quien busca novedades las hallará con más facilidad en los antiguos" (II, 190). This is Borgesian alchemy. The timid, inchoative *quizá* is overwhelmed by the adverb *siempre*, diacritically emphasized in the text. "Always," here, has the negative meaning of never, that is to say, one can never learn anything from his contemporaries. Such a claim may, of course, be debated, but Borges is making a point: the esthetic resolutions of the old masters overshadow the pretenses of history.

Notes

[1] Mead, p. 173.

Waiting for the Present

The vicissitudes of our meaningful perception of the present are best expressed in "Biografía de Tadeo Isidoro Cruz." Says Borges about Cruz:

> Lo esperaba, secreta en el provenir, una lúcida noche fundamental: la noche en que por fin vio su propia cara, la noche en que por fin oyó su nombre. Bien entendida, esa noche agota su historia; mejor dicho, un instante de esa noche, un acto de esa noche, porque los actos son nuestros símbolos.
>
> II, 43–44

Borges continues:

> Cualquier destino, por largo y complicado que sea, consta en realidad de *un solo momento*: el momento en que el hombre sabe para siempre quién es.
>
> II, 44

Tadeo Isidoro Cruz, like Tzinacán, "se vió a sí mismo" (II, 44). Whoever wishes to understand Borges' art, to grasp the meaning of Borges' seemingly abstracted literary protagonists and their social dislocation, has to begin by accepting his statement about Tadeo Isidoro Cruz as pivotal. Visual infirmity aside, Borges' preference for the short story over lengthier narratives finds its eloquent expression here. Borges, to use the words that he himself applies to H. G. Wells, presents in his concise stories an "essential humanity" (II, 244). All of Borges' characters, wittingly or unwittingly, wait for a present, for the one which justifies their humanity, and all of them justify their humanity in fulfilling that present. With the notable exception of Funes, whose relentless perception of the present is without emotional emphasis, the Borgesian protagonist imposes itself to the attention of the reader through an existential act.[1] While in the case of Tadeo Isidoro Cruz the essential existential act is not anticipated, in that of most Borgesian protagonists the significant present is foreseen or planned. This is a Borgesian constant. In this respect, the chronology of Borges' short stories is irrelevant: any compilation will do. "La espera," "Emma Zunz," "Muerte en el umbral," "El jardín de los senderos que se bifurcan," "La muerte y la brújula," "El milagro secreto," all but Borges' last volumes in prose, where the expectation replaces the existential act, are collections of stories in which the protagonist waits for the essential present.

The story in which waiting for the present, with all the attendant implications, comes to the fore, is "El fin." The title itself is highly significant, because the end—*el fin*—does not bespeak the death of the protagonist, only the meaninglessness of his life, once the act of existential self-justification is committed. A black man presents himself at a country store and stays on, as if waiting for someone ("como a la espera de alguien," I, 521). Days pass by without affecting his consciousness. Absent-mindedly playing the guitar, he waits for the "right" present. From the endless plain, a horseman finally materializes and enters the store:

> Sin alzar los ojos del instrumento, donde parecía buscar algo, el negro dijo con dulzura: —Ya sabía yo, señor, que podía contar con usted./ El otro, con voz áspera, replicó: —Y yo con vos, moreno. Una porción de años te hice esperar, pero aquí he venido./ Hubo un silencio. Al fin, el negro respondió:—Me estoy acostumbrando a esperar. He esperado siete años.
>
> I, 522

In the ensuing knife fight, the black man kills Fierro. The man is finished:

> Cumplida su tarea de justiciero, ahora era nadie. Mejor dicho era el otro: no tenía destino sobre la tierra y había matado un hombre.
>
> I, 524

Having justified himself in a meaningful present, the black man is dead, his consciousness indifferent to the series of presents awaiting him. "El fin" was published in 1944, in *Artificios*. There is another story, "Avelino Arredondo," which appeared in Borges' last prose volume, *El libro de arena* (1975), that echoes the "waiting for the present" theme. Arredondo's only vital ambition, his *raison d'être*, is that of assassinating Juan Idiarte Borda, president of Uruguay, who is ruining the country in an endless egotistical war. With singularity of purpose, Arredondo will sacrifice all his successive presents—largely unsolicited moments—to his aim, will mobilize all his vital and spiritual reserves in order to plan and live the only present which matters to him. Saturdays spent at the Café del Globo, the friends who accepted his reserved presence, even Clara, his fiancée, all recede from his consciousness in order to accommodate a chosen present:

> Sabía que su meta era la mañana del día de veinticinco de agosto. Sabía el número preciso de días que tenía que trasponer. Una vez lograda la meta, el tiempo cesaría, o mejor dicho, nada importaba lo que aconteciera después.
>
> II, 524

Borges' meaning is clear, exemplary. He does not claim that time would stop, any more than he traversed the waters of time upstream during his celebrated hallucinatory night in Buenos Aires. In the first instance, only the expectation of what time can bring ceases to impinge upon his consciousness. In the second, Borges understands the meaning of a word, eternity, not eternity itself. Until the desired present arrives, Arredondo has to fill up his time, "Para poblar el tiempo" (II, 525). On occasion, Arredondo achieves mystical moments of detachment:

> Para el encarcelado o el ciego, el tiempo fluye aguas abajo, como por una leve pendiente. Al promediar su reclusión Arredondo logró más de una vez ese tiempo casi sin tiempo.
>
> II, 526

When the desired day finally arrives, Arredondo's dream comes true: *"Adiós a la tarea de esperar"* (II, 526–27). His present is at hand. He calmly kills the president, calling the fact an act of justice under the sole determination of his will. The political reason for Arredondo's act is unimportant here; his need to justify himself through a single, essential act is not. It is not another triviality that fills up his time, it is the deed which gives meaning to his life, the only present that matters.

There is no need to observe a rigid chronology while dealing with the "right" present in Borges. The theme surfaces tenaciously. "El milagro secreto," for instance, was written in 1943. In this literary dream of Borges, Hladik awaits his present. Prague, where the protagonist, Hladik, lives, is being occupied by the Panzer divisions of the Third Reich. Denounced to the Gestapo, Hladik, as we know, will be shot by a firing squad. Borges' words are indispensable here:

> El primer sentimiento de Hladik fue de mero terror. Pensó que no lo hubiera arredrado la horca, la decapitación o el degüello, pero que morir fusilado era intolerable. En vano se dijo que el acto puro y general de morir era lo temible, no las circunstancias concretas. No se cansaba de imaginar esas circunstancias concretas: absurdamente procuraba agotar todas las variaciones. Anticipaba infinitamente el proceso, desde el insomne amanecer hasta la misteriosa descarga.
>
> I, 508

Borges continues: "Miserable en la noche, procuraba afirmarase de algún modo en la sustancia fugitiva del tiempo" (I, 508). Far from wishing to lose himself in time, Hladik seeks a consequential moment in it, the moment that can justify him and God (I, 510). It is the completion to perfection of a drama, "Los enemigos," which coincides with his death by Nazi bullets. Hladik needs that moment, a year in the psychological time of his consciousness, "la posibilidad de rescatar (de manera simbólica) lo fundamental de su vida" (I, 510). Death, the inevitable death, will signal to Hladik that his work is finished. When the anticipated death becomes actual death, Hladik's imagining comes to an end, his "vana tarea de imaginar" (I, 509) ceases to serve a purpose.

There is little to be gained from analysing other stories, like "Emma Zunz" o "El jardín de los senderos que se bifurcan," in terms of waiting for the present. This is what Emma Zunz and Yu Tsun conspicuously do. What should be emphasized, however, is that the waiting in question is not the passive waiting for Godot, to mention Beckett's play, but the forging of a "present" which will be isolated from reality. In other words, Borges' characters would have invented a Godot and would have imposed him on reality, oneirically or otherwise. The old man in "Las ruinas circulares" does precisely that. When Borges speaks of Hladik's "vain task of imagining," the adjective applies to the outcome rather than to the process of the activity. To be sure, Hladik cannot avoid his death, for that is extraneous to his will. What he can do and does, however, is to infuse meaning in his life, to create a present that can stand up to death. Sometimes the present sought does not correspond to the dream that generated it, and such failures are inherently human. Benjamín Otálora ("El muerto") or Lönnrot ("La muerte y la brújula") create dreams that reality does not accommodate, presents that fail to become *the* present.

The short story as literary format of expression lends its brevity to the intention of the author.[2] Since the Borgesian protagonists focus their vitality on the redemption of a single act of identity, the story cannot but be short. The series of presents which follow the capital one is of no interest, as the protagonist, an Avelino Arredondo or an Emma Zunz, for example, ceases to be existentially active, ceases to insert his or her humanity into the circumstance. The *yo*, to avail ourselves of Ortega y Gasset's formula of "yo soy yo y mi circunstancia," voluntarily detaches itself from the circumstance. One cannot make literature with someone whom the reader is unable to recognize as a human being, with ghosts. Death, in the case of Avelino Arredondo, to give but one example, will be a mere fact. To concatenate all the presents that lead to the essential one is either to deal in trivia or to suggest a determinism which detracts from the individuality of the character. "No modifica nuestra esencia los años, si es que alguna tenemos" (II, 471).

Such an essence, latent in the course of routinary life, is thrust to the fore by an extraordinary circumstance or a willed act. How the black man waits for Martín Fierro in "El fin" is of negligible literary value. "Se pasaba las horas con la guitarra," Borges notes flatly. Before receiving the letter notifying her of her father's death, Emma Zunz is a non-entity. This is poignantly brought forth when the issue of Emma's sentimental life surfaces. When Elsa, and the youngest daughter of the Kronfuss discuss dates, the vital preoccupation of young people, nobody expects Emma to comment:

> Luego, se habló de novios y nadie esperó que Emma hablara. En abril cumpliría diecinueve años, pero los hombres le insipiraban, aún, un temor casi patológico . . .
>
> II, 47

If Borges had capitalized on Emma's pathological fear of men, if such a fear were central to causal determinism, then Borges would have written a different story. The Emma of the story, as we know, in a complete about face, seeks out a man and allows herself to be possessed in order to build an alibi. The natural causal process is the result of "incontrolables e infinitas operaciones" (I, 170). To deal in it is to resort to psychological simulation (I, 170). Borges eschews such a simulation. He prefers another causal process, a magic one, "donde profetizan los pormenores, lúcido y limitado" (I, 170). In "Emma Zunz" and elsewhere, Borges remains faithful to such a process. As he puts it, it is a matter of honesty (I, 170). Nothing significant would be learned from Yu Tsun's career as a high school teacher of English in Tsingtao, or even from his reluctant career as a spy for Germany. Only after he finds out that his comrade, Runeberg, has been arrested by the British police, only when he knows that he will have a similar fate, does Yu Tsun decide on the present that will justify him in his own eyes. The fate that awaits him after the assassination of Stephen Albert, which gives the Germans the name of the British artillery park, is of no importance to Yu Tsun and to the reader. Borges, diffident of psychological simulation, mentions

Yu Tsun's "innumerable contrición y cansancio" (I, 473) but does not elaborate on it literarily.

Borges' preference for a significant present exhibits two characteristics. At the level of action, he circumscribes an event that leads the protagonist to the deliberate choice of a present, a present not foreseen by rigorous causality. Once the protagonist imposes such a present on himself and on reality, he ceases to be of interest to himself or to Borges. The other characteristic manifests itself in the structure of the story. "El fin" is short, exhausting itself in the ephemeral duration of a significant present. "Emma Zunz" is a more extensive short story, but follows the same pattern. In "El jardín de los senderos que se bifurcan," instead, there is the novelty of a doubly preserved present, so to speak. First, there are two narrators: Borges, who briefly informs us about an important World War I battle described in Liddell Hart's *History of European War*, and about Yu Tsun's manuscript. Thus we perceive that for his story Borges chooses the present which Yu Tsun chose for himself. With or without a formal division between narrators, the significant present emerges as an individual projection. "La otra muerte" is another case in point. The general information about Pedro Damián, the information that provides a specious continuity, is sketchy and not noteworthy. Pedro Damián lived uneventfully as a peasant on a farm in Río Negro or Paysandú, and was surprised by the revolution in 1904:

> Combatió en algún entrevero y en la batalla última; repatriado en 1905, retomó con humilde tenacidad las tareas del campo. Que yo sepa, no volvió a dejar su provincia. Los últimos treinta años los pasó en un puesto muy solo, a una o dos leguas de Ñancay.
>
> II, 55

Nothing memorable, thus far. Only the war obsesses Damián: "El sonido y la furia de Masoller agotaban su historia" (II, 55). To follow Borges' reasoning in matters that affect consciousness, what constitutes Damián's obsession is not the entire battle of Masoller, but a fraction of it, the moment which witnessed his cowardice. Damián had behaved like a man in various skirmishes, but when the two armies confronted each other, Damián weakened. Such is the version told not without soldierly sympathy by colonel Tabares, Damián's field commander. This is the "present" that Damián wishes to commit to oblivion. There is another version, narrated by Juan Francisco Amaro, the physician:

> Pedro Damián murió como querría morir cualquier hombre. Serían las cuatro de la tarde. En la cumbre de la cuchilla se había hecho fuerte la infantería colorada; los nuestros la cargaron, a lanza; Damián iba en la punta, gritando, y una bala lo acertó en pleno pecho. Se paró en los estribos, concluyó un grito y rodó por tierra y quedó entre las patas de los caballos. Estaba muerto y la última carga de Masoller le pasó por encima. Tan valiente y no había cumplido veinte años.
>
> II, 57–58

The "present" with which Pedro Damián lived since 1904 is replaced by the "present" that matters to him; this was his only hope. "La trajo," Borges tells us, "en forma de delirio pero ya los griegos sabían que somos las sombras de un sueño. En la agonía revivió la batalla, y se condujo como un hombre y encabezó la carga final y una bala lo acertó en pleno pecho" (II, 60). Pedro Damián died in 1946. In the agony of death, he relived the battle—his battle—and died under the hooves of the cavalry charge. As in "El sur," the protagonist dies at the very moment when the present that his dream is coincides with the physical death. Destiny surprises Damián in his desired—and earned—present. The exact opposite occurs in "La forma de la espada," where the protagonist abandons the reassuring heroic present that he invented, accepting the "old" present that he had been trying to conceal.

Borges does not explore the possibilities of the "waiting for the present" theme only in order to expand the limits of his literary craft. Profound, tentative metaphysical questions accompany the technical virtuosity: the meaning of life, death, life after death, redemption and damnation, etc. These are the "presents" that Borges wishes to explore. The fictitious characters are replaced by issues in the essays. We are closer to essays than to short stories. The Christian Eternity, in Borges' view best formulated by St. Augustine in his *Confessions*, is based on the mystery of trinity. The polemical or dogmatic aspects of the matter—Father, Son, and the issuance of the Holy Ghost by the two—do not engage our attention here. What is important is that the generative process involves in the act the past, the present, and the future (I, 323). Borges, of course, could have avoided the tripartite terminology in order to indicate that Trinity occurred outside time, but he does not. Irenaeus' elucidation, extolled by Borges as a form of hope, puts the issue differently: *"Aeternitas est merum hodie, est immediata et lucida fruitio rerum infinitarum"* (I, 323). That eternity is a today—a present—Borges tellingly adds, is of great emotional importance. Borges does not lose sight of his own humanity, and that of others: "No paso ante la Recoleta sin recordar que están sepultados ahí mi padre, mis abuelos y trasabuelos, como yo lo estaré" (II, 290). The temporality of the trinity may mean in terms of faith different things to different people, and contradictory perspectives are not devoid of interest. The mention of hell as physical violence ("violencia física," I, 323) throws the human condition and the issue of redemption into the forefront. In Borges' view, it would be highly arbitrary—and disconcerting, we add—to separate the concept of redemption from Trinity. The temporality of the Trinity—past, present, future—that is to say, its peculiar eternity, is directly related to the problem of redemption. Trinity may be atemporal, but redemption is not:

> Entendemos que renunciar a la Trinidad—a la Dualidad, por lo menos—es hacer de Jesús un delegado ocasional del Señor, un accidente de la historia, no el autor *imperecedero*, continuo de nuestra devoción. Si el Hijo no es también el Padre, la redención no es obra directa divina; si no es eterno, tampoco lo será el sacrificio de haberse denigrado a hombre y haber muerto en la cruz.
>
> I, 323–324

The matter is of the utmost importance, for Jesus is the author of *our* (my emphasis) continuous devotion. While

Borges' intellectual curiosity is amply in evidence, what prevails in this statement is his all too human interest in the Son,
on whose authenticity, divinity, and eternity our own, and
Borges', salvation depends. Beyond the actual and potential
speculations and debates on the matter, Borges ponders redemption with justifiable concern. "Los manuales de teología,"
he notes wrily, "no se demoran con dedicación especial en la
eternidad. Se reducen a prevenir que es la intuición contem-
poránea y total de todas las fracciones del tiempo, y a fatigar las
Escrituras hebreas en pos de fraudulentas confirmaciones,
donde parece que el Espíritu Santo dice mal lo que dice bien el
comentador" (I, 325). Borges' irony borders here on sarcasm. It
is not generalities that the human being needs, not the misguided and misleading egotism of the commentator, but reassurance, an embodiment of hope. This is not the traditional
anticlericalism of a Quevedo, but the disconcerting realization
that one is essentially alone with the question of redemption.
The erudition implicit in the lengthy catalog of scholarly
opinions, from Moses to Boethius to Hans Lassen Martensen,
fails to satisfy Borges' concern: "La eternidad quedó como
atributo de la mente de Dios" (I, 326).

Borges finds such formulations disheartening, for man cannot hope to understand or penetrate the divine mind. The
hope, once again, rests with Jesus, whose humanity is accessible to us, whose present is ours. There is no other choice:

> Nosotros percibimos los hechos reales e imaginamos los posibles (y los
> futuros); en el Señor no cabe esa distinción que pertenece al descono-
> cimiento y al tiempo.
>
> I, 327

Our consciousness is rooted in perception, and our perception
actualizes itself in the present. The future interests man only to
the degree to which it becomes the present, a significant
present. Thus redemption is not merely a hypothetical possibility, something of trivial interest, but a matter of vital concern. We dedicate to it our temporal reality. For Borges pre-
destination is nothing more than a glorious deformation

(I, 327), for it invalidates the significance of our present. The Christian Eternity appeals to Borges because it admits individual destinies (I, 329–30). When Borges seeks the best example to elucidate metaphysical perplexities, he does not choose a generic life—a composite of lives—but a concrete one, his own ("la mía, verbigracia," II, 290). For better or worse, his life appears real ("yo, desgraciadamente, soy Borges," II, 300). The various experiences which constitute such a life are real, not experience in general. Experience, as the sum total of a person's life, does not exist. Borges, quoting G. B. Shaw, states: "la tal suma no existe" (II, 291).

Redemption and the humanity of the Redeemer are at the center of Borges' preoccupation in "Tres versiones de Judas" as well as the future as a possible present. Nils Runeberg's speculations about the true identity of the Redeemer begin with what he construes to be factual reality, the humanity of the Redeemer:

> El Verbo, cuando fue hecho carne, pasó de la ubicuidad al espacio, de la eternidad a la historia, de la dicha sin límites a la mutación y a la muerte.
>
> I, 516

Space, time, humanity: the present; to negate these is to negate the humanity of the Redeemer, and the feasibility of redemption, of the significant present for which we wait. Runeberg completes the humanity of the redeemer by adding to it the concept of evil: He is Judas. Runeberg wanted to be with Judas. The unquestioning Christian wants to be with Jesus. The dissolution of our humanity will occur in a present, at our death. The Redeemer will lead the way. In Borges' words, speculations of the kind entertained by Runeberg may be scholastic frivolities (I, 178), but our interest in the temporality of the redemption is not. We fear Hell because if it becomes our present, it will be eternity without purpose (I, 179).

Notes

[1] Agheana, *The Prose of Jorge Luis Borges,* pp. 41–47.

[2] Enrique Anderson-Imbert, *Teoría y práctica del cuento* (Buenos Aires: Ediciones Marymar, 1979), p. 32.

La hora sin sombra

In the long and intricate commerce of human affairs, righteousness has always played a predominant role and has always sought the legitimacy of objectivity. Wars, revenge, punishment, conquests, etc., throughout history have been justified in terms of objective needs. Humanity has pursued and pursues the purification and the exoneration of its deeds in objectivity. While love, sympathy, hatred, and so on, are acknowledged as manifestations of subjectivity, impartiality is claimed as the chief attribute of objectivity. Thus objectivity, not always with the worst of intentions, pretends to put human matters above humanity. Yet, unfailingly, objectivity at best remains a subterfuge. Borges has given this matter coherent attention and expression.

Characteristically, Borges does not deal with the issue only intellectually. Next to the abstract matter there is always a proposition fecund in literary possibilities. "Los teólogos," for instance, is not only a work which concerns itself with heresies, with the orthodoxy or the heterodoxy of an Aurelianus or a John of Pannonia, with conflicting ideologies. It is also, and to a larger extent, a story of personalities in conflict, a study of the intrinsic limitations of man, of the hubris of righteousness, of the mirage of objectivity. The two lines run parallel for a while, then intersect each other at the end, exchanging intentions: the philosophical one acquires literary possibility, while the literary one takes on a philosophical aura. On the first plane, the essay, bursting with philosophical and religious erudition, speaks of the lethal enmity between Christianity and heresy, between Aurelianus and John of Pannonia. Initially, however, the two belong firmly to the orthodox camp. The twelve books of St. Augustine's *Civitas dei*, miraculously spared by the flames to which the Huns had irreverently consigned them, the text that reiterates the Platonic theory of the Eternal Return, spurred the founding of many sects.

One such sect, that of the *monótonos* or *anulares*, Borges informs the reader, which was corrupting the Christian doctrine with the Pagan emblems of the Wheel and the Serpent, attains alarming power and influence. The inherent fear is alleviated by the knowledge that John of Pannonia, who has distinguished himself with a treatise on God's attributes, would refute such a theory. The irrefutable eloquence of John of Pannonia accomplishes the task. Euforbus, the heresiarch of the Wheel and the Serpent, is condemned to be burned at the stake. Yet another heretical movement, that of the *especulares*, who had inverted the cross and replaced the image of Christ with that of the mirror, worried the Christian world. Perhaps contaminated by the previous sect, Borges tells us, the *especulares* imagined that every man is two men, and that the one whose Platonic image is in heaven is the real one. They also believed that the two men represented opposite states of each other: when one is asleep, the other one is awake, if one is parsimonious, the other is generous, etc. Dead, the two will become one again. In his report to the emperor, Aurelianus attributes the proliferation of heresies to John of Pannonia. John of Pannonia is condemned to die at the stake.

Underneath the probity with which the charges are made, however, lurks the green head of envy. Aurelianus, it is now clear, had coveted the theological fame of John of Pannonia. His denunciation of John of Pannonia denounces him. He is at an impasse. Borges resolves it brilliantly. Faced with the prospect of being either the accused or the accuser, of making a commitment, Aurelianus chooses neither. He prefers, instead, to create the illusion of objectivity. Making a commitment implies a subjective organization of reasons. Affective considerations, also, are unavoidable. Aurelianus has to remove himself from subjectivity or ambiguity. He resorts to the symbolism of dark-light. John of Pannonia will be burned at the stake at noon. Why in broad daylight, why precisely at noon?

From the tradition of *A Thousand and One Nights*, to Provençal poetry, to the theatre of the Spanish Golden Age, dark has come to symbolize the basic humanity of man, while light symbolizes his social persona, social authority. Thus in Tirso de Molina's *El burlador de Sevilla* social order is represented by light (the viceroy of Naples makes his entrance surrounded by lights), while Don Juan Tenorio's primordial humanity is represented by darkness. Don Juan does not step forward into the limelight. When the monarch asks the intruder to identify himself, Don Juan replies: "Un hombre sin nombre." In "El incivil maestro de ceremonias Kotsuke no Suke," a tale of honor, justice and vengeance, the head of the trangressor is exposed to the public in plain daylight, "a la luz sincera del día" (I, 281). In the case of the story under consideration, the question remains: why has John of Pannonia's immolation been set for noon? C. Wheelock focuses on the high noon time frame, but, moved by a different interest, gives it another interpretation.[1]

The light of the day underscores the legality of Aurelianus' enterprise: justice is being served. The noon hour suggests absolute clarity. The light of morning or that of the afternoon produces shadows which detract from its clarity. A shadow may be compared to an opinion, while pure light may be compared to the truth. In our context, the truth, the objective truth, would unavoidably be obscured by the shadow of any subjective opinions. This is precisely the effect sought by Aurelianus. Noon is the hour without shadows, pure light. Aurelianus stands at noon, without shadows. The burning at the stake of John of Pannonia appears as the embodiment of absolute justice, as objective necessity untainted by envy: "Aureliano presenció la ejecución, porque no hacerlo era confesarse culpable" (II, 36). The text continues: "Un ministro leyó la sentencia del tribunal. Bajo el sol de las doce, Juan de Panonia yacía con la cara en el polvo, lanzando bestiales aullidos" (II, 36). John prays first in Greek, then in an unknown language. The flames engulf him. Without the symbolism of dark-light, purity-impurity and its ethical implications, noon as the hour of John's execution would be a fortuitous or whimsical choice.

His revenge consummated, Aurelianus wanders aimlessly through the confines of the Roman empire:

> En una celda mauritana, en la noche cargada de leones, repensó la compleja acusación contra Juan de Panonia y justificó, por enésima vez, el dictamen.
>
> II, 37

In the darkness of his conscience, in the darkness that allows him no visual distractions, Aurelianus knows that his righteousness was illusory, that the noon hour of John's death was not without shadows. This process of self-examination completes itself with Aurelianus' own death. The scene is repeated, this time as reality rather than illusion. Divine justice will be served. This time the need for the noon hour is self-evident, in marked contrast to the deceptive probity of Aurelianus' choice.

> En Hibernia, en una de las chozas de un monasterio cercado por la selva, lo sorprendió una noche, hacia el alba, el rumor de la lluvia. Recordó una noche romana en que lo había sorprendido, también, ese minucioso rumor. Un rayo, al mediodía, incendió los árboles y Aureliano pudo morir como había muerto Juan.
>
> II, 37

In the obsessive night, John agonizes over the unjust death of John of Pannonia. Justice comes precisely at noon, Aurelianus' death paralleling that of John of Pannonia. He dies by fire, like John, but through divine or cosmic justice. Like the wild lions who face Don Quijote, beasts incapable of being moved by the hero's madness or courage, the lightning which ignites the forest is a phenomenon, a nonrational entity. This is not human justice; it is divine justice. In heaven, we are told, Aurelianus finds out that he and John of Pannonia are one and the same person, but only in heaven. In the realm of heaven, which, Borges insists, he can only attempt to describe metaphorically, Aurelianus and John are the same person, thus confirming, however tenuously, the validity of one of the heresies. This is Borges.

The symbolism of noon, with all its outlined implications, is also to be found in "La escritura del dios." Tzinacán, the high priest of the Quahalom pyramid, has been jailed indefinitely by the Spanish conquistador Pedro de Alvarado. The stone jail is in the shape of an almost perfect hemisphere. It is divided in two: one half is occupied by Tzinacán; the other, by a jaguar. Except for a brief period, Tzinacán and the jaguar live in complete darkness. That period is noon:

> En la hora sin sombra (el mediodía), se abre una trampa en lo alto y un carcelero que han ido borrando los años maniobra una roldana de hierro, y nos baja, en la punta de un cordel, cántaros con agua y trozos de carne.
>
> II, 86

Over the years, man and beast have caught a glimpse of each other at the hour without shadows:

> He perdido la cifra de los años que yazgo en las tinieblas; yo, que alguna vez era joven y podía caminar por esa prisión, no hago otra cosa que aguardar, en la postura de mi muerte, el fin que me destinan los dioses. Con el cuchillo de pedernal he abierto el pecho de las víctimas y ahora no podría, sin magia, levantarme del polvo.
>
> II, 86

Pedro de Alvarado is indeed the man who has put Tzinacán in chains, but the destiny that Tzinacán awaits is not that ordained by Alvarado but by the gods. This the essential framework. Pedro de Alvarado and the Spanish conquistadors play a negligible role in Tzinacán's destiny. His destiny is in the hands of the gods. Significantly, Tzinacán is not without power; the magic that he knows can infuse some vitality into his decrepit body. He can move about. But his power is useless against that of the gods. At the end of the story, when Tzinacán has a mystical experience which allows him to see the face without a face of the god behind the gods, he becomes one of the gods. He has been given the magic formula:

Me bastaría decirla para abrir esta cárcel de piedra, para que el día entrara en mi noche, para ser joven, para ser inmortal, para que el tigre destrozara a Alvarado, para sumir el santo cuchillo en pechos españoles, para reconstruir el imperio. Cuarenta sílabas, catorce palabras, y yo, Tzinacán, regiría las tierras que rigió Moctezuma.

II, 90

What has brought Tzinacán in possession of such power, what has altered or influenced his consciousness? The process is one of enlightenment.

Tzinacán's previous life had been one of appearances, of shadows, of illusions as a young man, as an adult, as a priest. He has acted without understanding himself, without understanding the gods. He was in the dark, as he was to be, literally, years later in jail. In prison, however, every day, at noon, the light falls vertically in the cell. There are no shadows, no distractions. This is not Plato's allegory of the cave, such as we know it. There is no artificial light in Tzinacán's prison, no man-made shadows deceiving the senses of the imprisoned. Tzinacán does not believe that shadows are his only reality, for he does not see any. The Socratic freed prisoner, drenched in the brightness of the sun, aware that the sun is the cause of all he sees, pities those left below for their ignorance, and prefers, like Achilles, to be the "poorest hired servant on earth" rather than return to the cave. Not so Tzinacán, whose enlightened abnegation is translated into total acceptance of his fate. Tzinacán has ceased to see only with his eyes. There is no external process of education to turn the soul away from the changing world to the immanent reality of the Good. There is no "leading forth," to refer to the etymological root of the verb to educate. What we witness in "La escritura del dios" is a process of self-realization. Tzinacán is in jail without human company. Every day he sees the jaguar. Suddenly, the revelation visits him. The mystery of his destiny is not to be found in another human being, not in another deluded dreamer, but in the jaguar—one of God's attributes:

Entonces mi alma se llenó de piedad. Imaginé la primera mañana del tiempo, imaginé a mi dios confiando el mensaje a la piel viva de los jaguares, que se amarían y se engendrarían sin fin, en cavernas, en cañaverales, en islas, para que los últimos hombres lo recibieran. Imaginé esa red de tigres, ese caliente laberinto de tigres, dando horror a los prados y a los rebaños para conservar un dibujo. En la otra celda había un jaguar; en su vecindad recibí una confirmación de mi conjetura y un secreto fervor.

II, 88

Tzinacán dedicates countless years to the mystery of the jaguar's skin, in the pure, ephemeral, noon light: "Cada ciega jornada me concedía un instante de luz" (II, 88). This pure light without shadows induces the miracle, a miracle that comes from within and that takes shape in his imagination. He accepts his destiny, he accepts the light, rather than the shadow of reason:

Un hombre se confunde gradualmente con la forma de su destino; un hombre es, a la larga, sus circunstancias . . . Bendije su humedad, bendije su tigre, bendije el agujero de luz, bendije mi viejo cuerpo doliente, bendije la tiniebla y la piedra.

II, 89

Tzinacán finds his destiny not in the infatuation of the intellect (*descifrador*) or in implied advantage of his profession (*sacerdote del dios*), but in the reconciliation with his present circumstance, with his destiny, with the pure light that illuminates it. It is reconciliation rather than resignation, because reconciliation does not mean rejection or passive acceptance, but participation. The old man in "Las ruinas circulares" would perhaps have phrased the issue differently, but would not have departed significantly from its philosophy. Tzinacán's is an act of self-redemption. "El perdón," says Borges elsewhere, "es un acto ajeno y sólo yo puedo salvarme" (II, 362). "Imaginé la primera mañana del tiempo, imaginé a mi dios," says Tzinacán, thus existentially assuming responsibility for his redemption. The degree of such a responsibility is couched in Socratic terms. The eyes, in Socrates' view, need a "third thing" to be used, they need light. For Socrates, the sun is to the visible world what the Good is to the invisible world. The matter imposes itself as a conclusion. Borges does, in this instance, carry the matter to a philosophical horizon; he leaves it open as a possibility. The light helps Tzinacán understand his present. Between the lines of the Aztec priest's realization, one reads, with Borges, Schopenhauer's words:

> Si a veces me he creído desdichado, ello se debe a una confusión, a un error. Me he tomado por otro, verbigracia, por un suplente que no puede llegar a titular, o por el acusado en un proceso por difamación, o por el enamorado a quien esa muchacha desdeña, o por el enfermo que no puede salir de su casa, o por personas que adolecen de análogas miserias. No he sido esas personas; ello, a lo sumo, ha sido la tela de trajes que he vestido y que he desechado.
>
> II, 278

This could well be Tzinacán's statement. Both Tzinacán and Schopenhauer speak in the first person, in confessionary tones. Both convey their pre-enlightened confusion in the past tense. The confusion and the error of mistaken identity belong to the past, to the shadows, to the discarded cloth. We are not what we were or thought that we were. We are what we are. References are misleading. The Socratic miracle happens, Tzinacán transcends himself, achieving mystical union, attaining the present of presents, so to speak:

> Ocurrió la unión con la divinidad, con el universo (no sé si estas palabras difieren). ¡Oh dicha de entender, mayor que la de imaginar o la de sentir! Vi infinitos procesos que formaban una sola felicidad y, entendiéndolo todo, alcancé también a entender la escritura del tigre.
>
> II, 89

Tzinacán, if we can retrieve the statement from the commonplace, has seen the light. He returns to the present that he is. It is a triumph:

> Por eso no pronuncio la fórmula, por eso dejo que me olviden los días, acostado en la oscuridad.
>
> II, 90

It is not merely a rationalization, an intellectual exercise, the rationalization of impotence. It is that, and much more. It is all that Tzinacán is all about.

Nowhere in the prose of Borges is the present more dramatically exemplified than in "La escritura del dios" and "Dos teólogos en la muerte." Nowhere do the philosophical and the theological implications of the present find more recognizable human embodiment, more vital awareness and immediacy, than in these two short stories. Zoroastrianism and Manichaeism, Platonism, Neo-Platonism, and Christianity, the movements which to a greater or lesser extent have attempted to rest cosmogony, theogony, and genealogy on the duality of light-darkness, reverberate in the narratives of Tzinacán, the Aztec priest condemned to solitary confinement by the Spanish conquistadors, and the theologians Aurelianus and John of Pannonia, fatefully uncertain of their orthodoxy. Man is at the center of the drama. For Zoroaster, man is forever torn between the creative force of light and all that is pure and good (Ahura Mazda), and the force of destruction, darkness and death (Ahriman). Manichaeism, the main Zoroastrian development in our era, whose syncretism accommodates Buddha, Zoroaster, and Jesus, posits the entire matter of conflict and redemption, of good and evil, religiously and ethically, on the light-darkness polarity. The Paulicians, the Cathari, the Albigensians, other minor sects under the spell of Manichaeism, which sought redemption in the pure but not all-powerful light, have clashed with orthodoxy within and without their conscience.[2] There is a vague resemblance between the Paulician Jesus, who becomes the Christ through his voluntary suffering rather than through divine paternity, and Tzinacán, the Aztec priest of "La escritura del dios." There are Socratic echoes in Tzinacán, and Christian intimations of the sanctification of the baptismal through light. There are human claims to righteousness dispelled by divine light in "Dos teólogos en la muerte." There is the esthetic consideration of noon light as the pure present of consciousness in both short stories.

Notes

1 Wheelock, p. 63.
2 *Dictionary of Philosophy and Religion*, p. 643.

The Forms of Passion

To speak of the passion of the Borgesian protagonist, a protagonist which traditional criticism has seen as a disintegrating identity,[1] would seem at first unwarranted, for passion is an individualizing force, not a depersonalizing one. But the Borgesian protagonist, to paraphrase the Argentine author himself, is demonstrably an individual, if he is anything at all (II, 461), and the force which galvanizes him is passion. Critics like Amado Alonso,[2] Gómez de la Serna,[3] and Ronald Christ,[4] have pointedly underscored Borges' emotive inclination, but their voices have been less resonant than those of critics who overintellectualize the Argentine author. Why, then, has this aspect remained largely unacknowledged by critics? Two reasons can be readily identified. The first is that of looking at passion through the eyes of Eros, thus wittingly or unwittingly limiting its range and autonomy. Eros, self-admittedly, is an exceptional presence in Borges' prose: "El tema del amor es harto común en mis versos; no así en mi prosa, que no guarda otro ejemplo que el de "Ulrica" (II, 536). The second, less conspicuous but equally misleading, lies in the apparent peculiarity of passion in the Argentine's prose works. The passion that permeates Borges' stories is passion *for* someone or something, rather than passion *between* two human beings. No ambiguity or ironic intention can be attached to an utterance that sustains the action in a story published in the later years of Borges' literary career: "La vida exige una pasión" (II, 410).

It is a statement whose fundamental reality, poetic aura, and philosophical import, are almost diffused by its topicality. It is, significantly, not lost in the middle of a Ciceronian phrase, but emphasized as the inchoative part of a paragraph. Borges, the cerebral Borges, the maker of labyrinths, the redeemer and perpetrator of metaphysical perplexities, with the authority of conviction, tersely states that life needs a passion. Human life needs a passion in order to be human life. Passion. The term, depending upon who entertains it, has been affected by various reductions. In order to understand it, etymological clarity must be sought.

What is passion? A lexicon, *A Comprehensive Etymological Dictionary of the English Language*, defines passion as follows: "passion, n.-ME., fr. OF(=F.) fr. L. passionem, acc. of passion, suffering, passion, affectation, fr. passus, pp. of pati, to suffer." *Webster's Third New International Dictionary* enlarges the etymological significance affectively and spiritually, by placing the term *fervor* in the context of emotion and feeling: "the man who seizes on one deep-reaching idea, whether newly found or rediscovered, and with single fervor forces it upon the world." Passion, then, is a form of action. The deep-reaching idea that generates passion is not qualified, thus lending itself to endless possibilities. This is the crux of the matter. Eros, the impoverished eros of common understanding, not that of Hesiod's *Theogony*, "the informing God of all things,"[5] with the exception stated, does not animate Borges' stories. Love, whether as *amor* or as *sexus*,[6] can be passionate, but it is not passion itself. Eros, for instance, does not figure at all in Homer.[7]

Borges diversifies passion into numerous meanings. He quotes Schopenhauer, for whom music is passion (I, 90). He considers the *kenningar*—the first literary manifestations in Iceland—to be cold aberrations which do not evoke passion (I, 336). However incongruously it may strike us, Sturluson, one of the first poets and compilers of *kenningar*, wishes to cultivate the passion of moderation (I, 339). In Alexandria, theology used to be a popular passion (I, 148). Vincent Moon is driven by the passion of fear (I, 487). Runeberg, the renegade theologian who commits suicide, has a "singular pasión intelectual" (I, 515). The origin of passions is always mysterious (II, 412). Not without irony, Borges marvels at the "curiosa pasión americana de la imparcialidad" (II, 521). Such a diversification of the term passion buttresses Borges' signal realization: "La vida exige una pasión" (II, 410). Borges, as any reader of his poetry knows, extolls fervor, and fervor is the chief attribute of passion.

It is without surprise that Borges notices the indifference with which the literary supplement of *The Times* speaks of Herbert Quain's death. The salient reason, in Borges' view, is the absence of passion in Quain's work: "Percibía con toda lucidez la condición experimental de sus libros: admirable tal vez por lo novedoso y por cierta lacónica probidad, pero no por las virtudes de la pasión" (I, 449). The "experimental" nature of Quain's books is to be linked to lack of passion, for without passion human life lacks credibility. Quain could not have written great literature. Literature which ignores or falsifies passion is bound to degenerate into caricature or artificiality. Borges observes: "Martín Fierro, (pese al proyecto de canonización de Lugones) es menos la epopeya de nuestros orígenes—¡en 1872!—que la autobiografía de un cuchillero, falseada por bravatas y por quejumbres que casi profetizan el tango" (II, 256). It would be preposterous to improve upon Borges' words. They are as clear as the intention which generates them.

If Borges imputes anything to Argentine literature, indeed to Argentine life, it is lack of imagination and fervor: "la novela argentina no es ilegible por faltarle mesura, sino por falta de imaginación, de fervor. Digo lo mismo de nuestro vivir en general" (I, 171). The readability of the Argentine novel is impaired by a verbal laboriousness which stifles fervor. This is not one of Borges' celebrated ambiguities. It is not occasional literary criticism. It is a serious statement, a vital one, for it refers not only to the Argentine's esthetics, but to Argentine life itself. Fervor, whether in life or in its literary rendition, is essential. The Argentine novel lacks imagination and fervor, the passion and the esthetic authenticity which could give it world resonance. The question is inevitable. Would Borges, then, so aware—and defensive—of the shortcoming of Argentine literature, commit the same mistake in his literary praxis? True, Borges does not write novels, but the issue here is not one of genre distinctions but of the dynamics of literature. Has his work gained world fame only through dazzling erudition and stylistic virtuosity? He, who defends the passion that the Argentine has for friendship, would he deprive his characters of feeling alive, of finding out who they are? The answer, demonstrably, is negative.

Borges, however, tends to be unidirectional rather than reciprocal in dealing with passion and its manifestations. When Borges sings about "la aceptada costumbre de estar solo" (*Obras*, 73), it is easy to extrapolate on his essential solitude. The verifiable truth, however, is that Borges in his poetry, and his protagonists in his prose works, may be solitary but not *alone*. Passion, intensified by mood, intuition, and surroundings, projects itself with marked singleness of purpose. Examples from Borges' poetry are adduced only in order to illustrate thematic continuity. The first poem in *Fervor de Buenos Aires* begins with a declaration of faith: "Las calles de Buenos Aires/ ya son mi entraña" (*Obras*, 17). It is the language of passion. And then: "Son para el solitario una promesa/ porque millares de almas singulares las pueblan/ únicas ante Dios y en el tiempo/ y sin duda preciosas" (*Obras*, 17). In the second poem of the volume, "La Recoleta," we read: "Vibrante en las espadas y en la pasión/ y dormida en la hiedra, sólo la vida existe" (*Obras*, 18). Even in "Sala vacía" there is a suggested live presence: "Los muebles de caoba perpetúan/ entre la indecisión del brocado/ su tertulia de siempre" (*Obras*, 27). Absence is also a presence: "Tu ausencia me rodea" (*Obras*, 41). In "Cercanías" we read: "He nombrado los sitios/ donde se desparrama la ternura/ y estoy solo y conmigo" (*Obras*, 45). Again, Borges may be solitary, but not alone. Borges' blindness is not loneliness, and he extolls the dignity of his mysterious condition: "Nadie rebaje a lágrima o reproche/ Esta declaración de la maestría/ de Dios, que con magnífica ironía/ Me dio a la vez los libros y la noche" (*Obras*, 89). "Si entre las cuatro/

Paredes de la alcoba hay espejo,/ Ya no estoy solo. Hay otro" (*Obras*, 814). Indeed the theme of the "other," sinuously present in Borges' work, underscores the metaphysical reassurance of the "double."

Borges' prose fiction is passion in action. There is the passion of machismo, the passion of fear, of patriotism, of friendship, or religion, of justice, even of snobbery. Yu Tsun and Cpt. Madden, in "El jardín de los senderos que se bifurcan," are moved by two different forms of passion, nationalism and patriotism. Vincent Moon, in "La forma de la espada," is possessed by the "pasión del miedo" (I, 487). In the same story, Borges calls patriotism "la menos perspicaz de las pasiones" (I, 486). Benjamín Otálora ("El muerto") is propelled into action by an "infatuación del coraje" (II, 24). Glencairn, the cruel judge in "El hombre en el umbral," dies without fear: "en los más viles hay alguna virtud" (II, 110). "Tema del traidor y del héroe" is a story of passions, like "El milagro secreto," "Tres versiones de Judas," "El sur." Even Otto Dietrich zur Linde, the Nazi of "Deutsches Requiem," had two passions, music and metaphysics, before embracing the horrid aberration of fascism.

In almost every short story by Borges there is a character moved by passion, passion as an expression of an inner need for affirmation, as individualizing action, if not as a reciprocal manifestation. Lukács, in an essential work, *The Theory of the Novel*, speaking of the archetypal map, in which the inside and the outside, the self and the world, the soul and the deed are eventually reconciled, writes that "passion is the way, predetermined by reason, toward complete self-being."[8] At the level of action, Lukács' words aptly describe the Borgesian character's pointed need for self-realization, a need that materializes itself through Protean forms of passion. Its consummation satisfies—for better or worse—the needs of an individual conscience, not of appetites or social desiderata.[9] This circuitous internal tension renders circumstantial interference inconsequential, which is why society has only a spectral presence in Borges' fiction. The external factors may make the resolution of an inner passion more pathetic, but they will never arrest it. Every vital act, states A. Tilguer, is an act of separation from the infinite, an individuation.[10] Properly understood, this statement accurately describes the dynamics of the Borgesian protagonist, his incessant need for essential affirmation, consciously or subconsciously. It is an affirmation of individuality, not its dissolution.

Borges may philosophize about such a matter, but he does not resolve it philosophically. His mistrust of philosophy is well known. Yet he does not reject philosophy only because it is an unreliable human construct, a mere coordination of words. He also opposes it because philosophers tend to regard the emotions that move us as vices, as—what is worse—traps of our own making. Spinoza makes this edifying statement in his *Tractatus politicus*.[11] Borges simply does not wish to go that far. He retrieves the Argentine, for whom, say, friendship is a passion, from the dictates of citizenship in order to allow him to be an individual, in order to maintain the purity of his sentiments. Borges stops at the gates of philosophy as he does at the gates of conventional morality. Such as it can be identified in Borges, passion is not a hedonistic pursuit but, as E. Cioran puts it, a form of punishment, the price for existing.[12] Vincent Moon, in "La forma de la espada," exemplifies such a reality.

While the unfolding passion is affected by circumstances and in turn affects circumstances, in essence it is not transformed by them. Nothing deflects the Borgesian protagonist from individualizing passion. Hladik's literary passion is not deterred by the importune invasion of Czechoslovakia by the Third Reich, or his own detention. If anything, these circumstances accelerate and intensify the resolution of his passion. The story, quite simply, is not about the barbarous invasion of a country by the Nazis, nor about the death of a man because of racial intolerance, but of self fulfillment. As the deputy director of the concentration camp in Tarnowitz, Otto zur Linde reluctantly carries out the extermination of Jews. He does it because he considers Nazism an intrinsically moral act (II, 65). He needs the (immoral) morality of Nazism, the perfection of indifference. He achieves it through the forced suicide of a poet, David Jerusalem. Otto zur Linde's confession is brutally unambiguous: "Ignoro si Jerusalem comprendió que si yo lo destruí, fue para destruir mi piedad. Ante mis ojos no era un hombre, ni siquiera un judío; se había transformado en un símbolo de una detestada zona de mi alma. Yo agonicé con él, yo morí con él, yo de algún modo me he perdido con él; por eso fui implacable" (II, 66). Otto zur Linde continues: "No hay hombre que no aspire a la plenitud, es decir, a la suma de experiencias de que un hombre es capaz" (II, 66).

While political doctrines do not amount to a novelistic condition, ethics do. Borges' preoccupation with ethics has been lifelong, steady but not obsessive. The backbone of his prose fiction is an ethical one. Borges notes and appreciates G. B. Shaw's ethical strain, lamenting the Argentine's disregard for ethics. Philosophy does not interest the Argentine: "La ética tampoco: lo social se reduce, para él, a un conflicto de individuos o de clases o de naciones, en que todo es lícito, salvo ser escarnecido o vencido" (II, 274). We now understand the Argentine's aversion for things social, for the sterile conflict which erodes his individuality. Such as he conceives it, the Argentine cannot find self-fulfillment in society. The Argentine, as an act of will, as a vital choice, does not wish to be a social animal. It is an asset and a liability as well. When Borges praises the individualism of the Argentinean he praises a salutary instinct, not an absolute model.

The essence of Borges' ethics is Aristotelian, teleological. Aristotle gradually became convinced that the universe is a complex of organisms, each striving to attain the purpose assigned to it by Nature; hence the teleological connotation. In such an universe organisms fulfill their nature.[13] Unlike Aristotle, however, Borges does not consider ethics a branch of politics. He prefers to focus on Aristotle's startling accomplishment of grounding ethics in psychology.[14] Thus ethics, based on the workings of the human soul, makes its way into Borgesian literature. Borges does not go as far as to say that happiness is the ultimate goal of our conscious acts, but he would agree with Aristotle that what we pursue must be final and self-sufficient.[15] Aristotle allows man a lifetime to seek happiness, Borges an act, a single redeeming act. A Borgesian character's self-sufficiency, as distinct from the larger Aristotelian context, is a solitary affair. He seeks participation, not fusion, through passion, not through love. The Borgesian protagonist is not interested in the theory of self-fulfillment; he is a man of action, as is Aristotle's man.[16] The Borgesian protagonist simply does not ask the question if the need for self-fulfillment is a divine prescription or an idiosyncratic choice, for both aspects disregard the adversities of fortune. Critics of Borges have noted that, with minor exceptions, his characters are not particularly emotional. A more accurate assessment, however, is that the Borgesian character is emotional but not sentimental. Sentimentality plays itself out in fantasy rather than in action.[17] Interestingly, in Aristotelian ethics neither virtues nor vices are feelings.[18] Aristotle says it best: "By 'feelings' I mean desire, fear, daring, envy, gratification, friendliness, hatred, longing, jealousy, pity and in general all states of mind that are attended by pleasure or pain."[19] Virtue, Aristotle tells us, is a disposition, an attitude about feelings.[20] In Borges, feelings are subordinated to disposition. Borges does not make the distinction that a bad virtue is a vice. In his literary praxis, he does not go beyond this point. He does, however, in his conscience: "Desconocemos los designios del universo pero sabemos que razonar con lucidez y obrar con justicia es ayudar a esos designios, que no nos serán revelados" (II, 363).

Significantly, the first virtue listed by Aristotle is courage. No reader of Borges' prose fiction would fail to descry this virtue in virtually every Borgesian protagonist. Fergus Kilpatrick is a traitor, not a coward. The title of the story, "Tema del traidor y del héroe," pits treason against heroism, not cowardice against valor. Pedro Damián ("La otra muerte") redeems his cowardice. Vincent Moon, whose cowardice is irreparable, to use Borges' own words, is one of the exceptions ("La forma de la espada"). Rosendo Juárez, both in "El muerto" and "Historia de Rosendo Juárez," is another one. Sometimes courage is shown in relation to pleasure or pain, as in Aristotle. In the *Seven Pillars of Wisdom* Lawrence lauds the courage of a German platoon, writing in Borges' translation: "Entonces, por primera vez en esa campaña, me enorgullecí de los hombres que habían matado a mis hermanos" ("El pudor de la historia," II, 283). At the end of "El jardín de los senderos que se bifurcan," Yu Tsun, who had temerariously transmitted a message to the Germans and killed Stephen Albert in the process, a propós of his boss in Berlin, states: "No sabe (nadie puede saber) mi innumerable contrición y cansancio" (I, 473).

Magnanimity is also present, even if it is in the form of a *beau geste*, as in the case of Martín Fierro. Justice—the term and the concept—appears frequently in Borges' prose work. The hope that Glencairn, the implacable judge in "El hombre en el umbral," would be a man of justice ("Todo tendrá justificación en su libro." II, 108) is soon dispelled by crass arbitrariness. Justice is restored when he is killed. Aurelianus, under the guise of justice and religious orthodoxy, has John of Pannonia killed, only to be killed in turn in the name of divine justice (II, 30-07). In this respect, "Los dos teólogos" represents an exception. If we are ignorant of God's literary preferences, as Borges puts it, we know even less about His justice.

The issue of Justice surfaces here and there, always tentatively. At the level of action, in the short stories proper, justice is corrective or emendatory. Aristotle recognizes such justice as a form of justice, but he disagrees with the Pythagoreans that it is simply a matter of reciprocity.[21] Involuntary actions do not carry the same weight as voluntary ones. In Borges, justice appears more often than not in the form of equity. Aristotle warns that justice and equity are not absolutely identical, and Borges is implicitly sympathetic to such a point of view. Aristotle states: "What puzzles people is the fact that equity, though just, is not the justice of the law courts but a method of restoring the balance of justice when it has been tilted by the law."[22] The statement fits almost perfectly Borges' literary view of the matter, but in his prose fiction the restoration of the balance of justice occurs not when there has been an infraction of the law, but when an arbitrariness has been perpetrated. We recall that Borges at eighty thinks that the only justice is private justice.[23]

Borges' contexts are not sociological. Benjamín Otálora is killed because he wishes to usurp the leadership and manly authority of Azevedo Bandeira ("El muerto"); Kilpatrick meets his orchestrated death because he has betrayed an Irish revolution ("Tema del traidor y del héroe); Martín Fierro dies in a knife fight with a black man, whose brother he had killed seven years before ("El fin"); Tadeo Isidoro Cruz, the head of a posse, abandons his men and joins the man he was hunting in order to even the odds ("Biografía de Tadeo Isidoro Cruz"); Emma Zunz seeks the demise of the man who had driven her father to suicide ("Emma Zunz"); the Arab king delivers the Babylonian king to die in the desert, an infinitely bigger labyrinth than the one to which the Babylonian monarch had proscribed him ("Los dos reyes y los dos laberintos"); Villari pays with his life for an act which remains a mystery to us ("La espera"); the Nielsen brothers sacrifice the wife of one of them in order to restore fraternal harmony ("La intrusa"); Uriarte kills Duncan as a dare in a duel ("El encuentro"); Tía Florentina kills her landlord not as much in order to avoid eviction, as to restore the honor of her defunct husband, Juan Muraña ("Juan Muraña"); the Gutres crucify Baltasar Espinosa in order to save themselves from a deluge ("El evangelio según Marcos"); Avelino Arredondo assassinates the president of Uruguay as a supreme act of dissidence ("Avelino Arredondo"), etc.

It has been stated that Borges' protagonist is not a social animal, which, as everybody knows, is true. The Argentine is an extreme example. Like his real life counterpart, he regards the state as an impersonal entity. Hegel's aphorism, "El Estado es la realidad de la idea moral," is but a sinister joke to him. All the protagonists mentioned above enact a personal, supra-social, morality. When Aristotle says that equity is not the justice of the law courts, we are closer to understanding the Borgesian protagonist. Aristotle considers equity a necessity:

> The need for such a rectification arises from the circumstance that that law can do no more than generalize, and there are cases which cannot be settled by a general statement. So in matters where it is necessary to make a general statement, and yet the statement cannot exclude the possibility of error, the law takes no account of particular cases, though well aware that this is not a strictly correct proceeding.[24]

To the Argentine every case is particular. To seek the justice administered by the State is, essentially, to be misunderstood, for the State does not cater to the particular. On the rare occasions when the State is present in Borges' work, it is only in a punitive capacity. In "Hombre de la esquina rosada," the death of the Corralero brings the police on the scene, an unwanted presence: "Quien más, quien menos, todos tendrían razón para no buscar ese trato" (I, 295). The brigand Juan Moreira is unceremoniously killed by the rural police ("La noche de los dones," II, 500). In "El acercamiento a Almotásim," a riot involving Muslims and Hindus is indifferently put down by police: "Atronadora, semidormida, la policía del Sirkar interviene con rebencazos imparciales" (I, 394). Aristotle sees the remedy of ethical imbalance in education. In Borges, education is a fount of sterility. For all of Borges' immense erudition, his literary children remain more committed to action than to knowledge. It is an action propelled by Protean passion.

Notes

[1] See Part I, *The Point of View*, notes 2-6

[2] "Borges, narrador," in *El escritor y la crítica*, p. 50.

[3] "El fervor de Buenos Aires," in *El escritor y la crítica*, p. 25.

[4] "Borges Justified: Notes and Texts toward Stations of a Theme," in *Prose for Borges*, p. 61.

[5] Joseph Campbell, *The Masks of God: Occidental Mythology* (New York: The Viking Press, 1964), pp. 227, 234.

[6] Rollo May, *Love and Will* (New York: W.W. Norton & Co. Inc., 1969), p. 72.

[7] Joseph Campbell, *The Masks of God: Oriental Mythology* (New York: The Viking Press, 1962), p. 235.

[8] Georg Lukács, *The Theory of the Novel* (Cambridge: The M.I.T. Press, 1971), p. 30.

[9] Erich Fromm, *The Art of Loving* (New York: Harper and Brothers Publishers, 1956), p. 10. The intensity of love and passion depends "on the degree of individuation which an individual has reached."

[10] Adrian Tilguer, *Moralità*, (Roma: Libreria di Scienze e Lettere, 1938), p. 20.

[11] Baruch Spinoza, opening chapter of *Tractatus Politicus*, quoted in *The Practical Cogitator*, ed. by Charles P. Curtis, Jr. and Ferris Greenslet (Boston: Houghton Mifflin Co., 1962), p. 399.

[12] Emile M. Cioran, *The Fall into Time*, (Chicago: Quadrangle Books, 1970), p. 137.

[13] Aristotle, *Ethics* (Baltimore: Penguin Books, 1953), p. 19.

[14] Ibid, pp. 22–23.

[15] Ibid., p. 37.

[16] Ibid., p. 41.

[17] Erich Fromm, p. 100.

[18] Ibid., p. 63.

[19] Ibid., p. 62.

[20] Ibid., p. 63.

[21] Ibid., p. 151.

[22] Ibid., p. 166.

[23] *Borges at Eighty*, p. 19.

[24] Aristotle, pp. 166–67.

Part II

The Literary Experience

The Point of View

In "Paul Groussac" Borges makes a statement whose candor and essential accuracy cannot be put in doubt:

> Soy un lector hedónico: jamás consentí que mi sentimiento del deber interviniera en afición tan personal como la adquisición de los libros, ni traté fortuna dos veces con autor intratable, eludiendo un libro anterior con un libro nuevo, ni compré libros—crasamente—en montón.
>
> I, 171

The statement bears closer scrutiny, for it sheds considerable light not only on Borges the reader, but on Borges the critic and writer as well. Above all, Borges is a genuine reader. To be a genuine reader is to establish a direct esthetic relationship with a work, to share in its vital experience without mediation, without prejudice. It is the only way to enjoy a work and to do it justice critically.

Borges' hedonism is not frivolity. What Borges objects to is not critical awareness but doctrinaire criticism. When Borges, in "Kafka y sus precursores," writes that every writer "creates" his precursors, the anachronism implied is neither gratuitous nor reduced to shock value. He deliberately uses the verb *crear* rather than *recrear* in order to accredit a point of view. To create, in the sense considered here, is to organize the literary matter according to one's own criteria, to recreate, is to organize such matter from someone else's point of view. Only as a "creation" does an author's work modify our concept of the past and of the future.[1] By refusing to subordinate his reading to a dogmatic critical purpose, Borges enjoys the freedom of seeking self-sustaining insights, of formulating hypotheses, of drawing vital nourishment from a work, in short, of adding to his own individuality. Borges' considerations have a vision of their own.

The statement also evidences an aspect that is essential in any rigorous evaluation of Borges' cultural configuration—his implacable determination not to deal with unreadable writers. While Borges does not itemize the attributes which integrate readableness(sic)—that most desirable, elusive quality of a written work—we must assume that readability means the totality of an esthetic experience. For Borges, then, rereading is never a remedial experience but an act of walking a little farther the paths that he has walked before. We recall the derisive incredulity with which the man from the future reacts to Borges-Acevedo's claim that he owns two thousand books. The judgement is concise and to the point: "Además no importa leer sino releer" (II, 512). In the prolog to *Artificios* (1944), Borges tells us about his reading preferences: "Schopenhauer, De Quincey, Stevenson, Mauthner, Shaw, Chesterton, León Bloy, forman el censo heterogéneo de los autores que continuamente releo" (I, 476). To most, the answer of a man in whose face someone threw a glass of wine during a heated literary or religious discussion, *"Esto, señor, es una digresión, espero su argumento"* (I, 404), would be nothing more than witty trivia. To Borges, however, it is sufficient cause for immortality (I, 404). So is Miguel de Servet's remark. Condemned to be burned at the stake, he says to Calvin: *"Arderé, pero ello no es otra cosa que un hecho. Ya seguiremos discutiendo en la eternidad"* (I, 404). Borges' fondness of quintessential statements, paradoxes and metaphysical perplexities reveals his keen interest in originality, however fragmentary and puzzling that originality may be. "Soy muy sensible a los halagos (de lo patético y de lo sentencioso)," has declared Borges recently.[2] Borges' own writing reflects and exemplifies such a concern. A literary work, writes Borges, "es un espejo que declara los rasgos del lector y es también un mapa del mundo" (II, 210).

The range of Borges is encyclopedic, and the list of authors who inform his writings is seemingly endless. Yet a careful reading of Borges reveals some preferences, the recurrent presence of names and onomastically related themes, whether in earnest or anecdotally. Borges may be overwhelmingly indebted to De Quincey, as he claims in an essay (II, 213), but he does not dedicate to him a single essay. Cervantes, Shakespeare, Whitman, Shaw, Quevedo, Valéry, in turn, are names both heading essay titles and resurfacing in a variety of themes, spanning virtually Borges' entire literary career. After Cervantes, John Barth writes, "Shakespeare is the name most often used by Borges."[3] The first essay that Borges dedicates to Walt Whitman, "El otro Whitman," dates back to 1929, while the last written remarks are to be found in *Elogio a la sombra* (1969), and *El oro de los tigres* (1972). Quevedo and Shaw are celebrated in *Otras inquisiciones* (1952), and, anecdotally, in the same breath, in the prologue to *El informe de Brodie* (1970): "Dios te libre, lector, de prólogos largos. La cita es de Quevedo, que, para no cometer un anacronismo que hubiera sido descubierto a la larga, no leyó nunca los de Shaw" (II, 371).

Some of Borges' most interesting statements, like the conclusion of "Nueva refutación del tiempo," can be thematically traced to the authors who have been Borges' constant intellectual companions. How Borges transfigures thematically an idea already transfigured by a Quevedo, for instance, how he grasps a Cervantine essence and dilutes it into various literary possibilities, how he sagely leaves the process open-ended, is one of the benefits that we derive from Borges' cultural and literary virtuosity.

Notes

[1] Ion. T. Agheana, "Borges, 'Creator' of Cervantes; Cervantes Precursor of Borges," *Revista de Estudio Hispánicos*, IX (1982), p. 17.

[2] In "Adolfo Bioy Cesares, un relato admirable." *El País*, 17 de Marzo de 1986: 9.

[3] "Literatura del agotamiento," in *El escritor y la crítica*, p. 180.

Cervantes

While Borges mentions Shakespeare and Cervantes with more or less the same frequency, his tone and attitude toward Cervantes differ from those towards the English dramatist. If Borges, as we shall see, is formally obsequious and virtually uncritical of Shakespeare, he is rather familiar and affectionately critical of Cervantes. The cultural certainty obvious in Borges' critique of Cervantes is understandable—both belong to the Hispanic world, to a common way of looking at the world. Borges' critique of Cervantes is both intellectually more rigorous and emotionally more intense than that of the English bard.

Interestingly but not surprisingly, Borges' first direct mention of Cervantes is an emotional one. When attempting to explain the notorious Argentine individualism and to justify it in terms of intellectual and ethical duty and promise, Borges resorts to a Cervantine utterance of scarce literary interest but of significant, if topical, moral import. It is Don Quijote's conciliatory remark: "allá se lo haya cada uno con su pecado" (I, 91-02). Borges writes: "El argentino hallaría su símbolo en el gaucho y no en el militar, porque el valor cifrado en aquél por las tradiciones orales no está al servicio de una causa y es puro" (I, 91). The supreme example of this inherited trait is a particular night immortalized by Argentine literature, the night in which a sergeant of the rural police sides with the deserter whom he is supposed to capture, in order to better the odds (I, 92). Much later, in "Nuestro pobre individualismo," Borges resurrects Don Quijote's quotation and buttresses it with another one: "no es bien que los hombres honrados sean verdugos de los otros hombre, no yéndoles nada en ello."[1]

Forbearance, understanding, autonomy, and a keen sense of humor, are the essential attributes inherited by the Argentines from the Spanish, attributes that, in Borges' view, reveal more honestly the true nature of the human being. The normative prescriptions of "isms," be they social, political, or religious, that is to say, supraindividual, cannot but falsify the inner configuration of individuality. Suffice it to say that to Borges' Argentine Hegel's assertion, "El Estado es la realidad de la idea moral," is nothing but a sinister joke (II, 162). The Argentine, like Don Quijote, is an individual, not a citizen (I, 91). D'Artagnan's exploits, Borges tells us, are more spectacular, but we perceive better Don Quijote's courage (II, 272). If Don Quijote continues to win posthumous battles, it is undoubtedly because of the peculiar individuality that courage and faith confer upon him. It is in Cervantes' work, more specifically in Don Quijote's statement, that Borges found a previously doubted affinity with Spanish culture.

Many of Borges' literary considerations and some aspects of his literary praxis draw their impetus from the *Quijote*. Foremost among them is the issue of realism. As distinct from that of the Picaresque novel, Cervantes' realism is not a view of the world limited by a single point of view.[2] Closer to life, Cervantes' realism does not reject or favor certain aspects of reality. As C. B. Aguinaga aptly puts it, the world that Cervantes presents is always—of necessity, we add—fragmentary, though complete in every fragment.[3] Any adventure of Don Quijote proves this point. Adventures viewed cumulatively may diversify some aspects of Don Quijote's character, but do not add or detract from its basic configuration. The episodic fragmentation contains an essential totality. The same, without reservations, can be said of Borges' prose work. The brevity of his writings is consonant with an expressed belief: "Cualquier destino, por largo y complicado que sea, consta en realidad *de un solo momento*: el momento en que el hombre sabe para siempre quien es" (II, 44). It is not even a night but the moment of a night in Tadeo Isidoro Cruz' life that interests Borges. In doing so, Borges seeks more a possible truth than an elusive novelty (II, 172).

When Borges writes "La postulación de la realidad," in which classical and romantic modes of expression are analyzed, the name of Cervantes is in attendance again. The essay carries both Borges' refutation of Croce, who emphasizes the identity of the esthetic with the expressive, as well as some of his own original, if not critically rigorous, views on the subject. Briefly, Borges details the matter as follows. The romantic, he states, wishes to express incessantly. The classical writer, in contrast, avoids laborious expression, often dispensing with preliminaries. We are now in the realm of Borgesian alchemy. As an example of classical writing, Borges quotes rather extensively from Gibbon's *Decline and Fall of the Roman Empire*. Borges tells us that the author, like his text, is not expressive: he records, rather than represents, reality (I, 154). Human experience may be inferred from the text but it is not in it: "Dicho con mejor precisión: no escribe los primeros contactos de la realidad, sino su elaboración final en concepto" (I, 154). He then adds: "Es el método clásico, el observado siempre por Voltaire, por Swift, por Cervantes" (I, 154).

Two observations are in order. The first is that a history text is adduced in order to illustrate a literary matter. By removing formal distinctions, Borges treats history and fiction alike. The second is that he adduces a literary figure in order to exemplify a historical contention. The writer is not Swift or Voltaire, but Cervantes. The text is a fragment of "El curioso impertinente," the short story interpolated in the *Quijote*. Is this an invitation to the reader to invent his perspective, that is to say, to view history literarily and literature historically? "Pasajes como los anteriores," says Borges about Gibbon's and Cervantes', "forman la extensa mayoría de la literatura mundial" (I, 155). There are, of course, problems with such a sweeping statement. The *Quijote*, to begin with, stands in marked contrast to the stylized Italian *novella* of which "El curioso impertinente" is an imitation. Borges is speaking of the wrong Cervantes, so to speak. This, paradoxically, is the same Borges who, we recall, insists that we perceive Don Quijote's courage better than D'Artagnan's (II, 272). The operative word here is "perceive", the experiential recognition of courage, not only its intellectual acknowledgement. Don Quijote experiences a defeat, not only rationalizes it. When one of his ears is half cut off, it hurts.

Cervantes, author of the *Quijote*, is neither a classical writer nor a romantic one, to follow Borges' distinction, for he neither abstracts his characters nor divorces them from action. Don Quijote's adventures are not conceptual, forgone conclusions. The reader does perceive Don Quijote's and Sancho's contact with reality. There is inherent imprecision in the vital experiencing of reality, and therefore in its literary rendition. Cervantes' *baci-yelmo* perspectivism is not a literary invention. Borges writes: "Vemos y oímos a través de recuerdos, de temores, de previsiones" (I, 155). "El mismo hecho de percibir, de atender, es de orden selectivo: toda atención, toda fijación de nuestra conciencia, comporta deliberada omisión de lo no interesante" (I, 155). This is, however oblique, a definition of individuality. Life is not a conceptual simplification. Our perception of it frequently is. In Borges' words: "Nuestro vivir es una serie de adaptaciones, vale a decir, una educación del olvido" (I, 155). Each adaptation is a dynamic interaction with reality. Given the loose concatenation of adaptations, rendered coherent by the presence of the individual, and the blurring effect of oblivion, the autonomous moment acquires an air of uniqueness. It is on such moments that Borges capitalizes.

Certain inherent limitations notwithstanding, Borges' approach to fiction bears measurable resemblance to Cervantes' approach to the *Quijote*, and the critical mechanism that he applies to the Spanish author's work can be readily applied to his own. Borges, like Cervantes, knows his characters. The situation in which they find themselves or which they provoke, may or may not be well conceived, it may or may not be convincing, but the individuality of a character, accentuated by the peculiarity of the circumstance, is always recognizable.[4] Borges delights in putting the character in a vital situation.

Borges, we recall, is not interested in Tadeo Isidoro Cruz' life, only in the moment of meaningful self-revelation. The inherited or imperceptively acquired ideality and the past recede; man is essentially alone in his circumstance. Virtually any example from Borges will do, but perhaps "La noche de los dones" is more poignantly illustrative. Moreira, a legendary bandit, is ambushed and killed early in the morning, while attempting to escalate a wall. Says the sergeant who administered the *coup de grâce*: "Moreira, lo que es hoy de nada te valió disparar" (II, 500). No fame, no words can alter the situation in which Moreira finds himself and by which he is overwhelmed.

The Borgesian protagonist, like Don Quijote, is never really defeated. He may put himself in an untenable situation whose outcome may be death, he may even fear such an outcome, but he is not defeated. Almost every Borgesism protagonist can appropriate Don Quijote's statement after the adventure with the lions: "Bien podrán los encantadores quitarme la ventura; pero el esfuerzo y el ánimo será imposible" (I, XV). The Borgesian protagonist is determined, self-propelled, brave. The seemingly timeless old man's remark in "El hombre en el umbral" is to the point. Speaking of an English judge ceremoniously tried and executed by Hindus and Sikhs, he says: "Murió sin miedo; en los más viles hay alguna virtud" (II, 110). Even curiosity triumphs over fear (I, 491). There is only one conspicuous coward in Borges' fiction, in the story aptly titled "El indigno."

Borges may discount, as he does, the verisimilitude of many of the adventures in the *Quijote*, but he does not quarrel with the haphazard fashion in which they occur. "Mi complaciente precursor", writes Pierre Menard, "no rehusó la colaboración del azar" (I, 430). This, of course, is obvious to the most casual reader of the *Quijote. Azar*, the Persian word for dice, is a term much favored by Borges, who believes that chance is an integral part of reality, and that acknowledging it is a matter of intellectual honesty. The people of Babylonia are forced out of the certainty of logic and symmetry in which they complacently live by the introduction of the lottery (I, 443), this intensification of chance (I, 445). When it was rumored that the hexagonal, that is to say, symmetrical library of Babel contained all knowledge, the first feeling was one of extravagant felicity, as Borges puts it (I, 459). The universe, it was thought, was justified, which brusquely usurped the unlimited dimensions of hope (I, 459). Alas, it was only an illusion. Chance redressed the balance.

If we dream the world, let us honestly say that it is a dream and not an objective form of reality. Borges is unambiguous on this point:

> Lo hemos soñado resistente, misterioso, visible, ubicuo en el espacio y en el tiempo; pero hemos consentido en su arquitectura tenues y eternos intersticios de sinrazón para saber que es falso.
>
> I, 204

It is instructive to see how Borges' Cervantes, the real Cervantes, and Borges himself view chance and "sinrazón," that is to say, the non-rational. From Borges' argumentation there emerges, if not a coherent body of literary theory, a clearer idea of his probing of the subject. Next to Homer's *Iliad*, Virgil's *Aeneid*, Lucan's *Farsalia*, and Shakespeare's dramas, as examples of literary realism, Borges places the *Quijote*. He hastens to add that this realism, as distinct from that of the 19th century, admits the supernatural but separates it from everyday reality. Cervantes himself relegates the depiction of reality to history.[5] He plays with the interaction between reality and fiction, but on a literary plane.

Initially, Américo Castro gave a marked philosophical orientation to Cervantes' preoccupation with reality, an orientation to which later on he applied corrective focusing. Cervantes, he stated upon reconsideration, was not really interested in the nature of reality, but in knowing how reality is always an integral part of one's subjective experience.[6] It is a significant statement. Predmore enlarges its seminal possibilities. He notes that Cervantes, when reviewing or explaining various adventures, more often than not uses expressions in which the word truth is prevalent; "and such was the truth", etc.[7] Truth, not reality. Cervantes, in the *Quijote*, is consistent in this respect. Allen keenly observes that Cervantes frequently overlooks aspects of Don Quijote's life, not because they are imaginings but because they are not worthy of note.[8] In doing so, Cervantes reveals his own interests, which are more literary than philosophical.

It is on this particular matter that Borges' point of view fluctuates. In "Magias parciales del *Quijote*" Borges writes that Cervantes sets antithetically "un mundo imaginario y poético," against "un mundo real prosaico" (II, 172). He illustrates the point: "A las vastas y vagas geografías del Amadís opone los polvorientos caminos y los sórdidos mesones de Castilla" (II, 172). The antithesis imaginary-poetic, real-prosaic is symmetrical, logically consistent. The reality of the world is not questioned philosophically, only discounted poetically. The focusing is, then, a question of artistic preference. Borges' Cervantes makes literature this way. If, however, the logical symmetry works in "Magias parciales del *Quijote*," in "Parábola de Cervantes y de *Quijote*" it does not. Borges states:

Para los dos, para el soñador y el soñado, toda esa trama fue la oposición de dos mundos: el mundo irreal de los libros de caballerías, el mundo cotidiano y común del siglo XVI.

II, 336

"Real" and "unreal" are opposites, "unreal" and "quotidian" or "common" are not. Common and uncommon are aspects of reality, not its substitutes.[9] The faulty antithesis prepares us for the point that Borges wishes to make:

No sospecharon que los años acabarían por limar la discordia, no sospecharon que la Mancha y Montiel y la magra figura del caballero serían, en el porvenir, no menos poéticas que las etapas de Sinbad o que las vastas geografías de Ariosto.

II, 336

The issue of reality-unreality is not posited philosophically but literarily. Time will add a poetic aura to Don Quijote, but not reality. Don Quijote remains a *soñado*. By contrast, La Mancha and Montiel are not figments of Cervantes' imagination but real topographical locations rendered poetic by time. Reality for Cervantes is something non-poetic, not something that exists or does not. The end of the essay is unambiguous: "Porque en el principio de la literatura está el mito, y asimismo en el fin" (II, 336). Borges himself in discussing Cervantes does not credit his argument with a philosophical purpose: "la discusión de su novedad me interesa menos que la de su posible verdad" (II, 172). This is an etymological intimation of verisimilitude. Borges ties Cervantes' use of the supernatural to this point:

> El plan de su obra le negaba lo maravilloso; éste, sin embargo, tenía que figurar, siquiera de manera indirecta, como en los crímenes y el misterio en una parodia de la novela policial. Cervantes no podía recurrir a talismanes o a sortilegios, pero insinuó lo sobrenatural de un modo sutil, y, por ello mismo más eficaz.
>
> II, 173

There is little doubt that we are in the realm of literary considerations. We have the first inkling that the *maravilloso* is more a literary category than a metaphysical one when Borges likens its oblique presence to the parodic presence of crimes and mystery in a detective story. It is not really the fear of being put on the index by the inquisition that causes Cervantes not to deal in commonplace symbols of the supernatural—talismans, magic spells—but a different interest, that of probing the limits of poetic and non-poetic expression. For the supernatural in Cervantes does not transcend human nature. Cervantes' supernatural is the poetic fruit of imagination. It is a device which, in spite of its great promise, ultimately fails to liberate Don Quijote. Marthe Robert's observation is as incisive as it is accurate: "The supernatural world that Don Quijote invents for his consolidation is then in the image of the natural world that he tries to escape."[10] This is at the heart of his disequilibrium. We begin to understand the fundamental question facing Borges. Is Don Quijote, through his presence and adventures, bringing idealism into reality, or is he introducing reality into idealism? Naturally, each postulate leads to a different conclusion about Cervantes' literary theory and praxis. The question does not find us unprepared. Borges tells us that the supernatural in the *Quijote* is the literary idealism of pastoral and chivalric works. He quotes Paul Groussac: "la cosecha literaria de Cervantes provenía sobre todo de las novelas pastoriles y las novelas de caballerías, fábulas arrulladoras del cautiverio" (II, 173). He also tells us that Cervantes delights in confusing the objective and the subjective, the world of the reader and that of the book (II, 173). But Borges' Cervantes, it is clear, stays squarely within the bounds of literature. Reality spills into idealism, rather than the opposite. This explains why Borges thinks that the *Quijote* is more a nostalgic farewell to the romances of chivalry rather than an antidote against them. It is the same ship changing direction, not a different ship.

Borges' critical instinct is unerring here. Ramón Menéndez-Pidal's rebuttal of Lord Byron, who claimed that with the *Quijote* Cervantes destroyed the Spanish spirit of chivalry and eventually the country, is certainly justified.[11] Equally valid is Menéndez-Pidal's observation that Menéndez y Pelayo, while basically accurate, overstated the case of not only Cervantes' transfiguration, but of his exaltation of the chivalric genre.[12] Cervantes, writes Levin, undermines romance with realism.[13] Gilman and Wicks agree that Cervantes discredits Avellaneda's spurious *Quijote* not by denying its existence—the book is out, Tarfe does exist, etc.—but by negating the authenticity of the characters it portrays.[14] Wicks, fittingly, compares Cervantes' treatment of the matter with a refraction in a Borgesian mirror.[15]

The "magic realism" of the Quijote, to use Serrano-Plaja's felicitous term, is not supernatural.[16] The "magic realism" in question is an *ensueño*, a culturally induced dream.[17] There is no such realism in Part I.[18] The interesting thing about Don Quijote is that he seeks the evidence of chivalric magic in everyday life.[19] This, ultimately, foreshadows his disillusion.[20] By making Don Quijote seek chivalric magic in life Cervantes does much more than indulge his character's penchant for illusion. He probes the possibilities and the limitations of art. "El arte—siempre—requiere irrealidades visibles" (I, 204), Borges writes in "Avatares de la tortuga." Borges inserts his statement in the middle of a philosophical consideration. His intention is clear. Since philosophy is nothing but a coordination of words (I, 204), since the consolation of scientific certainty is denied to man, Borges opts not for a questionable ultimate truth but for a possible truth, that of literature. So does Cervantes. The moment that Don Quijote gets out of the *sueño dirigido* that literature is in Borges' expression, (I, 177), a process of demythification begins. The man who dies, Alonso Quijana, is not Don Quijote; he has forfeited his literary validity. Don Quijote cannot think literarily anymore.[21]

Why does Borges insist that Cervantes had to insert, however indirectly, *lo maravilloso* (II, 173). For Borges to do so is a matter of probity. Here is how Borges sums up his consideration of causal processes:

> He distinguido dos procesos causales: el natural, que es el resultado incesante de incontrolables e infinitas operaciones; el mágico, donde profetizan los pormenores, lúcido y limitado. En la novela, pienso que la única posible honradez está con el segundo. Quede el primero para la simulación psicológica.
>
> I, 170

Enough said.

Early on in his career, discussing the genesis and evolution of the tango, Borges writes: "El tango puede discutirse, y lo discutimos, pero encierra, como todo lo verdadero, un secreto" (I, 94). It is a statement of signal importance. If *lo verdadero* inherently contains a secret, then verisimilitude—not the ultimate truth—is the only attainable goal. For Borges, aspiring at verisimilitude, at the incomplete but possible truth, is, then, not only a matter of feasibility but one of intellectual honesty as well. We are in the presence of a different interpretation of verisimilitude. Borges' refutation of some aspects of Menard's *Quijote* is illustrative in this sense. Menard, who "fails" to perceive Cervantes' rhetorical intention, writes:

. . . la verdad, cuya madre es la historia, émula del tiempo, depósito de las acciones, testigo de lo pasado, ejemplo y aviso de lo presente, advertencia de lo por venir.

I, 432

Borges, for whom truth is the equivalent of an incompletely perceived reality, cannot accept history as the origin of truth (I, 432). Truth precedes history, one of its unreliable manifestations (I, 432). It precedes literature too, but literature does not make the exorbitant claims of history.[22] In Borges' approach, resemblance and lack of resemblance are complementary rather than authentic. Emma Zunz' story (II, 51), Unwin's version of events in "Abencaján el Bojarí, muerto en su laberinto" (II, 97) are indeed incredible in Borges' words, but they impose themselves as substantially true. They are, like the variation of a legend in "Formas de una leyenda," made of "verdad sustancial y de errores accidentales" (II, 266). The verisimilitude that Borges speaks about is not, then, the verisimilitude of logic. It cannot be, if we examine the issue honestly. The verisimilar version of Don Quijote's reaction to a homicide in "Un problema" is logically plausible but useless literarily:

> Muerto aquel hombre, Don Quijote no puede admitir que el acto tremendo es obra de un delirio; la realidad del efecto le hace suponer una pareja realidad de la causa y Don Quijote no saldrá nunca de su locura.

II, 327-28

When Borges insists that Cervantes had to include *lo maravilloso* in his work, he credits him with intellectual honesty. Talismans and sorcery would have been crude devices, unworthy of Cervantes' genius (II, 173). He resorted instead to chivalric literature.

Borges' *maravilloso* is the *azar*, whose presence restores verisimilitude to reality, as well as mysterious objects. As we have seen, the Argentine author prefers to posit the issue in terms of common-uncommon rather than real-unreal. For him there are no opposites, only the known and the unknown, the explained and the unexplained coexisting in a dynamic relationship. The mystery often transcends humanity. "El misterio", writes Borges, "participa de lo sobrenatural y aun de lo divino" (II, 97) but infrequently, the mystery is simply the unexpected. Offering a possible interpretation of the enigma of Edward Fitzgerald, after considering some metaphysical versions, Borges asserts: "Más verosímil y no menos maravillosa que estas conjeturas de tipo sobrenatural es la suposición de un azar benéfico. Las nubes configuran, a veces, formas de montañas o leones" (II, 201). All the key terms for the understanding of Borges' outlook on the matter—verisimilar, supernatural, beneficial chance—are here. The verisimilar and the wondrous are not mutually exclusive.

Nor is the extraordinary necessarily a matter of human invention in Borges' work. Like the phantom in *Hamlet*, the unexplained secures part of the consciousness whether objectified or not. More often than not, however, the unexplainable is objectified: an Aleph, a book of sand, a one-faceted disc, a cone of unearthly metal, etc. By virtually eliminating the antithesis real-unreal, by blurring formal genre distinctions, Borges both expands and enriches the realm of human awareness, like Pierre Menard's reading and "writing" of the *Quijote*. Borges educed his essential ambiguities from Valmiki's *Ramayana*, from *Thousand Nights and One Night*, from Shakespeare, from Cervantes (I, 175).

Notes

[1] *Quijote*, I, xxii; Borges, (I, 162).

[2] Carlos Blanco Aguinaga, "Cervantes and the Picaresque Mode: Notes on Two Kinds of Realism," in *Cervantes*, ed. by Lowry Nelson, Jr. (Englewood Cliffs: Prentice Hall, Inc., 1969), p. 139.

[3] Ibid., p. 151.

[4] Gene Bell-Villada, p. 43.

[5] Arturo Serrano-Plaja, *"Magic" Realism in Cervantes* (Berkeley and Los Angeles: University of California Press, 1970), p. 12.

[6] Cf. Richard L. Predmore, *The World of Don Quijote* (Cambridge: Harvard University Press, 1967), p. 53.

[7] Ibid., p. 56.

[8] John Allen, *Don Quijote: Hero or Fool?* (Gainsville: University of Florida Press, 1969), p. 15.

[9] Ion T. Agheana, "Borges, 'Creator' of Cervantes; Cervantes, Precursor of Borges," p. 20.

[10] Marthe Robert, *The Old and the New* (Berkeley, Los Angeles, London: University of California Press, 1977), p. 163.

[11] Ramón Menéndez-Pidal, "The Genesis of *Don Quijote*," in *Cervantes Across the Centuries*, ed. by Angel Flores and M.J. Benardete (New York: The Dryden Press, 1947), p. 35.

[12] Ibid., p. 35.

[13] Harry Levin, "*Don Quijote* and *Moby Dick*," in *Cervantes Across the Centuries*, p. 223

[14] Stephen Gilman, "The Apocryphal Quijote," in *Cervantes Across the Centuries*, p. 246; Ulrich Wicks, "Metafiction in *Don Quijote*," in *Approaches to Teaching Cervantes*, ed. by Richard Bjornson (New York: MLAA, 1984), p. 75.

[15] Wicks, p. 75.

[16] Predmore, pp. 50–53.

[17] Serrano-Plaja, p. 100.

[18] Ruth S. El Saffar, *Novel to Romance* (Baltimore and London: The Johns Hopkins University Press, 1974), p. 5; Serrano-Plaja, p. 131.

[19] Henry K. Ziomek, *Reflexiones del Quijote* (Madrid: Gráficas Molina, 1969), p. 84.

[20] Predmore, p. 81.

[21] Serrano-Plaja, p. 12.

[22] See José Ortega y Gasset, *Meditaciones del Quijote* (Buenos Aires: Espasa Calpe, S.A., 1942), p. 114.

Shakespeare

Borges' references to Shakespeare are numerous, interesting, and largely uncritical. Few attentive critics would fail to notice that Borges, ultimately, is not critically interested in the English bard's literature, in the esthetic realities and possibilities of his work, but in the nature of his creativity. There is no coherent Borgesian criticism of Shakespeare's work, not even a succinct analysis of a particular aspect. What we have, instead, is brief judgments of encomiastic intention and circumstantial validity: the work of Shakespeare, along with that of Balzac and Whitman, the epitome of the plenitude of life (I, 85); Shakespeare, in Hazlitt's formulation, as an infinite entity resembling all human beings (I, 526); Shakespeare, together with Cervantes and Virgil, an author of enduring appeal; Shakespeare, in Victor Hugo's poetic vision, an ocean forever changing its configuration (II, 261), a Protean diversification which, like Brahms' music, suggests the infinite variety of the world (II, 63); Shakespeare as a literary variation of Spinoza's infinite God (II, 261).

Only sporadically does Borges emit a judgment of discernable critical import. In one of the many disparate remarks on literary theory, Borges tell us that Hamlet's definition, "quintessence of dust," does not help us understand man in general but a particular man, Prince Hamlet (II, 217), just as the definition *roseau pensant* informs us about Pascal the man, not Pascal as a generic specimen (II, 217). Thus Borges eschews a philosophical consideration of the issue in favor of a literary one. Valéry, the lucid, cerebral Valéry, obsessed by Platonic purity, accuses Pascal of "dramatización voluntaria" (II, 217).

But what for Valéry is a philosophical terminus, for Borges is a beginning fertile in interpretative possibilities. Moreover, Shakespeare's voluntary dramatization, his centripetal interest in the individuality of the human being, appeals to Borges. Parolles, the *miles gloriosus* of *All's Well That Ends Well*, when the secret of his fraudulent promotion to captain is exposed, utters words which transform him from a conventional character of farce into a recognizable individuality, Man and man. Here are Parolles' words in Borges' translation: *"Ya no seré capitán, pero he de comer y beber y dormir como un capitán; esta cosa que soy me hará vivir"* (II, 277). Shakespeare's text reads:

> . . . Captain I'll be no more,
> But I will eat and drink, and sleep as soft
> As captain shall: simply the thing I am
> Shall make me live.
>
> IV, 3

Thus Parolles for the first time "dramatizes" himself, rather than the *dramatis persona* that he pretended to be. Borges is evidently more interested in Shakespeare than in one of his characters, Parolles. By uttering the known words, Parolles tells us more about Shakespeare than about himself. Shakespeare, Borges writes, intervenes and puts in Parolles' mouth the memorable statement. The name of the play is not even mentioned.

Hamlet, Macbeth, and *Julius Caesar* are the only Shakespearean dramas identified by title in Borges' prose works. "El Aleph," the story, begins with a verse from *Hamlet*: "O God, I could be bounded in a nutshell / and count myself a King of infinite space" (*Hamlet*, II, 2). Borges sees in Hamlet's nutshell what he sees in Pascal's sphere and in his own *Aleph*, a confirmation of a postulate refined by Giordano Bruno, that all the universe is a center, or that the center of the universe is everywhere and its circumference nowhere (II, 136). Bruno, in the light of the Renaissance, as Borges puts it, had drawn from a long tradition of metaphorical elaborations on the infinity of the divine. Hamlet is quoted again, this time in conjunction with Schopenhauer's view on suicide. Asks Borges' Schopenhauer: "¿Es el monólogo de Hamlet la meditación de un criminal?" (II, 214). It is interesting—but not surprising—that Borges, dealing, as he habitually does, with fragmentary projections, imparts to Hamlet's "to be or not to be" deliberation a philosophical intention that was, by today's standards, alien to Shakespeare. Having added to the statement of Epictetus ("Recuerda lo esencial: la puerta está abierta") Schopenhauer's question, Borges raises the issue of Jesus Christ's death as a voluntary act—the only logical assumption, to John Donne's mind (II, 215). By his paradigmatic use of Christ's death, Borges, ever so subtly, switches the problem from moral grounds to logical and legalistic ones. In the background, Schopenhauer's question looms large: "Is Hamlet's monolog the meditation of a criminal?" Would Shakespeare have seen it as such? Borges is now precisely where he wishes to be: in a grey zone in which he can speak about Shakespeare, with Shakespeare, and, on occasion, for Shakespeare.

Borges' philosophical variations on Shakespearean literary themes have measurable originality. There is no coherent philosophy in Shakespeare, no unitary view on life.[1] Even his preoccupation with time does not transcend the boundaries of traditional medieval thought. Some of Shakespeare's most striking love passages demonstrably coast on established rhetoric.[2] Shakespeare's genius, at the conceptual level, was to center drama not on verbal interest but on experience, on the human situation, on the character.[3]

Borges seizes upon this idea and plays constructively with it. In critiquing Hawthorne, Borges underscores what he considers to be the New England author's chief weakness, that of placing emphasis on the circumstance, not on the character: "Hawthorne primero imaginaba, acaso involuntariamente, una situación y buscaba después los caracteres que la encarnaran" (II, 182). In short, Hawthorne did not believe in his characters, which is why his characters are not entirely credible. They are, Borges insists, in Conrad, in Cervantes' *Quijote*, in Shakespeare's *Hamlet*. Thus with one stroke Borges removes the genre distinctions, which elsewhere he calls superstitions, and addresses himself to the issue of literary creation. Hamlet is as real as Don Quijote. Borges is explicit:

> Qué importan hechos increíbles o torpes si nos consta que el autor los ha ideado, no para sorprender nuestra buena fe, sino para definir a sus personajes. Qué importan los pueriles escándalos y los confusos crímenes de la supuesta Corte de Dinamarca si creemos en el príncipe Hamlet.
>
> II, 182

Faith makes Hamlet real to us, real, as it were, in terms of verisimilitude, esthetically not philosophically.

Edward Armstrong calls Hamlet's musings "man-in-the-street" philosophy.[4] The splendor of the human being, epitomized by "What a piece of work is man," is completely neutralized by the image of man as "quintessence of dust."[5] Hamlet will find himself not in metaphysical speculations but in action.

Traversi has energetically underscored Hamlet's loathing of physical processes, particularly of reproduction.[6] Propelled by this fundamental aversion, Hamlet, as everybody knows, wishes to hear no more of marriages and sarcastically advises Ophelia to go to a nunnery—the Elizabethan colloquial term for brothel. In other words, Ophelia's retreat to a house of ill repute is to complete the process of degradation. For all its philosophical possibilities, Hamlet's situation is not essentially philosophical. As a play, Stoll reminds us, *Hamlet* is not a drama of the mind but of characters.[7] Hamlet's conflicts are emotional.[8]

Although Borges knows *Hamlet* very well, it would be difficult to establish an unmediated connection between the Argentine's work and this drama by Shakespeare. Yet it would be equally difficult not to discern the similarity of certain seminal points. Hamlet saw in the physical process of reproduction an aggravated form of corruption. Borges plays, philosophically this time, with the same issue. Anyone acquainted with Borges' work will recall the statement that Bioy Casares "finds" in the volume XXVI of the 1917 *Anglo-American Cyclo-paedia*, a reprint of the *Encyclopedia Britannica*: "*Los espejos y la paternidad son abominables* (mirrors and fatherhood are hateful) *porque lo multiplican y lo divulgan*" (I, 410). Borges considers Bioy's recollection, "copulation and mirrors are abominable," literarily superior to the encylopedic entry. If indeed the world is adrift because the God that created it, disappointed with the results, committed suicide, if indeed the imperfection that he left behind threatens to multiply itself meaninglessly and indefinitely ("Biathanos"), the concern recorded by the *Anglo-American Cyclopedia* and unearthed by Bioy Casares is justified. As usual, Borges raises an issue, gives it a philosophical dimension, and leaves its problematic resolution to the reader.

Hamlet, we have seen, abhors reproduction and the social entity that sanctions it. He could not imagine any happiness in them. Neither does Borges' Shakespeare. The Shakespeare of "Everything and Nothing," a young man, suddenly made aware of his disconcerting uniqueness, seeks generic consolation, recognizable communality. What does he have in common with his fellow men? What confers meaning upon his own humanity? Learning, as more often than not is the case in Borges' works ("El milagro secreto," "Tlön, Uqbar, Orbis Tertius"), fails to satisfy Shakespeare, who barely retains some rudimentary Greek and Latin. Sex, equally, falls short of the promise: "después consideró que el ejercicio de un rito elemental de la humanidad, bien podía ser lo que buscaba y se dejó iniciar por Anne Hathaway, durante una larga siesta de junio" (II, 341). Only in acting and writing does Shakespeare encounter a measure of identity and gratification. Borges makes Shakespeare's disaffection with sex implicit in the following statement: "Las tareas histriónicas le enseñan una singular felicidad, acaso la primera que conoció" (II, 341).

No critic ignores the fact that Shakespeare's drama, *Julius Caesar*, figures prominently in Borges' "Tema del traidor y del héroe." Superimposed on the basic structure and thematic configuration of Shakespeare's Roman play, Borges' story follows a recognizable thread. A conspiracy, for the sake of illustration placed in Ireland, brings about a reversed perspective on the theme of the traitor and of the hero. Kilpatrick, the protagonist of the story, is reminiscent of Brutus, the hero of Shakespeare's drama, and like Brutus, is divided against himself.[9] Kilpatrick, the leader of the insurrection, is also its traitor. The facts are known. Confronted with the truth, Kilpatrick alters the factual reality of complying with the staged assassination hastily organized by Nolan, and his own image, by enlarging through sincerity and courage his appeal as a martyr. "Kilpatrick, arrebatado por ese minucioso destino que lo redimía y que lo perdía, más de una vez enriqueció con actos y palabras improvisadas el texto de su juez" (I, 494). Borges adds tellingly: "En la obra de Nolan los pasajes imitados de Shakespeare son los *menos* dramáticos" (I, 494). Borges' preoccupation with the cyclical nature of history, which obliterates the distinction between fiction and non-fiction, has been the object of numerous studies and needs no further elaboration. The transparent parallelism between *Julius Caesar* and the story, does.

Why does Borges choose *Julius Caesar*, why has Shakespeare chosen a Roman subject and followed Plutarch very closely? Borges' explanation that expediency alone dictated Nolan's choice is wrapped in an irony that conceals a larger and more interesting reason. Nolan's familiarity with Shakespeare's most important plays, which he had translated into Gaelic, while inherently a factor in the decision, is not the determing one. He was equally familiar with the Swiss Festspiele, on which he had written an article. Yet all that he drew from the Festspiele was the idea of a vast show enacted by vast participating masses. Why did Shakespeare avail himself of Plutarch's accounts? Shakespeare dramatized Plutarch because in Plutarch's historical accounts he found moral paradigms of exemplary clarity.[10] So does Nolan, within the story, so does Borges outside of it, in Shakespeare's dramas.

The action of the story could have taken place in any oppressed country (Poland, Ireland, the Republic of Venice, Borges suggests), but once Borges chooses Ireland, the peculiarity of the plot makes the presence of Shakespeare's *Julius Caesar* a natural choice. Culturally, a Swiss Festspiel—the concept, its arguments—extraneous to Ireland, would have had little impact on the Irish. Not so Shakespeare and his dramas. Ryan, Kilpatrick's great grandson, author of a work on the Irish revolution, thinks at first that the key to the elucidation of the events is to be found in Condorcet's decimal system, in the morphologies of Hegel, Spengler, and Vico, or in the theory of the transfiguration of the soul. He is, evidently, on a false track. He breaks out of the circularity of these abstractions thanks to a disconcerting discovery: some of the words that Kilpatrick exchanged with a beggar the day of his death had been prefigured by Shakespeare in *Macbeth* (I, 492). Once in the proper cultural ambience, Ryan succeeds in elucidating the mystery, even if later, for personal and patriotic reasons, he alters the facts.

By cultural ambience we mean, of course, cultural awareness, whether such an awareness be informed by fact or fiction, implicit and explicit elements of a cultural vision. Without this cultural awareness, of which he is part, Ryan would not have recognized the beggar's words as vague echoes of *Macbeth*, and without *Macbeth* he would have not thought of Shakespeare and of Julius Caesar as the seminal idea for Kilpatrick's real-life drama. Both the aware and the unaware participants in the events were culturally predisposed to understand Kilpatrick's fate, aware of the meaning of the unfolding drama. Moreover, the events surrounding Kilpatrick's death are a case in point. "Las cosas que dijeron e hicieron", Borges tells us, "perduran en los libros históricos, en la memoria apasionada de Irlanda" (I, 494). Recorded by history or retained by legend, the former as unreliable as the latter, the facts become an intrinsic part of the cultural awareness of Ireland. The facts, of course, attest to the factuality of the event, not to its originality. Nolan knew well the works of the English "enemy" William Shakespeare, and the people of Ireland, however generally, must have been acquainted with them. Like a Greek audience watching an anonymous, loose recasting of, say, Sophocles' *Oedipus*, Nolan's Irishmen must have been vaguely familiar with Shakespeare's dramas and the moral tenor of certain events resembling them. Whether the people who witnessed Kilpatrick's assassination were instantly reminded of *Julius Caesar* or not is unessential. That they were culturally receptive to the moral and political significance of the events is what matters.

Plutarch's Brutus is more dramatic than Shakespeare's, just as Nolan's Kilpatrick is more dramatic than Shakespeare's Brutus. Borges writes: "En la obra de Nolan, los pasajes imitados de Shakespeare son los *menos* (Borges' emphasis) dramáticos; Ryan sospecha que el autor los intercaló para que una persona, en el porvenir, diera con la verdad" (I, 494). They are, however sketchily, the image of reality, not images of images, literary variations. In others words, the less Kilpatrick resembles a literary character the more dramatic he is, which gives us a glimpse into Borges' view on literature and life. Borges, here and elsewhere, finds life—the situational unfolding of a will in action, with all its foreseen and unforseen vicissitudes—more dramatic than literature. Lived experience is more dramatic than an imagined one. Shakespeare's dramas are not adduced by Nolan in order to substitute reality but in order to interpret it, to impart to it a desired direction, not to lead to the facts, but in order to understand them. Facts, we are given to understand, are not dramatic—the truth is. This is why Nolan's "drama" is more dramatic than Shakespeare's.

Shakespeare is more than a casual presence in Borges' work. In "Everything and Nothing," he again engages Borges' critical attention. "Everything and Nothing" is a clever piece of writing, a masterpiece of transparent ambiguities. The title of the essay is deliberately ambiguous. "Everything" and "Nothing" refer to the materiality, or lack of it, of being, not to the awareness of the human condition, to identity. The materiality in question does not differentiate between animate and inanimate, rational and non-rational entities ("La penúltima postulación de la realidad"). Borges' emphasis is clear. The materiality or immateriality of the magus' son in "Las ruinas circulares," for instance, is not a central point. Awareness of such materiality or immateriality is. Like the God of "Everything and Nothing," who dreams Shakespeare, the magus dreams his son and imposes him on reality. Oblivious to his true condition, he knows himself to be real, with a definite identity, a reality and an identity confirmed by this participation in the universe. Borges, however unreliably and unfortunately, is Borges (II, 300).

While the essay begins with "everything" and "nothing," it ends with *muchos* and *nadie*, thus shifting the issue from physics to metaphysics. We are now on a different plane. God's statement, "yo tampoco soy," is one of identity not one of materiality. God, simply, like the God of Schopenhauer or of the Buddhists, does not have—cannot have—a definite identity. The subsequent divine classification is to the point: *"yo soñe el mundo como tú soñaste tu obra, mi Shakespeare, y entre las formas de mi sueño estás tú, que como yo eres muchos y nadie"* (II, 342). *Muchos y nadie*, not "everything and nothing." It is the spirituality of his human condition that likens man to God—the only likeness possible. Temporality and atemporality both separate and unite them. Judged in a context of materiality, Shakespeare is ultimately nothing—biblical dust. One cannot do literature with this sort of thing. Not surprisingly, Borges resorts to "somebody" and "nobody" as terms indicative of a supraphysical reality, even of a possible immortality, unaffected by material metamorphoses.

Borges' Shakespeare is not "everything" or "nothing," but "something" and "someone"—a fundamental need. "La indentidad fundamental de existir, soñar y representar le inspiró pasajes famosos" (II, 342). Borges writes, "Tenía que ser alguien" (II, 342), he reiterates. In order to become one, to be conscious of his identity, Shakespeare has to act, whether theatrically or otherwise. "To be or not to be" remains a question only as long as Hamlet is paralyzed by inertia.

Hamlet now defines himself by deed. He has resolved his conflictive emotions. This is the crux of the matter. Emotions, ultimately, affect not our reason but our will. Reason cannot generate reality—the will does.[11] In Shakespeare's early plays, reason is pitted against passion. In later dramas, the emphasis is on the good-evil antithesis, posited not morally but as an imbalance.[12] In either case, the will is central to man's dilemma of identity. We are not far from Schopenhauer's voluntarism, much commented upon by Borges.

Borges plays with ambiguity up to the last lines of "Everything and Nothing." He tells us that, like Proteus, Shakespeare exhausted all the appearances of being (II, 342). Not the being, we repeat, but the appearances of being. There is no denial of the being, only of the reliability of its appearances. Borges's Shakespeare, then, does not participate in nothingness, if one can accept this oxymoronic incongruity. By virtue of his participation in existence, dream, and representation, Shakespeare is a fluid "someone," an identity. Borges develops the argument masterfully. He tells us that either before or after his death Shakespeare appeared before God and, wishing to be himself, asked who he was. God, from a whirlwind, thunderously answered: *"yo tampoco soy; yo soñé el mundo como tú soñaste tu obra, mi Shakespeare"* (II, 342). The ambiguity is not insoluble. It is not that God does not exist, but that He does not exist as a single anthropomorphic entity. "I am not anybody in particular, either." Borges' God seems to say, "I am that I am" (II, 277). That God acknowledges Shakespeare is, of course, a recognition of the dramatist's existence, real or fictitious, but an existence nevertheless. God never tells Shakespeare that he is "nothing," only that he is no one.

Interestingly, the encounter with God does not resolve Shakespeare's dilemma. Shakespeare's uncertainty was somehow more reassuring before finding himself in front of God than after. Before, he felt the need to be somebody, and he was. After, he remains someone, but this someone is a figment of God's dream. We find Hamlet, spectator of *Hamlet*, disconcerting because such a inversion blurs the distinction between reality and fiction, putting in doubt not reality itself but the nature of reality. It is like Carlyle's universal book of history, in which we write and in which we are written (II, 175).

The elucidation of a fundamental mystery, such as the nature of one's reality, becomes a crushing burden. Characteristically, Borges places such moments near death—the extinction of temporal consciousness. Death removes the burden of knowledge. If Shakespeare met God at the end of his life, then his subsequent death rendered the truth tolerable. If immediately after, the knowledge is inconsequential. In the agony of death, Dante finally found out "who" and "what " he was, and blessed his misfortunes. Tradition has it, according to Borges, that upon awakening Dante felt (*sintió*) that he had gained and lost something infinite. Death, of course, obliterated even this residual feeling (II, 345-46). Hladik ("El milagro secreto") has to die when he achieves perfection, and so does Tzinacán ("La escritura del dios") after describing the mystery of life and his life in the Aleph that the high wheel his prison is.

Borges puts Shakespeare on a pedestal, reverentially pays his intellectual respects, and, in the most sincere form of flattery, recasts some of his ideas.

Notes

[1] Derek A. Traversi, *An Approach to Shakespeare*, 2nd ed. (Garden City: Doubleday and Co., 1956), p. 10.

[2] Ibid., p. 15.

[3] Ibid., p. 59.

[4] Edward A. Armstrong, *Shakespeare's Imagination* (Lincoln: University of Nebraska Press, 1963), p. 108.

[5] Ibid., p. 108.

[6] Traversi, p. 93.

[7] Elmer Edgard Stoll, *Art and Artifice in Shakespeare* (New York: Barnes and Noble, 1951), p. 108.

[8] Traversi, p. 83.

[9] Derek Traversi, *Shakespeare: The Roman Plays* (Stanford: Stanford University Press, 1963), p. 15.

[10] Traversi, *Shakespeare: The Roman Plays*, 11.

[11] Traversi, *An Approach to Shakespeare*, p. 160.

[12] Ibid., p. 127; Theodore Spencer, *Shakespeare and the Nature of Man* (New York: The MacMillan Co., 1942), p. 93.

Quevedo

More than a man of letters, more than a literary phenomenon, Quevedo is a literature (II, 211). Borges, who vindicates Quevedo on the basis of such a distinction, finds the Spanish author's omission from the compendium of world writers an extravagance (II, 164). The absence of conspicuous sentimentality from Quevedo's work, of communicable warmth, partially explains such an oversight. Quevedo simply does not give himself to flights of effusion, and his work rarely inspires pathetism. Even a casual but perceptive reader can readily notice that Quevedo does not speak to man, to the delicate microcosm that man is, but about him. Quevedo is essentially lonely, steeped into what Naumann calls "inhumana soledad."[1] If he fails to establish an eternal dialogue with the reader, to engage his imagination, Borges believes, it is not because of inferior talent but because somehow he did not manage to coin an universal symbol. Homer has Priam, Sophocles has Oedipus, Lucretius the infinite, Dante the concentric circles, Shakespeare his violence and music, Cervantes the dynamic relationship between Don Quijote and Sancho. Swift, Mallarmé, Kafka, Góngora, Melville, Whitman, also figure in Borges' pantheon of writers who have committed an explicit or implicit symbol to the memory of man (II, 164-65). Quevedo, instead, projects the image of a literary caricature. Borges quotes the trenchant judgment of Leopoldo Lugones (*El imperio jesuítico*, 1904, p. 59): "El más noble de los estilistas españoles se ha transformado en un prototipo chascarrillero" (II, 165). Such as Borges envisages the matter, sentimentality—in literature or in life—is not a prerequisite for greatness; creating a symbol, an enduring one, is. Borges, of course, is also speaking about himself.

The magnitude of Borges' admiration for Quevedo can be educed from his assessment of Quevedo as a writers' writer: "Para gustar de Quevedo hay que ser (en acto o en potencia) un hombre de letras; inversamente, nadie que tenga vocación literaria puede no gustar de Quevedo" (II, 165). Borges is rather precise here. When he says that in order to enjoy Quevedo one must be either virtually or potentially a man of letters, he enlarges considerably Quevedo's appreciation. Whoever has literary vocation cannot help but like Quevedo, not necessarily Quevedo's opus or Quevedo the man, but Quevedo the literato. For Quevedo is above all a virtuoso of the word, a man who, like Borges himself, always found refuge and solace in books.[2] When Borges writes that Quevedo's greatness is verbal (II, 165), he does not mean the latter's celebrated mordacious humor, for humor in Borges' view is perhaps an oral genre (II, 273). Rather, seeking something more enduring, he states that Quevedo is a man of letters, a generator of literature; not a philosopher, a theologian, or a statesman, but a man of letters. To say, like Leopoldo Lugones, that Quevedo is the noblest of Spanish stylists, is not sufficient (II, 165). Borges adds that Quevedo redeems almost everything with the dignity of language (II, 166). Diffident of philosophy, when he has to choose between the arbitrariness of a method and the triviality of conclusions, Quevedo opts for a third alternative, a stylistic one of illusory precision (II, 166).

Quevedo, in Borges' interpretation, was uncomfortable with trivialities in poetry (II, 167). Borges' phrasing is careful. His Quevedo is not reticent about poetry as a genre, only about the hackneyed, often false, images routinely transmitted from generation to generation. "Olvidó, al censurarlas," says Borges, "que la metáfora es el contacto momentáneo de dos imágenes, no la metódica asimilación de dos cosas . . ." (II, 167). When Quevedo perceives not a fleeting contact but a methodical assimilation of things, we are not far from logic.

Indeed, Borges tells us that for Quevedo language was, essentially, a logical instrument (II, 167).

It is the only serious criticism that Borges levels at Quevedo. But the desire to vindicate Quevedo is also present in the statement. Quevedo, we are given to understand, with his vast erudition surely knew how metaphors are born and how they function, but such knowledge must have been obscured by his critical temperament. While such a temperament did not hamper Quevedo in his anticlerical works, in which, however brilliantly, he merely observed a literary tradition (II, 167), it did affect his creative process in poetry. Here Borges' judgment becomes highly personal and slightly anachronous. Terry points out that modern criticism of Quevedo often ignores the vagaries of the term metaphor in different cultural periods:

> La concepción de la metáfora en los siglos XVI y XVII insiste en su capacidad de envolver al lector en un proceso de abstracción, algo bien distinto, hay que decirlo, de la moderna tendencia a mirarla en términos de exactitud sensórea.[3]

The acceptance of the term in the 16th and 17th centuries differs from that of modern times. Borges, of course, does not ignore the difference, but tends to lend uniqueness to Quevedo's propensity. Quevedo, however, was not the only Baroque poet to have challenged the muse in Petrarchan terms. Borges writes about Quevedo's amatory poetry: "Considerados como documentos de una pasión, los poemas eróticos de Quevedo son insatisfactorios; considerados como juego de hipérboles, como deliberadoes ejercicios de petrarquismo, suelen ser admirables" (II, 168).

First, to consider a poem a document of passion is to write with an obvious oxymoronic intention. We may not agree with Valéry that every work of art is a forgery, but a poem—of whatever nature—cannot be a document, an account of legal or historical precision.[4] Borges, as we can see, prefers to emphasize Quevedo's classical erudition and inspired verbal dexterity. There is, however, a marked difference between the Petrarchan use of hyperboles and oxymoronic images and that of Quevedo. Naumann incisively notes that in the Petrarchan tradition the union of opposites indicates renunciation of knowledge in a situation which seems incomprehensible. But Quevedo, in Naumann judgment, does not renounce knowledge, only the meaning of knowledge.[5] This is why Quevedo, while frequently using classical models, improves in imagery upon the model used.[6] Durán observes that however contradictory a Quevedian reality may be, the context always elucidates it.[7] Not infrequently, Quevedo works by reductions, by inversions; the image becomes an object, a meaning is rendered absurd (II, 167). In a work that is merely an extension of a literary tradition, like Quevedo's anticlerical pieces, the personality of the author is thematically overshadowed. Not so in a work of thematic originality. Borges is emphatic on this matter. The personal Quevedo is not to be found in, say, *El Buscón* or some anticlerical tract, not in the vehemence with which he rejects passion, but in his reflective moods, in melancholy and the untranslatable *desengaño* (II, 168).

As in Whitman's case, Borges reproduces integrally some of Quevedo's sonnets. When from the Protean work of Quevedo Borges chooses a particular sonnet, the choice receives added significance. Let us read it with Borges:

> Retirado en la paz de los desiertos,
> Con pocos, pero doctos, libros juntos,
> Vivo en conversación con los difuntos
> Y escucho con mis ojos a los muertos.
>
> Si no siempre entendidos, siempre, abiertos,
> O enmiendan o secundan mis asuntos,
> Y en músicos callados contrapuntos
> Al sueño de la vida hablan despiertos.
>
> En fuga irrevocable huye la hora;
> Pero aquélla el mejor cálculo cuenta,
> Que en la lección y estudio nos mejora.
>
> II, 168

Why would Borges consider "Desde la torre" to be the quintessential Quevedo? Let us follow Quevedo—and Borges—

closely. The sonnet, of which there are two versions, we learn from James O. Crosby, is both a great poem and evidence of Quevedo's bettered poetic expression.[8] In the original version the last verse of the quatrain read *oigo hablar* instead of *escuchar*.[9] The choice is significant for it reflects active participation, not passive reception. This is not Hamlet's monolog before Yorick's skull, but a dialog, a dual participation. The wisdom that wafts towards Quevedo, like the music of Orpheus, originates in the land of the dead, the dead resurrected by an esthetic act. While the peace of the desert is suggestive of the studious quiet of a library, Quevedo's presence is not reduced only to reading. The key term in the first quatrain is conversation, an activity that, as opposed to reading, engages not only vision and intellect, but listening and speaking, a totality. Thus the dialogical presence of Quevedo in the sonnet acquires a marked dramatic interest. To hear, to see, to think, to speak, suggest of course an immediate individuality interacting with reality.

We can discern this in Borges. The myriad inscriptions on carts in Buenos Aires are not just lapidary sentences, but fragments of a dialogue in which the reader participates. "Pa la rubia, cuándo," "Quien lo diría," "No llora el perdido," are sentences which, in Borges' vision, aside from echoing delicately a Browning, a Góngora, or a Mallarmé (I, 74), constitute a premise for discussion, not a conclusion. Borges writes with conviction:

> Implican drama, están en la circulación de la realidad. Corresponden a frecuencias de la emoción: son como del destino, siempre. Son ademanes perdurados por la escritura, son una afirmación incesante. Su alusividad es la del conversador orillero que no puede ser directo narrador o razonador y se complace en discontinuidades, en generalidades, en fintas: sinuosas como el corte.
>
> I, 74

Borges' judgement is not incompatible with that of Quevedo in the sonnet. From Borges we learn that something dramatic is part of a dynamic reality (*circulación*), that it unfolds within the gamut of emotion, that it is an incessant gesture. Ignoring the temperamental configuration of the *orillero*, we must remember that he is a conversationalist—hence the incompleteness of his utterances.

If the first quatrain establishes the live presence of Quevedo, the second one accredits that of the books, of the authors who wrote them. The active voice, in the present, is predominant: *enmiendan, fecundan, hablan.* The contrapuntal intention is inescapable; *"hablan despiertos" "al sueño de la vida."* The double aspect of communication is perhaps best illustrated in Borges' "Kafka y sus precursores." Borges writes about Kafka: "A éste, al principio, lo pensé tan singular como el fénix de las alabanzas retóricas; a poco de frecuentarlo, creí reconocer su voz, o sus hábitos, en textos de diversas literaturas y épocas" (II, 226). It is an extraordinary statement. Kafka, according to Borges, is to be found in one of Zeno's paradoxes, in an apology of Han Yu by Margouliè, in a writing by Kierkegaard, in a poem by Browning, in two stories by León Bloy and Lord Dunsany. While the works cited do not resemble each other, they resemble Kafka's, which Borges finds significant (II, 228). He goes on to say that in each text there is a Kafkaesque idiosyncrasy; if Kafka had not written, we would not have recognized him in other authors. Borges' judgement: "El hecho es que cada escritor *crea* a sus precursores. Su labor modifica nuestra concepción del pasado, como ha de modificar el futuro" (II, 228. Borges' emphasis.). Borges uses the verb *crear*. To "create," of course, is to organize the literary matter according to one's own creative impulse and sensitivity, while to "recreate" is to do so from someone else's point of view. And it is only as a creation, not as a recreation, that an author's work can modify our concept of the past and of the future.[10] Borges exemplifies his theory in "Pierre Menard, autor del *Quijote*."

The tercet that follows is an encomium to the printing press, which frees (active voice) the great spirits of mankind from the constraining vicissitudes of age, that is to say, of mortality. The dialog is timeless. Describing the burning at the stake of Miguel de Servet in Calvin's Geneva, Borges quotes the Spaniard's memorable last words: *"Arderé, pero ello no es otra cosa que un hecho. Ya seguiremos discutiendo en la eternidad"* (I, 404. The emphasis is Borges'.). That the old masters are not only books is a fact, like Servet's death. That they are alive in the books, like Servet's argument, is what is essential. It is not by accident that Borges is forever receptive to this sort of verbal immortality. The last tercet of Quevedo's sonnet does much more than rhapsodize on the *tempus fugit* theme or the benefits of instruction. It inserts Quevedo into the continuity of his predecessors, it offers him the hope of an eternity. Quevedo himself, bettered by the dynamic contact with the past, by the wisdom gleaned from his forerunners, by the incessant dialogue, becomes the promise of a great book. Better yet, he became a literature (II, 211).

For Quevedo, such a dynamism is the true greatness of the past, not its static, archeological presence. And it is this mutual relationship that Quevedo maintains with the past that appeals to Borges, for the past, thus construed, is nothing but a present. The live past becomes a living present. This is one of the affinities that Quevedo and Borges have in common. Like Quevedo's sonnet, Borges' essays, however philosophical, have a conversational tone. The I of the author is prominent in the discussion of philosophical or metaphysical matters put forth by predecessors while engaging the attention of the reader. Borges refutes Kant's notion that space is a universal form of intuition, considering it an incident in time, and agrees in principle with Spencer's and Schopenhauer's assertion that some realities—sounds, odors, etc.—do not need space: one cannot look for the left side of a sound or imagine an inside-out odor (I, 132). Borges' contribution has the directness of a conversational rejoinder:

> Imaginemos que el género humano sólo se abasteciera de realidades mediante la audición y el olfato. Imaginemos anuladas así las percepciones oculares, táctiles y gustativas y el espacio que éstas definen. Imaginemos también—crecimiento lógico—una más afinada percepción de lo que registran los sentidos restantes. La humanidad—tan

afantasmada a nuestro parecer por esta catástrofe—seguirá urdiendo su historia. La humanidad se olvidará de que hubo espacio.

I, 133

Borges adds to the subject matter discussed by his illustrious predecessors, and repeatedly urges all participants to imagine (*imaginemos*) another possibility of being. As in "Historia del guerrero y de la cautiva," we are in the realm of literature rather than history. Following the Argentine's optics in "Kafka y sus precursores," one can easily discern Borges—a possible Borges—in Quevedo's sonnet.

In the sonnet, Borges finds a different Quevedo. In spite of some literary conceits destined to emphasize Quevedo's linguistic virtuosity, the sonnet, in Borges' view, is very efficacious. The poem is not a transcription of reality, because reality is not verbal (II, 168). Its force and significance reside in its mood. The words, uncharacteristically for Quevedo, recede into the mood that they create. They are not, as more often than not is the case with Quevedo, literary artifacts, "objetos verbales, puros e independientes como una espada o como un anillo de plata" (II, 171), not an end in themselves, but a means of conveying meaning. By contrast, a sonnet like "Harta la Toga del veneno tirio" is vintage Quevedo. It is in the context of this sonnet that Quevedo's best pieces exist beyond the notion that engendered them and the common ideas which informed them (II, 171). Quevedo transcends the obscurity of language by objectivising it.

What else has Borges learned from his own dialogue with Quevedo? "No pocas veces," says Borges, "el punto de partida de Quevedo es un texto clásico" (II, 169). It is as if Borges were speaking about himself. Even someone sporadically acquainted with Borges' work would not fail to acknowledge that most of his essays and prose fiction begins with an outside reference: a literary allusion, a philosophical proposition, a direct quotation. Speaking of Spencer's and Schopenhauer's theory about the avoidability of space, Borges writes: "Quiero completar esas dos imaginaciones ilustres con una mía, que es derivación y facilitación de ellas" (I, 133). The virtue of such a procedure resides in the immediate prestige that it confers upon the writer, who thus appears as a perpetuator of universal themes, not as a dilettante engaged in trivialities. The occasional—and, perhaps, inevitable, as Borges would put it—poetry dedicated to, say, a Duke of Osuna is one thing, and the sonnet inspired by a verse from Propertius' elegies, "Ut meus oblito pulvis amore vacet," is quite another. To begin a work with a classical reference is to make a statement of principle; it is, in a way, to aspire to classicism. And classicism is for Borges an accessible form of immortality. When Borges ponders the question as to what makes a literary work classic, he does not detach his name from those of universal fame:

> Yo, que me he resignado a poner en duda la indefinida perduración de Voltaire o de Shakespeare, creo (esta tarde de uno de los últimos días de 1965) en la de Schopenhauer y en la de Berkeley.
>
> II, 303

Whatever mutations intervene in Borges' point of view, he prefers to remain within the realm of universal writers and, like them, to win the mysterious loyalty of readers (II, 303). Borges has read the classics, has dialoged with them, has learned from them. He, like Quevedo, has preferred the select company of greatness. When Eudoro Acevedo, Borges' fictive *alter ego* in "Utopía de un hombre que está cansado" tells the man of the future that he has more than two thousand volumes in his library, the latter ironically retorts: "Nadie puede leer dos mil libros" (II, 512). He concludes emphatically: "Además no importa leer sino releer" (II, 512). Flaubert, we recall, nourished himself on the intensive culture of a half dozen disparate books (I, 211).

There is a lot of Borges in Quevedo, and vice versa. Borges' most notable, if facetious, attempt at pure poetry is that of the *kenningar*, "objetos verbales, puros e independientes como un cristal o un anillo de plata" (I, 352). It is an almost literal description of Quevedo's poems (II, 171). The *kenningar*, the first deliberate verbal enjoyment of an instinctive literature (I,

335), are at first divine utterances. In Snorri Sturluson's *Edda Prosaica* a certain Aegir or Hler, well versed in the occult arts, cultivates the friendship of Bragi, the god of poetry. During a protracted conversation between man and god, promoted by vast quantities of mead, the latter dictates to the former a list of metaphors indispensable to poetry (I, 339). The metaphors are the god's reality, while for Hler they are a metaphorical equivalent of it. Modern man does not possess the magic to understand this. Our metaphors are not like Hler's. It is an opinion that has not changed in Borges' enduring literary career. Hler and Bragi figure in an essay written in 1933. Thirty nine years later, in the prolog to *El oro de los tigres*, he expresses essentially the same point of view:

> En el principio de los tiempos, tan dócil a la vaga especulación y a las inapelables cosmogonías, no habrá habido cosas poéticas o prosaicas. Todo sería un poco mágico. Thor no era el dios del trueno; era el trueno y el dios.
>
> II, 439

Bragi is not reality and metaphor, but reality. The metaphor is a concession, an invented compromise, that he makes for his friend Hler. It becomes art. It becomes art when we pass from a natural order to a magical one, say from birds to literature as in "La busca de Averroes," or from earth to heaven, as in "Los teólogos."

Quevedo's vast work is predominantly comprised of variations on the same theme. The theme is not man, but the endless verbal diversification of the *ingenio*. Quevedo dealt with skeletons, linguistically and emotionally. Unlike the old magus in "Las ruinas circulares," Quevedo did not look for a live soul to participate in the universe. Even in "Amor constante más allá de la muerte," according to Durán the best Spanish sonnet ever written, the immortality sought is not that of the soul but of the body.[11]

Of the seemingly endless number of outstanding literary and philosophical figures that have claimed Borges' curiosity, few have endured more in Borges' attention than Quevedo. One of

Borges' last stories, "Utopía de un hombre que está cansado," begins with a reference to Quevedo: "*Llamóla* Utopía, *voz griega cuyo significado es* no hay tal lugar" (II, 510). Borges, of course, could have chosen an etymological explanation from a lexicon or a reference to a Greek philosopher. Instead, he quotes Quevedo. In the prolog to *El informe de Brodie* (1970), Borges mentions Quevedo anecdotally (II, 371). The reason is clear: "Trescientos años ha cumplido la muerte corporal de Quevedo, pero éste sigue siendo el primer artífice de las letras hispánicas" (II, 171). Borges admires Quevedo's linguistic virtuosity, the extraordinary range of his versatility, the biting humor that lingers with the persistence of aphoristic wisdom. Notwithstanding his deficiencies, Quevedo remains, in the judgment of Luis Astrana Marín, the greatest master of language that Spain has ever produced.[12]

Notes

[1] Walter Naumann, "Polvo enamorado: Muerte y Amor en Propercio, Quevedo y Goethe," in *Francisco de Quevedo*, ed. Gonzalo Sobejano (Madrid: Taurus, 1978), p. 335.

[2] Manuel Durán, *Quevedo* (Madrid: Edaf, 1978), p. 25.

[3] Arthur Terry, "Quevedo y el concepto metafísico," in *Francisco de Quevedo*, p. 67.

[4] Durán, p. 96.

[5] Naumann, p. 337.

[6] James O. Crosby, "Quevedo, la antología griega y Horacio," in *Francisco de Quevedo*, p. 274.

[7] Durán, p. 51.

[8] Crosby, *En torno a la poesía de Quevedo* (Madrid: Castalia, 1967), p. 40.

[9] Ibid., p. 40.

[10] Agheana, "Borges, 'Creator' of Cervantes; Cervantes Precursor of Borges," p. 17.

[11] Durán, p. 99.

[12] Luis Astrana Marín, *Ideario de Don Francisco de Quevedo* (Madrid: Almagro, 1940), p. 22.

Shaw

Judging by the number and the content of references to George Bernard Shaw, and by Shaw's enduring presence in his work, Borges holds the Irish master in great admiration. Shaw's vigorous philosophical thinking, his theory and practice of literature, his irrepressible corrosive wit, have appealed to Borges, implicitly and explicitly, throughout his entire literary career. Why, among the seemingly endless figures of world literature who inhabit Borges' literary world, is Shaw an exemplary writer? What is Borges' Shaw like? Previous, casual mention notwithstanding, the first essay that Borges dedicates to Shaw is "Nota sobre (hacia) Bernard Shaw," written in 1951, but published in 1960, in *Otras inquisiciones*. There is both certainty and tentativeness in the title, which reveals Borges' intellectual honesty about Shaw. Borges avoids formulating definitive judgments about the Irish author, avoids even casting a shadow of irony or doubt, as if desirous of keeping this literary relationship active, alive.

Curiously, Borges dedicates the inchoate part of his essay not to Shaw, but to a rather lengthy and eclectic list of writers. The names, however, with minor exceptions, are recognizable and can be readily organized around Borges' intention, that of providing a contrasting background to Shaw's originality. Raymond Lull, John Stuart Mill, and the imaginary Kurd Lasswitz, spanning centuries, are mentioned in order to illustrate the intellectual propensity of making out of metaphysics and literature a combinatory game. Borges' emphasis: "Quienes practican ese juego olvidan que un libro es más que una estructura verbal, o que una serie de estructuras verbales;

es el diálogo que entabla con su lector y la entonación que impone a su voz las cambiantes y durables imágenes que deja en su memoria" (II, 271). We are in possession of the main characteristic of Shaw's literary individuality, for Shaw, as distinct from those who indulge in pure structural virtuosity, engages the reader in a dialog.

Borges' attack against literature made with the help of dictionaries has prepared us for such a statement. This time, he makes it on behalf of Shaw. Literature is a live relationship between a literary work and its reader, a dialog, not merely an esthetic sample which we simply enjoy or critique. In short, literature is not a game. It is a dialog, an infinite dialog (II, 271). An interlocutor is not a fixed point of view or an abstraction. An interlocutor, in life or in a literary context, is a naturally polyvalent presence: "puede no hablar y traslucir que es inteligente, puede emitir observaciones inteligentes y traslucir estupidez" (II, 272). An example from literature: "d'Artagnan ejecuta hazañas numerosas y Don Quijote es apaleado y escarnecido, pero el valor de Don Quijote se siente más" (II, 272–73). Once again, the verb *sentir* makes its appearance in a literary consideration; not *notar* or *percibir*, but *sentir*. It refers to both the literary work and the reader; the purpose of the former is *hacer sentir*, the experience of the reader is *sentir*.

The introductory part of the essay leads to a question of universal scope. The question, in Borges' view, is an ethical one: "¿Puede un autor crear personajes superiores a él?" (II, 273). In spite of its topicality (Cervantes-Don Quijote, etc.), and of Borges' ironic claim to originality, the question is valid. Such a question, of course, affects the totality of literary expression, creator and creation. Borges' answer is negative, a negation that comprises not only the ethical aspect, but intellectual and moral ones as well (II, 273). Like father, like son? Borges' answer is affirmative, but qualified by a significant distinction. The discrepancy is not between literary father and son, but between son and other literary offspring, of generational differences. This brings forth Shaw's "anachronism." Borges is now in his element. Some of the characters created by Shaw—

Lavinia, Kreegan, Shotover, Richard Dudgeon, and, above all, Julius Caesar—surpass, in Borges' view, any modern literary protagonist: "Pensar a Monsieur Teste junto a ellos o al histriónico Zarathustra de Nietzsche es intuir con asombro y aun con escándalo la primacía de Shaw" (II, 273). Valéry and Nietzsche produce characters who transcend the differential traits of the I, whose personality dissolves into nothingness. They embody philosophical points of view more than they do individualized humanity. Borges' Shaw, in spite of his political militancy and philosophical allegiances, marches in the opposite direction. His characters are not ideologies dissembled by flesh and blood, but genuine human beings individualized by their experiences. Zarathustra is histrionic and pathetic as a human being, as a human being in literature, to be sure, but a human being nevertheless, not simply as a philosopher *manqué* or an utopian man of action. His humanity is not recognizable, vitally or literarily. As opposed to Hawthorne, Shaw does not subordinate literature to ethics. Readers familiar with Shaw's thematic preoccupation might feel inclined to take Borges to task, but Borges has taken pains to underscore that he is a hedonistic reader (I, 171). Not infrequently, a hedonistic critic as well.

When a writer is also a critic, his criticism is edifying not only in terms of other authors but of himself as well. Such is the case with both Shaw and Borges. Shaw, for instance, claims that Shakespeare never understood virtue and courage.[1] Shaw believes that the Shakespearean character does not operate under the purposeful guidance of an ethical system. Without virtue and courage, without an ethical purpose to justify and ennoble him, the Shakespearean *dramatis persona* can only be a protagonist but not a hero. It is not inaction that prevents the Shakespearean protagonist from attaining true heroic greatness, but action which does not transcend the desires of the I. Contrary to Soergel's assertion ("Bernard Shaw es un aniquilador del concepto heroico, un matador de héroes," II, 273), Shaw is not a killer of heroes. On the contrary, he is a sincere admirer of the heroic spirit, and, demonstrably, a creator of heroes. The Shavian protagonist exudes *élan vital* (to use Borges' term) and freedom, and these are the attributes that appeal to Borges. Shaw's work has the flavor of freedom, "sabor de liberación" (II, 274). The noun *sabor* is recurrent, the context similar. In "El pudor de la historia," whose title denotes the inability of history to recognize the true significance of certain dates and events, Borges ruefully remarks:

> Hay un sabor que nuestro tiempo (hastiado, acaso, por las torpes imitaciones de los profesionales del patriotismo) no suele percibir sin algún recelo: el elemental sabor de lo heroico.
>
> II, 282

Borges writes with clarity. He continues:

> Me aseguran que el *Poema del Cid* encierra ese sabor; yo lo he sentido, inconfundible, en versos de la *Eneida* ("Hijo, aprende de mí, valor y verdadera firmeza; de otros, el éxito") en la balada anglosajona de Maldon ("Mi pueblo pagará el tributo con lanzas y con viejas espadas"), en la *Canción de Rolando,* en Victor Hugo, en Whitman, en Faulkner ("La alhucema, más fuerte que el olor de los caballos y del coraje"), en el *Epitafio para un ejército de mercenarios* de Houseman, y en los "seis pies de tierra inglesa" de la *Heimskringla.*
>
> II, 282

This rather lengthy and seemingly eclectic enumeration has the virtue of showing unambiguously that Borges finds the heroic flavor in the epic tradition, and that such a tradition is not extinct.

The crude imitations of heroism perpetrated by the professionals of patriotism are, needless to say, a travesty of the heroic spirit. It is not the first time that Borges derides the self-deluding strictures of misunderstood patriotism. "Las ilusiones del patriotismo no tienen término," writes Borges about the ridiculous pretense that the moon of Corinth is more beautiful than that of Athens (II, 161). He sees an inherent contradiction in the attitude of nationalists who, on the one hand, extoll the capacity of the Argentine mind, and, on the other, limit the exercise of poetry of such a mind to a few poor, local themes (I, 220). Shaw, for reasons not dissimilar to those of Borges, strenuously objected to national patriotism.[2] While the epic condition is verbally exemplified in Borges' compilation of memorable utterings, it is realized in action.

When Borges states that Shaw's work is evocative of the *Portico*, the Greek world is brought to the fore. Borges, we recall, circumscribes philosophy and ethics as the fundamental themes of Shaw (II, 274). Against the background of Greek antiquity, virtue and courage, notions that Shaw's Shakespeare is supposed not to have understood, acquire added meaning. The Shavian hero is essentially cast in a Greek epic mold. It is, then, hardly surprising that a serious study, like A. W. H. Adkin's work on Greek values, begins with a prefatory quotation from Shaw: "I say that a man's first duty is to learn to fight. If he can't do that, he can't set an example; he can't stand up for his own rights or his neighbors'."[3] We are not far from Aristotle's assertion that drama is primarily ethical.[4] The Shavian hero is Sophoclean rather than Euripidean, for he prefers to act rather than suffer.[5] Octavius, in Shaw's *Man and Superman*, lamenting the death of his benefactor, unwittingly points out his inability to act: "I always intended to thank him."[6] Next to John Tanner, the main character, he is a meek, self-effacing presence. He cannot stand alone.

The Sophoclean hero acts in a vacuum, alone.[7] This is inevitably so, for the crisis in which he finds himself pits him against the *polis*. The Homeric culture is essentially a "shame culture" in which the utmost good is to be well spoken of.[8] Tanner, speaking of the society of his time—end of the 19th century, beginning of the 20th century—states that it is dominated by shame, so much so that even when people speak about virtue they feel shame. Tanner expresses forcefully the degree to which such a society has perverted its values: "The more things a man is ashamed of, the more respectable he is" (p. 52). To quote Tanner's—and Shaw's—irreplaceable expression, the human being has become "nonentitized" (p. 60). Fighting and asserting one's self, as Shaw puts it in Adkins' quotation, are, then, the only things that can transform man into an entity once more. For the Greek hero, to decry injustice is not enough; he must act.[9] But he must act in accordance with his conscience, for virtue for the hero is faithfulness to his ideas and ideals.[10] In the tragic hero, action springs from the very root of his individual nature, from his *physis*.[11] The Shavian hero, like his Greek counterpart, is a man in crisis. Yet, again like his Greek homologue, he does not respond to the crisis for purely selfish reasons. The Greek hero, whether an atheist or not, must, in Plato's view, possess a just character, an *ethos dikaion*.[12] And so it is with the Shavian hero.

No one acquainted with Shaw's *Man and Superman* ignores its ironic outcome. John Tanner, for all his heroic rhetoric, does not acquire genuine heroic stature. In spite of his conscience, he simply is not a doer. The quintessential Shavian hero is Undershaft, a man who transforms a vision into action.[13] Nor is there any discrepancy between vision and action. The judgment of C. H. Whitman on the heroic temper is illuminating: "The highest heroes are not men of delusion. They are men of clarity and purity."[14] They do things on their own spiritual terms. The Greeks had the genius of generalizing about the individual without destroying individuality.[15] So did Shaw.

The Shavian hero is a person of clarity of purpose and action. Borges notes that Shaw puts the illusions of eroticism, abnegation, glory, and pure love in hell, and the comprehension of reality in heaven (I, 232). Had Shaw not qualified the categories that he consigns to hell, we, like Soergel, would have considered him to be a killer of heroes (II, 273). The comprehension of reality is not affected by eroticism, abnegation, glory, and love, only by the illusions which we unwisely attach to them. In essence, we elevate illusions into absolutes. It is a serious, self-deluding flaw. There is no eroticism without commitment, no abnegation without sacrifice, and no love without suffering. Illusions, unmistakably, corrupt the integrity of reality, which is why Shaw places them in hell. Borges tellingly underscores the reason for Soergel's judgment on Shaw, his failure to accept other than romantic heroes (II, 273). A hat which is not

sanctioned by Paris is not a hat (II, 78). An illusion is misleading because it tampers with recognizable reality. Borges' Teodelina Villar, in "El zahir," is less interested in beauty than in
perfection (II, 77). Having considered this statement, the per-
spicuous reader already guesses Teodelina's flaw; her propensity to unreality, her gradually becoming part of it. Teodelina,
we read, "se plegaba a los azares de Paris o de Hollywood" (II,
78). Instead of being elegant she is merely pretentious. Unfa-
vorable circumstances lead her to the realization that her
"reality" is only an illusion. She wills herself to die (II, 78). The
narrator himself, with deliberate irony, confesses his own
infatuation with illusion: "¿Confesaré que, movido por la más
sincera de las pasiones argentinas, el esnobismo, yo estaba
enamorado de ella y que su muerte me afectó hasta las
lágrimas?" (II, 78). Snobbery as sincere passion epitomizes the
extent of self-delusion. In Borges, illusions end in death (Teodelina Villar in "El zahir," Benjamín Otálora in "El muerto,"
etc.). In Shaw they are consigned to Hell.

Borges installs Shaw's work in an epic framework. Shaw,
unlike Argentines in general, does not reduce ethics to a
conflict among individuals, classes, or nations (II, 274). Instead,
he makes it a matter of individual conscience—of conscience in
action. Borges characterizes the philosophies which appeal to
vanity—Heidegger's and Jaspers' existentialism—as immoral
(II, 274). In contrast, we are told, Shaw's work breathes
freedom, the freedom of the *Portico*, of the sagas (II, 274).
Interestingly, Borges criticizes Nietzsche's Superman but not
Shaw's. Nietzsche's Superman—the man capable of living
happily with immortality—cannot exist, or can exist only as a
mental nightmare (I, 360). Shaw's Superman exists, but he
exists only as John Tanner, not as Don Juan. In John Tanner's
metaphysical dream, Borges points out, the horror of Hell is its
unreality (II, 248). It is a fecund idea. This unreality of Shaw's
Hell helps Borges understand Nazism (II, 248). Hitler and the
exponents of Nazism cannot be heroes because they are blood
relatives of chaos ("consanguíneos del caos"). Borges writes:

Ser nazi (jugar a la barbarie enérgica, jugar a ser un vikingo, un tártaro, un conquistador del siglo XVI, un gaucho, un piel roja) es, a la larga, una imposibilidad mental y moral. El nazismo adolece de irrealidad, como los infiernos de Erígena. Es inhabitable; los hombres sólo pueden morir por él, mentir por él, matar y ensangrentar por él. Nadie, en la soledad central de su yo, puede anhelar que triunfe.

II, 248–49

Shaw puts Superman and hell in a metaphysical dream. Hitler attempted to put him on earth, thus ultimately rendering him totally unreal. That this unreality was not going to endure was made obvious by the defeat of Nazi Germany (II, 248). Descending upon the earth, Superman doomed himself. The ethical I of an individual cannot possibly desire the triumph of a horrendous unreality like Nazism any more than it wishes to converse with Nothingness (II, 274). The defeat of Nazism was not willed away by heroic rhetoric but by heroic action. As Borges writes in "El hombre en el umbral," "Hablar no basta" (II, 109). Shaw and Borges know this. A character is forged in the crucible of experience.

The primacy of Shaw is that of esthetic freedom. This is Borges' central point. *Man and Superman,* according to Pearson, a critic whom Borges himself quotes elsewhere (II, 204), was the first play by Shaw that had no reference to the stage conventions of his age.[16] The best Shaw is not that of the first works, preoccupied with civic issues, is not that of the dated humor of the *Pleasant Plays,* but that of the protagonists who transcend such matters without transcending themselves. The best Shaw is not a political writer or a moralist, but a man of letters, a creator of individualities. While there is ample social criticism in Shaw's work, a close scrutiny reveals that such criticism has more to do with the abuse of personal relationships than with social injustice as such.[17] Shaw eschews ideals that are purely conventional, deprived of any ethical significance.[18] There is, to be sure, a recognizable social backdrop to Shaw's work, but Shaw drew more from situational humanity, real or imagined, than from social realities or political ideas.[19] Are the best of Shaw's protagonists heroes? It depends on how closely we adhere to the spirit, rather than the letter, of the term. Let us follow Borges' reasoning. He points out that the understanding of *Martín Fierro*, for instance, is impaired by formal genre distinctions, to which some critics cling unduly. Borges underscores the novelistic nature of Hernández' poetic work:

> Dije que una novela. Se me recordará que las epopeyas antiguas representan una preforma de la novela. De acuerdo, pero asimilar el libro de Hernández a esa categoría primitiva es agotarse inútilmente en un juego de fingir coincidencias, es renunciar a toda posibilidad de examen. La legislación de la épica—metros heroicos, intervención de los dioses, destacada situación política de los héroes—no es aplicable aquí. Las condiciones novelísticas, sí lo son.
>
> I, 128

And so it is with Shaw's characters, who share in the epic or heroic condition, but who do not subordinate such a condition to a vogue. Shaw, the consequential Shaw, refused to falsify humanity. He was accused of being too close, not too removed from his characters. Soergel, it will be remembered, called Shaw a killer of heroes. Substituting *concepto heroico* and "matador de héroes" for "individuality" and "killer of individuality," the statement reads like some of the contemporary criticism on Borges.[20] Contrary to the romantic belief of the time, romanticism is not the only way of achieving individuality. Borges terms the romantic emphasis on personality a partial lie (I, 156). It is indeed the creation of memorable protagonists, of individualities free of literary prejudices or fashionable emphasis, that accredits, to Borges' mind, Shaw's literary greatness.

From Frank Harris' biography of G. B. Shaw, Borges quotes a letter by the Irish writer: "Yo comprendo todo y a todos y soy nada y nadie" (II, 273). From this nothingness ("tan comparable a la de Dios antes de crear el mundo, tan comparable a la divinidad primordial que otro irlandés, Juan Escoto Erígena, llamó *Nihil*," II, 273), Shaw educed many persons, or *dramatis personae*. A close textual analysis is essential here. The nothingness of Shaw is comparable to that of God, but not equal. Shaw created Superman; he was not Superman. Borges, with habitual subtlety, blurs the distinction. We do not know anything about the mysterious nothingness from which God created the world. We do know something about the nothingness from which Shaw drew his characters; it is that of human experience, an experience that he interprets esthetically. He draws his characters from the species. Borges' own words: "Bernard Shaw edujo casi innumerables personas, o *dramatis personae*" (II, 273). Or *personas* and *dramatis personae* are, in this Borgesian context, interchangeable. We are in the realm of Borgesian magic. The spell is temporary. Shaw's esthetic freedom does not really transgress the realm of human experience. Shaw's protagonists are memorable because they have an I, instead of fomenting the illusion of one, because they act congruously within that I, instead of spending themselves in inconclusive variations of the self (II, 274). For all its lapidary brevity, Borges' mention of the *Vedanta,* one of the quintessential Hindu theses, is illuminating. The *Vedanta* does not object to the true Self, only to the illusion of the self. The true Self is immortal and exists outside the rationalizing mind.[21] It is an absolute perceived by transcendental consciousness. The self, individuality, is perceived by the mind.[22] It is not the self's claim to individuality, to an ephemeral reality that is, that the *Vedanta* objects to, but to immortality, which for the imperfect human being can only be an illusion. Borges recalls Coleridge's observation that men are born either Aristotelians or Platonics. The discrepancy in their point of view is edifying:

> El platónico sabe que el universo es de algún modo un cosmos, un orden; ese orden, para el aristotélico, puede ser un error o una ficción de nuestro conocimiento parcial.
>
> II, 269

In the *Vedanta* such an illusion is a capital error (II, 274). Shaw, we are given to understand, does not incur in such an error (II, 274).

Literature, Borges tell us elsewhere, is not ecumenical,

impersonal (II, 141). Shaw's own social persona may well have been an invention of the Irishman, but this does not invalidate the existence of a "real" Shaw. As to Shaw as his own *dramatis persona*, Borges is clear: "la más efímera será, lo sospecho, aquel G. B. S. que lo representó ante la gente y que prodigó en las columnas de los periódicos tantas fáciles agudezas" (II, 273). Borges makes us see, in this respect, Shaw's similarity to Whitman. He reminds us that Whitman created a literary Whitman, no less authentic than the Whitman who was the director of the *Brooklyn Eagle*, who did not see action on the battlefields of Georgia (I, 197).

Shaw's social persona, however, is not what interests Borges, who prefers to deal with Shaw the playwright and his literary creations. For this is the Shaw from whom, with Borges, we learn:

> Lo que tú puedes padecer es lo máximo que pueda padecerse en la tierra. Si mueres de inanición sufrirás toda la inanición que ha habido o que habrá. Si diez mil personas mueren contigo, su participación en tu suerte no hará que tengas diez mil veces más hambre ni multiplicará por diez mil el tiempo que agonices. No te dejes abrumar por la horrenda suma de los padecimientos humanos; la tal suma no existe. Ni la pobreza ni el dolor son acumulables.
>
> II, 291

This is considerably more than just an incisive observation. It is a philosophical realization, and an esthetic credo. Society is made of individuals, not of masses; the individual is real, the masses are an abstraction. The suffering induced by a particular situation is real to the individual who perceives it, not so suffering in general, which is an abstraction. Shaw puts it beautifully: neither poverty nor suffering are cumulative.

Ethically, the premise is important because it brings forth the issue of responsibility. It is not that universal guilt does not exist. It does, but it is only an abstraction. Whoever kills a man destroys the world, as the Mishnah asserts in the *Sanhedrim* (II, 291). Whoever kills all men would be only as guilty as Cain (II, 291). We are, in Borges' own words, in the realm of magic (II,

291). If there is no plurality, to use again Borges' terminology, then the answer must be affirmative. There is plurality, however, but a plurality made of individualities, the former abstract, the latter concrete. This is reiterative in Borges' thought:

> Lucrecio (*De rerum natura,* I, 830) atribuye a Anaxágoras la doctrina de que el oro consta de partículas de oro; el fuego, de chispas, el hueso, de huesitos imperceptibles.
>
> II, 291

Gold, fire, bone, then, are abstractions. Not so the individualities—grains, sparks, tiny bones—which integrate them. In an allegory abstractions are personified (II, 270). Otherwise they are unintelligible. There is a double movement, not consummated. In an allegory there is something novelistic; in a novel, there is something allegorical. The novelistic character is potentially generic (II, 270).

Esthetically, the matter assumes the same coordinates. Of course literature exists, but, again, only as an abstraction. Literature is made of individual pieces of literature written by individual authors. Borges' own realization:

> Durante muchos años, yo creí que la casi infinita literatura estaba en un hombre. Ese hombre fue Carlyle, fue Johannes Becher, fue Whitman, fue Rafael Cansinos-Asséns, fue de Quincey.
>
> II, 141

Borges' characters exhibit the experiential immediacy suggested by Shaw. It is, in fact, their strength. We do not know exactly when Borges read Shaw, but the latter's presence can be identified in his prose writings, particularly in his fiction. "Nueva refutación del tiempo" appeared in *Otras inquisiciones,* in 1952. Well advanced in years, in his last prose volume, *El libro de arena,* Borges echoes Shaw's thesis. The story, significantly, is "El otro." In it, Borges exchanges bits of wisdom with the younger Borges, whom he "meets" near Charles River, in Cambridge. The young, idealistic Borges thinks of *littérature engagée,* of writing a volume of poetry, *Los himnos rojos,* which would extoll "la fraternidad de todos los hombres" (II, 461). The elder Borges' irony is unmistakable.

> Me quedé pensando y le pregunté si verdaderamente se sentía hermano de todos. Por ejemplo, de todos los empressarios de pompas fúnebres, de todos los carteros, de todos los buzos, de todos los que viven en la acera de los números pares, de todos los afónicos, etcétera.
>
> II, 461

The younger Borges thinks that he can be brotherly to an abstraction. Borges continues: "Me dijo que ese libro se refería a la gran masa de los oprimidos y parias" (II, 461). The elder Borges' answer is unequivocal, with the weight of conviction: "Tu masa de oprimidos y de parias no es más que una abstracción. Sólo los individuos existen, si es que existe alguien" (II, 461).

This is not one of Borges' ironies. The statement is not unlike Shaw's observation. Consciousness is individuality. Borges' Shakespeare may have believed at first that he was like everybody else, but the utter surprise of a companion with whom he discussed the matter freed him from his error (II, 341).

Literature committed to narrow doctrines is inherently limiting, for it deals more with the character of man, rather than with his experience. Wells was a case in point. Shaw's work, as judged by Borges, is different: "La obra de Shaw, en cambio, deja un sabor de liberación. El sabor de las doctrinas del Pórtico y el sabor de las sagas" (II, 274). The meaning of Borges' statement lies in the interpretation parables ("parábolas sociológicas," II, 211), reductions of freedom, concessions made to causes. The works that contain them do not appeal to Borges, only those which are permeated by mystery (II, 211). The doctrines of the *Portico*, the Greek flights of fancy and intellect, the Scandinavian sagas make man a part of the universe, not only a social entity. What Borges sees in Shaw is freedom and clarity with "ism" impurities filtered out, the freedom and clarity that ennoble and dignify human life. It is in this sense that Borges praises Shaw's fundamental thematic endeavors, philosophy and ethics (II, 274), philosophy and ethics estheti-cally conceived, as literature, not as political propaganda.

Borges himself lives and writes by such beliefs. In the prolog to *El hacedor* (1960) Borges speaks of one of his propensities, the propensity "a estimar las ideas religiosas y filosóficas por su valor estético y aun por lo que encierran de singular y de maravilloso" (II, 304). Borges the man is to be found in the confession that the prolog to *El informe de Brodie*: "No he disimulado nunca mis opiniones, ni siquiera en los años arduos, pero no he permitido que interfieran en mi obra literaria, salvo cuando me urgió la exaltación de la Guerra de los Seis Días" (II, 370). The research technique put forth by Borges in "Kafka y sus precursores" applies here: Shaw is a precursor of Borges, Borges is a precursor of Shaw.

Notes

[1] Alfred Turco, *Shaw's Moral Vision* (Ithaca and London: Cornell University Press, 1976) p. 31.

[2] Christopher Hollis, *The Mind of Chesterton* (Coral Gables: University of Miami Press, 1970), p. 80.

[3] Arthur W. H. Adkins, *Merit and Responsibility. A Study in Greek Values* (Oxford: Clarendon Press, 1960), p. A.

[4] Cf. Bernard M. W. Knox, *The Heroic Temper* (Berkeley and Los Angeles: University of California Press, 1966), p. 1.

[5] Adkins, p. 5.

[6] George Bernard Shaw, *Man and Superman* (Baltimore: Penguin Books, 1952), p. 43.

[7] Knox, p. 5.

[8] Adkins, p. 154.

[9] Ibid., p. 173.

[10] Knox, p. 57.

[11] Ibid, p. 5.

[12] Adkins, p. 308.

[13] Turco, p. 206.

[14] Cedric H. Whitman, *Homer and the Heroic Tradition* (New York: W. W. Norton and Co., 1965), p. 199.

[15] Whitman, p. 123.

[16] Hesketh Pearson, *G. B. S. A Full Length Portrait* (New York and London: Harper and Brothers, 1942), p. 199.

[17] Turco, p. 40.

[18] Ibid., p. 31.

[19] A. M. Gibbs, *The Art and Mind of Shaw* (New York: St. Martin's Press, 1983), p. 23.

[20] Ana María Barrenechea, *Borges. The Labyrinth Maker*, p. 144.

[21] Swami Prabhavananda, *The Spiritual Heritage of India* (New York: Doubleday and Co. Inc., 1964), p. 321.

[22] Ibid., pp. 330–31.

Whitman

When Borges, not known for encomiastic effusions, states that criticism has simplified Walt Whitman into a mere giant, we have a measure of his admiration for the American poet. Early in his career, after having sought freedom and himself in the *ultraista* movement,[1] in 1929, Borges recognized the overwhelming power of Walt Whitman. The title of the note, "El otro Whitman," sets a clear distinction between the poet's true greatness, and that assembled and misinterpreted by European criticism, mostly French. The French, in Borges' view exceedingly formal in their approach to literature, did not know what to make of Whitman. They praised his *licence majestueuse*, declared him to be a precursor of free verse poets, and suggested a rather lame comparison to Victor Hugo. Whitman's economy of expression baffled them. He remained misunderstood. Such misunderstanding was to be far reaching. Since South America informed itself about North America through Paris, as Borges ruefully puts it, Whitman did not fare any better in the Southern Hemisphere. The French, whose committee-governed culture does not admit spontaneity (I, 139), could not—or refused to—accept Whitman's rejection of intellectual schemes, his spontaneity, his peculiar morality. They could not share his view that the world is a contingency, and that it is precisely this contingency that generates rich possibilities. Borges, whose unceremonious dislike of the French cultural establishment is obvious, guides the reader to an exemplary reminder of where literary criticism tends to fail:

> Porque una vez hubo una selva tan infinita que nadie recordó que era de árboles; porque entre dos mares hay una nación de hombres tan

fuerte que nadie suele recordar que es de hombres. De hombres de humana condición.

I, 142

To speak in general terms of Whitman's poetry—of anything, for that matter—is not enough. When Borges speaks of the "other" Whitman, he focuses on three poems, whose translation he offers. The first one is "Once I Passed Through a Populous City." In it, Whitman declares that he committed to memory for future reference the experiences that he had while passing through a populous city: the unmediated human presence (*espectáculos*), the mediated one (*arquitectura, costumbres, tradiciones*). This is what Borges calls an esthetic fact. However, what remains central to such a fact is not an abstraction—the totality of the experience—but a particular memory, that of a woman whom the poet had met fortuitously. In short, he remembers their love, born out of two free wills but in fortuitous circumstances. Everything else has been forgotten. Whitman, significantly, affirms this love as a cycle of memory-experience. The poem ends *in medias res.*

> Pasé una vez por una populosa ciudad, estampando para futuro
>   empleo en la mente sus espectáculos, su arquitectura,
>   sus costumbres, sus tradiciones.
>
> Pero ahora de toda esa ciudad me acuerdo sólo de una mujer
>   que encontré casualmente, que me demoró por amor. Día
>   tras día y noche tras noche estuvimos juntos—todo lo
>   demás hace tiempo que lo he olvidado.
>
> Recuerdo, afirmo, sólo esa mujer que apasionadamente se apegó
>   a mí.
>
> Vagamos otra vez, nos queremos, nos separamos otra vez.
>
> Otra vez me tiene de la mano, yo no debo irme.
>
> Yo la veo cerca a mi lado con silenciosos labios, dolida y
>   trémula.

I, 140–41

One can recognize Borges in this poem by Whitman. Borges, whose linguistic conciseness is reflected in the choice of

genre—the poem, the essay, the short story—is always interested not in someone's entire life—an illusory totality—but in a
moment, a significant moment in which a person becomes
unmistakably aware of his identity. It is the moment epitomized by a particular night in Tadeo Isidoro Cruz' life. It is, so
to speak, the moment of truth. Even the memory-experience
cycle can be descried in short stories, like "La otra muerte,"
where Pedro Damián transforms a memory and imposes it on
unmediated experience—the present. Virtually all of Borges'
protagonists are like the Whitman of the poem, experientially
and esthetically engaged in only one act. Whitman, Borges tells
us, "fue poeta de un laconismo trémulo y suficiente," not
merely "un varón saludador y mundial" (I, 140). Borges
vindicates Whitman's brevity of expression, a brevity not
justified by ceremonial superficiality but by the concentration
on a single act of experience. Whitman declares having forgotten the oblique presence of man (architecture, customs, tradi-
tions, the populous city), retaining instead the live presence of
a specific woman in a specific context. It matters not that the
lady in question remains unnamed. Her name is not essential;
her emotive presence, experientially or esthetically, is. What
Borges celebrates in Whitman is his sufficient brevity, that is to
say, a brevity that accommodates an essential moment of
identity. The oblique presence of man is, as everybody knows,
conspicuously absent or barely recognizable in Borges' prose
work. It is occasionally implied but not explicit. Whitman,
however tenuously, has left his mark.

The second poem translated by Borges is "When I Read a
Book," in which Whitman muses over the esthetic fact, and the
experience which generates it. Not fortuitously, Whitman
ponders a specific form of literary expression, a biography. He
has read, he says, a famous biography, a biography which the
author called the life of a man (I, 141). Would his own
biography, Whitman asks, be referred to in the same way? The
negative answer is anticipated by Whitman's parenthetical
assertion:

(Como si alguien pudiera saber algo sobre mi vida;
Yo mismo suelo pensar que sé poco o nada sobre mi vida real.
Sólo unas cuantas señas, unas cuantas borrosas claves e indicaciones.
Intento, para mi propia información, resolver aquí.)

I, 141

This is the kind of intellectual honesty that Borges appreciates. Any biographical pretense is preposterous, for totalities are simply conventions, not the sum total of a life. Thus justified, Whitman's economy of expression is a deliberate choice, a matter of intellectual and artistic integrity. The meaningful clues are few. This is consonant with Borges' literary theory and praxis. "El otro" (Borges), the distillation of old and new experience into wisdom, is Borges' comparable statement.

The third Whitman poem rendered by Borges is "When I Heard the Learned Astronomer." The evidence of a totality which is the learned astronomer's conference, with all its trappings of figures, charts, maps, etc., oppresses Whitman's humanity with knowledge. For, indeed, it is knowledge, not wisdom, that the astronomer dispenses to public applause, suspicious knowledge. For knowledge is the generalization of individualities. Whitman, overwhelmed by this learned denial of his individuality, abandons the conference, releasing himself into the mythical, humid air of the night.

Qué pronto me sentí inexplicadamente aturdido y hastiado,
Hasta que escurriéndome afuera me alejé solo
En el húmedo místico aire de la noche, y de tiempo en tiempo,
Miré en silencio perfecto las estrellas.

I, 141

If Whitman wished to underscore the need for solitude of his poetic *alter ego*, he indeed succeeded. Whitman steps out into a night in which the indirect presence of man (buildings, etc.) is veiled by darkness. Only the stars above silently witness his quest for essential solitude. The last verse clinches the experience, and presents it as an esthetic fact: "Miré en silencio perfecto las estrellas" (I, 141). To use Newton Arvin's felicitous term, Whitman immerses himself in "material ideality." He humanizes the thought of deity in order to feel comfortable, not to sublimate it.² Whitman could not bring himself to believe that the universe was indifferent to man, that man did not transcend the natural order.³ He does not lock himself into hermetic idealism. He makes God human in order to trust him.⁴ Whitman relies not on introspective imagination, but on the outward flight of the spirit, of the spirit that wishes to be— and is—multitudinous. "I am large," proclaims Whitman, "I contain multitudes."⁵ He unfetters his spirit and lets it roam freely and draws his strength from the vitality of the time, by smelling real flowers and talking to real people, even if he does so through different versions of his *ego*, both experientially and esthetically. Whitman is not a forerunner of his time. He is, in every sense of the word, a contemporary of the time in which he lives. He declares with pride: "I take part."⁶

> Yo soy el hombre. Yo sufrí. Ahí estaba.
> El desdén y la tranquilidad de los mártires.
> La madre, sentenciada por bruja, quemada ante los hijos,
>   con leña seca;
> El esclavo acosado que vacila, se apoya contra el cerco,
>   jadeante, cubierto de sudor;
> Las puntadas que le atraviesan las piernas y el pescuezo,
>   las crueles municiones y balas;
> Todo eso lo siento, soy.
>
> I, 196

Borges' own words are indispensable here: "Todo eso lo sintió y lo fue Walt Whitman, pero fundamentalmente fue—no en la mera historia, en el mito" (I, 196). Cartesian logic: I feel therefore I am? It is not only about Whitman that Borges is speaking here, but of himself as well. The verb *sentir* occurs frequently in Borges' work. As late as 1973, past the age of seventy, he still ponders the meaning of feeling. He says about different moments of his family's history: ". . . am feeling them, which is another way of living them—and perhaps a deeper one, for what I know."⁷ Whitman is contemplating the stars. Is not this man also the Borges of the celebrated hallucinatory night in Buenos Aires? Borges' words: "Aspiré noche, en asueto serenísimo de pensar" (I, 331). Everything is diffused

by darkness: "los portoncitos—más altos que las líneas estiradas de las paredes—parecían obrados en la misma sustancia
infinita de la noche. The poignant statement: "Me quedé
mirando esa sencillez" (I, 331). We are not attempting to trace
Borges' possible sources of inspiration, only to emphasize the
unmistakable affinity between the two writers, their ways of
ascertaining esthetically an individuality. Borges may be solitary in this circumstance but he is not merely a spectator.[8] Like
Whitman, he is an esthetic participant. Borges, who only later
manages to define his imagining, states: "Es evidente que el
número de tales momentos humanos no es infinito" (I, 332). He
sums up this experience and its esthetic expression:

> Quede, pues, en anécdota emocional la vislumbrada idea y en la
> confesa irresolución de esta hoja el momento verdadero de éxtasis y la
> insinuación posible de eternidad de que esa noche no me fue avara.
>
> I, 332

Borges finds that the three poems—three confessions, he calls
them—translated from Whitman are thematically similar: "la
peculiar poesía de la arbitrariedad y la privación" (I, 142). He
sums up the theme as follows:

> Simplificación final del recuerdo, inconocibilidad y pudor de nuestro
> vivir, negación de los esquemas intelectuales y aprecio de las noticias
> primarias de los sentidos, son las respectivas moralidades de esos
> poemas. Es como si dijera Whitman: Inesperado y elusivo es el mundo,
> pero su misma contingencia es una riqueza, ya que ni siquiera podemos
> determinar lo pobres que somos, ya que todo es un regalo.
>
> I, 142

This is a lesson. Borges, whose answer is implicitly affirmative,
asks: "¿Una lección de la mística de la parquedad, y ésa de
Norte América?" (I, 142). Indeed. Whoever reads Borges' prose
fiction with his statement about Whitman in mind will not fail
to notice that the lesson was not lost on him. Borges writes
about the trees that make a forest, not about the forest. Quoting
Anaxagoras and Josiah Royce, he states that gold is made of
gold particles, fire is made of sparks, bone of tiny bones, etc,

(II, 291). In other words, Borges is not interested in gold, fire, and bone, in the nominal abstraction, but in the real particles which integrate such elements. The final statement of the essay is significant: "Esa proposición es compatible con la de este trabajo" (II, 291). And, one can defensibly add, with Borges' prose fiction in general.

Borges finds in Whitman a fecund source of critical awareness. He lucidly sees how and why traditional criticism misunderstands Whitman:

> Casi todo lo escrito sobre Whitman está falseado por dos interminables errores. Uno es la sumaria identificación de Whitman, hombre de letras, con Whitman, héroe semidivino de *Leaves of Grass* como Don Quijote lo es del *Quijote*; otro, la insensata adopción del estilo y vocabulario de sus poemas, vale a decir, del mismo sorprendente fenómeno que se quiere explicar.
>
> I, 194

In dealing with Borges, we should keep this statement in mind. Borges points out the cause of the critics' misunderstanding of Whitman. As distinct from other writers, from Appolonius of Rhodes to T. S. Eliot, Whitman chose one of his plenitudes, happiness. While in doing so Whitman is exhibiting his solidarity with man, he does not sacrify the singularity of happiness. He identifies himself with man by being a man. Says Whitman in Borges' translation: "Lleno de vida, hoy, compacto, visible, Yo" (I, 197). The very fact that such a state is temporally successive ensures individuality:

> A ti, que no has nacido, te busco.
> Estás leyendóme. Ahora el invisible soy yo,
> Ahora eres tú, compacto, visible, el que intuye los versos y
>   el que me busca,
> Pensando lo feliz que sería si yo pudiera ser tu compañero.
>
> I, 197

This is the vital regeneration of the I. Whitman again, in *Songs of Parting*: "¡Camarada! Este no es un libro;/El que me toca, toca a un hombre." (I, 197). Borges perceives Whitman's intention:

"Whitman deriva de su manejo una relación personal con cada futuro lector. Se confunde con él y dialoga con el otro, con Whitman (*Salut au monde*, 3): ¿Qué oyes, Walt Whitman?" (I, 198). Whitman speaks to the Whitman in each of us, and to each of us who is in Whitman.

Whitman celebrates the happiness of man, not of superman. Nietzsche's Superman, capable of eternal happiness, does not exist, cannot exist, Borges insists (I, 195). Whitman has courage and faith. Forty years after exalting Whitman's quest for the essence of human happiness, Borges returns to the theme. We, like the characters of James or Kafka, tend to be defeatist:

> Somos tan pobres de valor y de fe que ya el *happy-ending* no es otra cosa que un halago industrial. No podemos creer en el cielo, pero sí en el infierno.
>
> II, 446

Borges, ritually praised for his ambiguity, could not be any clearer. The statement puts forth a simple truth about Borges' fiction: no Borgesian character, whatever the nature of their enterprise, lacks courage and faith. Yu Tsun ("El jardín de los senderos que se bifurcan"), Hladik ("El milagro secreto"), Emma ("Emma Zunz"), virtually all of Borges' protagonists exhibit purposeful individuality and faith in that individuality. Borges does not infuse the term faith with any religious meaning. By it he underscores man's belief in the possibility of happiness, not only his inexorable demise. Mallarmé chose negative themes, Heidegger and Jaspers made their philosophies into exercises in vanity (II, 274). Not so Whitman, who had faith in happiness, and the courage to sing freely about it. Writers, from Heraclitus to Stefan George, have been attracted by pantheism. Whitman, instead, embraces a peculiar panhumanism that does not exclude the presence of God. He does not wish to define divinity or to play with the shadows of contrast, but to identify himself in endless tenderness with his fellow men; that is to say, with one person at a time, in dialog. Whitman, like a prophet, wished to maintain the flame of happiness forever burning.[9] The promise of happiness is over-whelmingly powerful:

> Una cosa es la abstracta proposición de la unidad divina; otra, la ráfaga que arrancó del desierto a unos pastores árabes y los impulsó a una batalla que no ha cesado y cuyos límites fueron la Aquitania y el Ganges.

> I, 198

Borges concludes: "Whitman se propuso exhibir un demócrata ideal, no formular una teoría" (I, 198). The term democrat here is innocent of any political connotations; it simply indicates a free man, aware of his freedom. However idealized such a *persona* may be, it is clear that we are dealing with a recognizable individuality not with an abstraction.

The American poet's *modus operandi* is clear: "Whitman redactó sus rapsodias en función de un yo imaginario, formado parcialmente de él mismo, parcialmente de cada uno de sus lectores" (II, 195–96). The reader has to distinguish the voice of the poet, as well as his own. The certainty of the known is blurred by the uncertainty of the unknown, and here is where critics habitually fail:

> De ahí las divergencias que han exasperado a la crítica; de ahí la costumbre de fechar sus poemas en territorios que jamás conoció; de ahí que, en tal página de su obra, naciera en los estados del sur, y en tal otra (también en la realidad) en Long Island.

> II, 196

From his point of view and that of the reader Whitman enlarges the human capacity for altruism, fervor, and happiness (II, 196). Borges concludes: "Vasta y casi inhumana fue la tarea, pero no fue menos la victoria" (I, 198). D. H. Lawrence's judgement on Whitman is significant: "What a great poet Whitman is: great like a great Greek."[10]

Whitman was a catalyst of experience. Next to him, a Hawthorne is vitally and intellectually a recluse, a man who voluntarily removed himself from "entire heartlessness."[11]

Passion and feeling give way to mere thought in Hawthorne's life.

Notes

[1] Thorpe Running, *Borges' Ultraista Movement and its Poets* (Lathrup Village: International Book Publishers, 1981), p.

[2] Newton Arvin, *Whitman* (New York: The MacMillan Co., 1938), p. 202.

[3] Ibid p. 214.

[4] Ibid p. 280.

[5] Ibid p. 219.

[6] Ibid p. 280.

[7] *Borges on Writing*, ed. Norman Thomas di Giovanni, Daniel Halpern, and Frank Shane (New York: E. D. Sutton & Co., 1973), p. 50.

[8] Alberto C. Pérez, *Realidad y suprarrealidad en los cuentos fantásticos de J. L. Borges* (Miami: Ediciones Universal, 1971), p. 177.

[9] Robert L. Stevenson, "The Gospel According to Walt Whitman," in *A Century of Whitman Criticism*, ed. by Edwin Haviland Miller (Bloomington, London: Indiana University Press, 1969), p. 64.

[10] D. H. Lawrence, "Whitman," in *A Century of Whitman* Criticism, p. 159.

[11] Newton Arvin, *Hawthorne* (Boston: Little, Brown, Co., 1929), p. 185.

Valéry

To include Valéry among the figures who have endured in Borges' attention, along with Quevedo, Shaw, and Whitman, would appear at first to be a rather unwarranted proposition. Valéry, as one can easily verify, is of rather brief mention in Borges' work. Three reasons, however, justify our decision: a) the fact that Borges considers Valéry to be a symbol, a distinction conferred only upon one other poet, Whitman, b) the fact that Valéry is antithetically contrasted with Whitman, and c) the fact that Borges and Valéry, their differences notwithstanding, share many affinities in their exploration of the fundamental problems of time, space, and movement.

Borges, the clarification is imperative, sees Valéry as a symbol, not as a model. His critical assessment of Valéry is not followed by prescriptive incitations. A brief consideration of the term symbol is useful. The Greek word *symbolon*-symbol, has differentiated itself into two rather distinct meanings, quite removed from the original one of two pieces that fit together.[1] In religion and myth, the symbol is a representation of a transcendent reality, while in logical and scientific thought it is understood as an abstract sign.[2] From a religious point of view the symbol "participates" in the reality that it represents.[3] The cross, for instance, is an obvious Christian symbol, an emblem of the central issue of redemption. To use Cassirer' explanation, a scientific symbol is extensive, while a symbol of myth and religion is intensive.[4] Russell calls the classes of "agreed-upon connotation" "incomplete symbols," replaceable by descriptions.[5] It is in the "scientific" sense that Borges assesses Valéry. To see someone or something as a symbol is to

formulate a critical judgment, a logical or scientific differentia-
tion, not an ethical conclusion. Valéry is not a model, not a
paradigmatic example to emulate. Borges admires Valéry critically, as a man whose greatness is intrinsic and contrastive at
the same time. He admires him for the horizon of possibilities
of his work, above all for his unfailing lucidity ("héroe de
lucidez," I, 138).

Borges' elaborate contrast of Valéry to Whitman explains the
reason. Borges defends such a comparison, however arbitrary
it may appear to be (II, 196). Valéry's lucidity, we learn, is a
scrupulous one. Two portraits emerge gradually, along two
coordinates. Valéry exalts the spirit, Whitman, the flesh:

> Valéry es símbolo de infinitas destrezas pero asimismo de infinitos
> escrúpulos; Whitman, de una casi incoherente pero titánica vocación de
> felicidad; Valéry ilustremente personifica los laberintos del espíritu,
> Whitman, las interjecciones del cuerpo. Valéro es el símbolo de Europa
> y de su delicado crepúsculo; Whitman, de la mañana de América.
>
> II, 195

Valéry and Whitman, in Borges' vision, are not facets of the
same coin, not psychological counterparts of the same entity.
They are two different ways of being part of the world, two
statements, and two promises. Valéry is the symbol of the
delicate twilight of Europe, of a past that is exhausting itself.
Whitman is that of the dawn in America, of a barely initiated
beginning. The word poet, Borges tells us, could not be applied
to two more disparate artistic temperaments.

There is a double contrast in Valéry's case. He symbolizes his
time not by participation but by isolation. His lucidity and
detachment set him apart from a century that adores, as Borges
puts it, the chaotic idols of the blood, of the earth, of passion
(II, 197). Valéry could never evince the vital claim of a Whitman, "I take part."[6] There is a deeper yet distinction between
the two writers. Whitman is an emblematic symbol, an active,
participating symbol, he is America. He is temperamentally
America. Valéry, in spite of certain identities, is *not* Europe.
Valéry's creations are personifications of the spirit; Whitman's

are celebrations of being. Monsieur Teste merely plays at being, Whitman vitally is. Whitman wishes to be happy, Valéry, to understand: "Este no magnifica, como aquél, las capacidades humanas de la filantropía, de fervor y de dicha; magnifica las virtudes mentales" (II, 196). Whitman's philanthropy and happiness, and the fervor with which he practices them, are realized in altruism, in the recognition of individualized otherness, in the exaltation of humanity. Whitman reaches to the humanity of others, and returns to his own through the humanity of others. Valéry's centrifugal intellectualism keeps him apart from the reassuring benefits of philanthropy. In each case, the choice is deliberate.

While Whitman abandons himself to life, Valéry dispassionately analyzes it. Under the relentless stare of his lucidity, the cosmetic self-delusion of the world loses its appeal:

> Proponer a los hombres la lucidez en una era bajamente romántica, en la melancolía del nazismo y del materialismo dialéctico, de los augures de la secta de Freud y de los comerciantes del *surréalisme,* tal es la benemérita misión que desempeñó (que sigue desempeñando) Valéry.
>
> II, 196

The statement has both the merit of circumscribing a world in which assorted "isms" lure man into surrendering his individuality, and of defining Valéry. Seduced by cheap romanticism, by ideological illusions, by the promise of transcending himself through surrealism or through Freud, man forfeits his critical faculty. The working principle of romanticism, to Borges' mind, is the emphasis, the partial lie (I, 156). In a period of low romanticism, as the one that Borges ascribes to Valéry's time, the emphasis is more pronounced, the lie, larger. The "isms" that Borges enumerates are all predicated on misleading emphases. Valéry's laudable mission is to keep that critical faculty alert. Borges' choice of words is significant, for it changes the grounds on which he—and we—assess Valéry.

A mission of critical conscience, however, deals with the human being by reduction. The advances of the "isms," which Borges groups under the term State, are possible only at the expense of individualism (II, 163). Borges' Valéry lives in a world of surrendered individuality, of lethargic complacency. The very nature of the mission limits the writer's scope, who subordinates his talent to a specific, extraliterary, purpose. Hawthorne made art into a function of conscience, which affected his work (II, 189). Borges readily admits that Yeates, Rilke, and Eliot have written more memorable poetry than Valéry. His literary judgment of Valéry is therefore clear. He admires Valéry for his uncompromising spirit, for his unity of purpose, for the nobility of attempting to redeem man by opening the eyes of his mind, for his tenacity, even for making himself into a *persona* of his own intellectual creation, but not for the greatness of his literature. Borges formulates his opinion unambiguously:

> Valéry nos deja, al morir, el símbolo de un hombre infinitamente sensible a todo hecho y para el cual todo hecho es un estímulo que puede suscitar una infinita serie de pensamientos.
>
> II, 196

One discerns some Borgesian alchemy in this statement. The sensorial connotation of sensitivity is discounted by what sensitivity generates in this context: not feelings or sentiments but thoughts. Thoughts that proceed from facts, from finished action, not from acts, action in the making. We are closer to philosophy than to literature, to a lucidity that, to paraphrase Cioran, is not consciousness.[7] Borges, as we can see, does not wish to detract from Valéry's greatness, only to suggest that his greatness is other than purely literary. Valéry was receptive to everything that stimulated his thinking. Borges' view on the matter:

> Mis amigos me dicen que los pensamientos de Pascal les sirven para pensar. Ciertamente, no hay nada en el universo que no sirva de estímulo al pensamiento; en cuanto a mí, jamás he visto en esas memorables fracciones una contribución a los problemas, ilusorios o verdaderos, que los encarnan. Las he visto más bien como predicados del sujeto Pascal. Así, como la definición *quintessence of dust* no nos ayuda a comprender a los hombres sino al príncipe Hamlet, la defi-

nisión *roseau pensant* no nos ayuda a comprender a los hombres pero sí a un hombre, Pascal.

II, 217

Borges' Valéry accuses Pascal of voluntary dramatization (II, 217). Indeed, he states—rather idiosyncratically—that Pascal abandoned exactitude for vagueness.[8] Borges' comment on Pascal: "el hecho es que su libro no proyecta la imagen de una doctrina o de un procedimiento dialéctico sino de un poeta perdido en el tiempo y en el espacio" (II, 217). Borges' judgment is sensibly closer to the mark than Valéry's. It is not surprising, then, that Valéry, the poet who wishes to see reality unpoetically, criticizes Pascal. Valéry strives to discern the essence of things.[9] It is also interesting to note that Pascal, who is making a philosophical assertion, defines space metaphorically. Would Valéry's Monsieur Teste do the same?

Valéry remains a symbol. The judgment accredits Valéry's faithfulness to his mission, to the mission of lucidity. Borges finds Valéry's texts admirable as a relentless statements of purpose. As in Pascal's case, whose *roseau pensant* helps us understand not man in general but a particular man, Pascal, Borges insists that Edmond Teste is not one of the myths of this century but a Doppelgänger of Valéry: "Para nosotros, Valéry es Edmond Teste" (II, 196). To a remarkable extent, indeed he is.[10] For Teste is not merely a duplication of Edgar Allan Poe's Chevalier Dupin (II, 196).

When Borges speaks of Valéry, he does not speak of works like *Introduction à la méthode de Léonard de Vinci, La jeune Parque,* or *Le Cimetière marin,* but *La soirée avec M. Teste,* and *Mme Emilie Teste.* In short, he speaks about M. Teste. Who is M. Teste? He is an intellectual figment, a character only tenuously recognizable as a human being. Mrs. Teste tells us that his head is a sealed treasure, and she is not sure if he has a heart.[11] There is a puerile obstinacy about him, an unwillingness to act and to accept human conventions. There is no humility in him, no tenderness, no love, only intellectual pride.[12] He is incapable of feeling. As Brodin aptly puts it, M. Teste *thinks* his pleasure and his suffering.[13] Valéry's own assessment of M. Teste is definitive: "Il n'y a pas un grain d'espérance dans toute la machine de M. Teste."[14] M. Teste is not human.

Was Valéry the victim of an illusion, or of excessive clairvoyance? Was he trying, as Cioran believes, to find in lucidity, as Wagner attempted in music, the means of capturing the essence of the world? His theory of art is utterly unpoetic. Inspiration and improvisation are cursed words for Valéry. Borges' oxymoronic statement is not without irony. Valéry preferred "los lúcidos placeres del pensamiento y las secretas adventuras del orden" (II, 197). Adventure and order are clearly antithetic, mutually exclusive, in fact. An adventure breaks a continuity, it does not affirm it. It is the unknown, rather than the known. Borges, ever so elegantly, tells us that Valéry put himself in an impasse. Valéry wished to acquire a unitary vision—*une vision d'ensemble*—through unencumbered lucidity. He went beyond the mark. Cioran's judgment is to the point:

> Et Valéry en effet ne sera jamais *entier*, il ne s'identifiera ni aux êtres ni aux choses, il sera à côté, en marge de tout, et cela non point par quelque malaise d'ordre métaphysique, mais par excès de réflexion sur les opérations, sur le fonctionnement de la conscience.[15]

Valéry's trajectory is centrifugal, away from any concrete element on which human experience can focus, a flight into an intellectual refuge. In his resolute pursuit of order, he ignores the unpredictable twists of destiny, he becomes marginal. Monsieur Teste is not a survivor. He will die, thinking that the society scrutinized by his incisive intellect will also die, while in reality it is only changing. Teste "the exceptional creature of the exceptional moment,"[16] fails to understand the meaning of life. As a Valéry critic puts it, Teste is no longer of this world, he is inhuman.[17]

Valéry is one of the writers whom Borges brings into the discussion of writing and the philosophy of literature. In "La flor de Coleridge" he quotes, in translation, from Valéry:

La Historia de la literatura no debería ser la historia de los autores y de los accidentes de su carrera o de la carrera de sus obras sino la Historia del Espíritu como productor de literatura. Esa historia podrá llevarse a término sin mencionar un solo escritor.

II, 138

While the statement advocates a literary pantheism in the service of the Spirit, a pantheism that Borges unmistakably discounts at the end of the essay (II, 141), we retain the injunction that the history of literature should not be the incidental history of the creators of literature. The vicissitudes of an author's life or those of his work, whether seen from the Spirit's or the reader's point of view, are extraneous to the distilled experience that a work of art is. Knowing that there were pirate editions of the *Quijote* or that a certain Torrigiani broke Michelangelo's nose does not contribute measurably to our esthetic appreciation of the author's work.

The basic misunderstanding of Walt Whitman, in Borges' estimation, resides in our fusing Whitman the writer with Whitman the man. Borges writes: "Pasar del orbe paradisíaco de sus versos a la insípida crónica de sus días es una transición melancólica (I, 194). Like a child born, after its genesis a work of art acquires autonomy. Laotse, we are told, wished to live secretly and not to have a name. Similarly, Flaubert aspired at anonymity: "Este quería no estar un sus libros, o apenas quería estar de un modo invisible" (I, 214). Borges continues: "el hecho es que si no supiéramos previamente que una misma pluma escribió *Salammbô* y *Madame Bovary* no lo adivinaríamos" (I, 214).

The impertinence of strictly biographical data in the assessment of a work of art is not one of Valéry's originalities. Chesterton, much quoted by Borges, underscored it before: "What a man's name was, what his income was, whom he married, where he lived, these are not sanctities; they are irrelevancies."[18] The matter is not of passing interest. It resurfaces, anecdotally, in "Sobre el 'Vathek' de William Beckford": "Wilde atribuye la siguiente broma a Carlyle: una biografía de Miguel Angel que omitiera toda mención de las obras de

Miguel Angel" (II, 250). The inversion implied in the joke does not detract from the seriousness of the issue. Borges is not unaware of the problem:

> Nadie se resigna a escribir la biografía literaria de un escritor, la biografía de un soldado; todos prefieren la biografía genealógica, la biografía económica, la biografía psiquiátrica, la biografía quirúrgica, la biografía tipográfica.
>
> II, 250

A specialized biography is in itself a contradiction, for it is fragmentation—a misleading fragmentation. The literary biography of a writer or the military biography of a soldier, while still fragmentary, are not interdisciplinary, do not define one reality with the lexical and conceptual terminology of another. Poe's restlessness is a case in point. So fascinated is a biographer of Poe by the poet's instability of domicile, that a matter of great literary importance, like the cosmogony of *Eureka*, barely survives parenthetically (II, 251). An author and his "biological" counterpart are two different entities. Borges, the man Borges, recognizes himself less in the works of Borges than in those of other authors (II, 347–48). The mere history of a work of art cannot infuse any meaning into a work of art. Borges pointedly quotes Herbert Quain's self-deprecating confession: *"No pertenezco al arte, sino a la mera historia del arte"* (I, 449). Borges' elucidation, without expressing any allegiance, is illuminating: *"No había, para él, disciplina inferior a la historia"* (I, 449). We are still within the coordinates put forth by Valéry.

Both Valéry and Borges explore the mysterious workings of language, the possibilities and limitations of the word. For Valéry myth is a verbal construct which only exists verbally: *"Mythe* est le nom de tout ce que n'existe et ne subsiste qu'ayant la parole pour cause."*[19] The word, like the myth it sustains, is a matter of faith. The social mechanism, in its diverse complexity, rests in fact on this faith in instituted words.[20] When the faith wavers, communication is impaired and it eventually breaks down. Language degenerates into a mere habit.[21] In "Parábola de Cervantes y de Quijote" creator and creation ("el soñador y el soñado," II, 336) represent two opposing worlds, the unreal world of the books of Chivalry, and the quotidian, ordinary world of the 17th century (II, 336). Leaving aside the fact that unreal is not the opposite of quotidian but of real, which leads to a specific consideration of the issue, we note that Borges underscores the eroding effect of time on the discord. In time, Mancha and Montiel acquire the same poetic aura as the travels of Sinbad or Ariosto's vast geography (II, 336): "Porque en el principio de la literatura está el mito, y asimismo en el fin" (II, 336). Between the two poles, literature assimilates reality and gradually transforms it into mythical matter, that is to say, into a reality sustained by the word and by the faith that we invest in it. At the end of "La muralla y los libros" Borges writes memorably that mythology, along with weathered faces, music, certain sunsets and places, tells us something, or is about to tell us something, and that the imminence of such a revelation, always incomplete, is an esthetic fact (II, 133). When language degenerates into a mere habit, as Valéry puts it, it empties itself of meaning. In Borges' "Utopia de un hombre que está cansado," it becomes a system of quotations (II, 514).

The trouble with contemporary literature is its propensity to emphasize (I, 138). A repeated emphasis, like a quotation, becomes a fossil. "Palabras definitivas," writes Borges, "palabras que postulan sabidurías adivinas o angélicas o resoluciones de una más que humana firmeza—*único, nunca, siempre, todo, perfección, acabado*—son del comercio habitual de todo escritor" (I, 138). Such a practice unwittingly leads to linguistic impoverishment. While the French "Je suis navré" may not exactly mean "no iré a tomar el té con ustedes," as Borges claims, it does point to a certain linguistic depreciation. And why has the verb *aimer* (to love) been demoted to *gustar* (to like)? Even a cerebral writer like Valéry, whom Borges calls a hero of organizing lucidity ("héroe de la lucidez que organiza," I, 138) indulges in the French penchant for hyperbole (I, 138). Salvaging some forgettable verses from Lafontaine, Valéry decrees them to be the most beautiful verses in the world ("ces plus beaux vers du monde," I, 138).

In Borges, the movement is centripetal, towards the recognizable concreteness of individuality. In Whitman there is a centripetal-centrifugal cycle that regenerates itself. All Borgesian protagonists wish to affirm themselves, and they do so in the brief intensity of a moment, of a situation. The fortuitous-*el azar*-always present in Borges' prose-fiction, accelerates and outlines the process of identity. It is the unpredictable, which may or may not cooperate with his designs, which removes the protagonist from the comfort of order, which thrusts his individuality into action.

Perhaps one of G. B. Shaw's witticisms, paraphrased, best describes Valéry and Borges; they are two authors separated by common affinities. Valéry dealt with metaphysics in order to discredit it, to negate its pretense as true discourse about being.[22] Borges himself considers philosophy to be a mere coordination of words, a verbal convention, but he is fascinated by the perplexities of metaphysics. Both authors are mesmerized by Zeno of Elea, the father of enduring paradoxes. Borges would not quarrel with Valéry's assertion that philosophy is nothing but mythology.[23] Valéry is dismayed by the fact that the body can function and accomplish things without the mediation of the intellect,[24] while Borges admires its incomprehensible autonomy (I, 155). Valéry is aware of the fact that reality is not produced by reason. Borges states that reality is not verbal (II, 168). Valéry deplores the fact that language as speech is degenerating into a habit.[25] In "Utopia de un hombre que está cansado" Borges presents us with a fictive situation in which speech has been reduced to a system of quotations (II, 514). Teste takes refuge in myth. Valéry defines myth as "le nom de tout ce qui n'existe et ne subsiste qu'ayant la parole pour cause."[26]

Valéry's detached lucidity, as we have seen, stands in contrast to his time, "un siglo que adora los caóticos ídolos de la sangre, de la tierra y de la pasión" (II, 197). Blood, land, and passion, the elemental imperatives of human life, are, of course present in Borges' fiction, but not as idols, not as ends in themselves. They call to action, but the action itself is always governed by an individual conscience and will. This is the hallmark of the Borgesian protagonist. One concludes with Cioran: "Lucidity is not consciousness." Valéry ignores the essence of such a thought. Borges does not.

Notes

[1] W. L. Reese, *Dictionary of Philosophy and Religion* p. 563.

[2] Ibid., p. 563.

[3] Ibid., p. 563.

[4] Ibid., p. 563.

[5] Ibid., p. 563.

[6] Cf. Arvin, *Whitman,* p. 280.

[7] Emile Cioran, *The Fall into Time*, p. 133.

[8] Albert Béguin, *Pascal* (Bourges: Editions du Seuil, 1967), p. 14.

[9] Pierre Brodin, "Paul Valéry," in *Les écrivains francais de l'entre-deux-guerres* (Montréal: Editions Bernard Valiquette, 1942), p. 113.

[10] Ibid., pp. 87–122.

[11] Ibid., p. 87.

[12] Ibid., p. 93.

[13] Ibid., p. 92.

[14] Ibid., p. 94.

[15] Emile Cioran, *Valéry face a ses idoles* (Paris: Editions de L'Herne, 1970), p. 40.

[16] Agnes MacKay, *The Universal Self. A Study of Paul Valéry* (Toronto: The University of Toronto Press, 1961), p. 82.

[17] Régine Pietra, *Valéry: directions spatiales et parcours verbal* (Paris: Minard, 1981), p. 270.

[18] G. K. Chesterton, *Varied Types* (New York: Dodd, Mead and Company, 1903), p. 4.

[19] Pietra, p. 279.

[20] Ibid., p. 279.

[21] Ibid., p. 182.

[22] Ibid., p. 188.

[23] Ibid., p. 183.

[24] Ibid., p. 199.

[25] Ibid., p. 282.

[26] Ibid., p. 279.

Literary Echoes

The brief note that appears in *El hacedor* (1960), "La trama," contains a thought which, by virtue of its Protean diversification, must be construed as a constant in Borges' work:

> Al destino le agradan las repeticiones, las variantes, las simetrías; diecinueve siglos después, en el sur de la provincia de Buenos Aires, un gaucho es agredido por otros gauchos y, al caer, reconoce a un ahijado suyo y le dice con mansa reconvención y lenta sorpresa (estas palabras hay que oírlas, no leerlas): ¡Pero che!
>
> II, 326

Borges offers a proposition and its illustration. Much earlier, in "El sur" (*Artificios*, 1944), he expressed the same thought: "a la realidad le gustan las simetrías y los leves anacronismos" (I, 531). The fragment which makes the *gaucho's* utterance essentially one with that of Julius Caesar has the merit of showing with exemplary clarity Borges' predilection for certain philosophical themes and their esthetic possibilities.

That history repeats itself, that such a repetition—cyclical rather than circular—affirms, like Marcus Aurelius' philosophy, the analogy, not the identity, of individual destinies, that such matters are among Borges' obsessive preoccupations, is something hardly in need of further elaboration.[1] How Borges deals esthetically with such matters, how he echoes them thematically in his work, is a field still fertile in interpretative possibilities.

Like the "visible" work of Pierre Menard (I, 427), the fragments and references which postulate or evoke symmetries—literary ones, in this context—are easily recognizable. "¡Pero che!", is an esthetic variation of Julius Caesar' wistful reprobation of Brutus, "¡Tú también, hijo mío" (II, 326). This is the quintessential Borges. Suffice it to recall works such as "Pierre Menard, autor del *Quijote*, " "Tres versiones de Judas," "Kafka y sus precursores," "Formas de una leyenda," or "Historia de los ecos de un nombre," to substantiate Borges' propensity for thematic and stylistic variations. The last work cited, "Historia de los ecos de un nombre" is, like "La trama," illustrative. It vindicates history esthetically. An obscure utterance, Borges informs us, is repeated (II, 275). The original declaration hails from the second book of Moses, *Exodus*. Moses asks God His name, and God answers: "Soy El Que Soy" (II, 276). Predictably, Borges discounts any idle curiosity or philological interest on Moses' part. The vital need for Moses is to know "who" or "what" God is. Like Scotus Erigena, like us, Moses operates within the expressive inadequacies of language, for language only allows us to think in terms of a "who" or a "what." Language, to use Schopenhauerian terminology, imperfectly reconciles the succession of time with the position of space.[2]

Having set the background, having buttressed it with the compendium of cross-cultural examples, Borges traces the interpretative fate of "Soy El Que Soy," with its anachronistic symmetries. Christian theology takes the utterance to mean that God alone is real, that the personal pronoun I can be legitimately pronounced only by Him. Spinoza, Borges writes, restates the same metaphysical point of view (II, 276). Martin Buber, by giving the original statement the possible versions of "Soy el que seré" or "Yo estaré dónde yo estaré" (II, 276), adds to God's pronouncement the notions of space and time. Philosophy, in many of the tongues of man, has consigned the matter to voluminous tracts of problematic coherence. Literature, whose esthetics and substance rest not on chronology but on factual or possible human experience, on real or imagined *quiddity*, has fared better. It has reflected it kaleidoscopically. The *gaucho* who dies oblivious to any similarity between his remark and that of Julius Caesar, is chronologically unaware that history repeats itself. From the visible reference we pass to the thematic presence.

> *Ich bin der ich bin, Ego sui qui sum, I am that I am*—, el sentencioso nombre de Dios, el nombre que a pesar de constar de muchas palabras, es más impenetrable y más firme que los que constan de una sola, creció y reverberó con los siglos, hasta que en 1602 William Shakespeare escribió una comedia.
>
> II, 277

The drama in question is *All's Well That Ends Well*. In it, as we have seen, Parolles, the quintessential *miles gloriosus*, states after being exposed as an impostor: *"Ya no seré capitán, pero he de comer y beber y dormir como un capitán; esta cosa que soy me hará vivir"* (II, 277). Only a person versed in both biblical scholarship and literary matters could descry in Parolles' words God's answer to Moses. Yet the answer is implicitly in it. In revealing its thematic substratum, Borges does much more than trace a verbal genealogy. He neatly circumscribes the ideal purpose of literature:

> Así habla Parolles y bruscamente deja de ser un personaje convencional de la farsa cómica y es un hombre y todos los hombres.
>
> II, 277

If Borges espouses any esthetic credo at all, this would be it. The business of literature, such as it emerges from Borges' comment on the significance of Parolles' words, is to confer individuality upon man, without invalidating Man. It is a thought of stunning clarity, which defines an artistic standard. No writer could have a higher aspiration. The issue surfaces again in Swift the man, and in his main work, *Gulliver's Travels*. Decrepit, deaf, afraid of madness, Swift receded into senility. Incapable of reading and writing, useless to others and himself, he asked for God's mercy in death. One evening, the dying old man was heard saying: "Soy lo que soy, soy lo que soy" (II, 278). Borges interprets his words:

> *Seré una desventura, pero soy*, habrá sentido Swift, y también, *Soy una parte del universo, tan inevitable y necesaria como otras*, y también *Soy lo que*

Dios quiere que sea, soy lo que me han hecho las leyes universales, y acaso
Ser es ser todo.

II, 278

While Borges ends his inquiry here, he adds, by way of an epilog, the words of a moribund Schopenhauer:

Si a veces me he creído desdichado, ello se debe a una confusión, a un error. Me he tomado por otro, verbigracia, por un suplente que no puede llegar a titular, o por el acusado en un proceso por difamación, o por el enamorado a quien esa muchacha desdeña, o por el enfermo que no puede salir de su casa, o por otras personas que adolecen de análogas miserias. No he sido esas personas; ello, a lo sumo, ha sido la tela de trajes que he vestido y que he desechado. ¿Quién soy realmente? Soy el autor de *El mundo como voluntad y representación*, soy el que ha dado una respuesta al enigma del Ser, que ocupará a los pensadores de los siglos futuros.

II, 278

In "Historia de los ecos de un nombre," Borges calls such echoes *versiones*.

In 1932 Borges wrote "Las versiones homéricas," an essay which explores translations as literary variations.[3] While esthetic differences—the experimental sorting of omissions and emphases (I, 181)—are inevitably more dramatic when originals and their translations are considered, they are not necessarily limited to such a context. Esthetic variations can—and do—occur in the same language (I, 181), and Borges brilliantly illustrates such a proposition in "Pierre Menard, autor del *Quijote*." The matter is further explored in Quevedo's poetry.

Borges warns us that the poetry of Quevedo cannot be construed as a document of passion (II, 168)—a potential error of interpretation. Quevedo's poetry, if anything, is literary virtuosity (II, 165). This throws the issue of inspiration in a different light. Not infrequently, Quevedo often receives the first poetical impulse from a classical text. A case in point is "Polvo serán, mas polvo enamorado" as a recreation (*recreación*, II, 169) of Propertius' "ut meus oblito pulvis amore vacet" (*Sexti Properti elegiarum Liber I*, xix).[4] The analysis requires a more extensive citation from Propertius' elegy:

Non ego nunc tristes vereor, mea Cynthia,
Manes, nec moror extremo debita fata rogo;
sed ne forte tuo careat mihi funus amore,
hic timor est ipsis durior exsequiis.
Non adeo leviter noster puer haesit ocellis,
ut meus oblito pulvis amore vacet.

I, xix

The unavoidable observation is that the poem is written from Cynthia's, not the poet's, point of view. Propertius, although alive, speaks as if he were already dead. Having removed himself from the equation of love with Cynthia, he is nothing but a spectral, inconsequential presence. Love is now only Cynthia's reality, for Propertius is unceremoniously hiding behind his hypothetical death. The poet is afraid that Cynthia's fickle love will not outlast the duration of his funeral pyre. His forgotten dust will lack Cynthia's love. The elegiac beauty of the poem cannot conceal Propertius' essential weakness, that of being a dependent—rather than a participant—in love.

Quevedo, ostensibly, writes his sonnet from his own point of view, from the unimpeacheable purity of his love, from his everlasting commitment to such a love. He writes from the only certainty that is in his power, that of his own feelings. Hence the sonnet's overwhelming force:

Alma a quien todo un dios pasión ha sido,
venas que humor a tanto fuego ha dado,
médulas que han gloriosamente ardido:
su cuerpo dejará, no su cuidado;
serán ceniza, mas tendrán sentido;
polvo serán, mas polvo enamorado.[5]

As opposed to Propertius, Quevedo is far from surrendering his love, and ultimately his humanity, to the will of his beloved. On the contrary, he affirms himself in the togetherness of love, a togetherness that will not dissolve because of the inconstancy of his feelings or his inexorable mortality. Thus framed, the sonnet speaks with the authority of conviction, for

Quevedo's notorious diffidence toward women is well known (II, 168). It matters little that he writes not about a passion but about *Passion*. Borges' reflexion: "Para la gloria, decía yo, no es indispensable que un escritor se muestre sentimental, pero es indispensable que su obra, o alguna circunstancia biográfica, estimulen el patetismo" (II, 164). This is precisely what happens with this sonnet by Quevedo.

Just as Borges says that he discerns Kafka's voice and literary habits in other literatures and periods of time (II, 226), we can state that we can find Borges in Quevedo, Shaw, or Milton. Speaking of man's inability to transcend himself, Borges cites a verse from Milton's *Paradise Lost*: "Which way I fly is Hell; myself am Hell" (I, 232). Quevedo, in an outburst of theological magic, as Borges puts it, writes: "Con los doce cené: yo fui la cena" (II, 169). Chronologically, Quevedo's verse precedes that of Milton, but that does not bear upon the discussion. What matters is that both authors are mentioned by Borges, that he quotes the thematically related verses, that he deals with this philosophical proposition and its esthetic rendition on his own terms. Here is Milton's line in its context:

> Me miserable! Which way shall I fly
> Infinite wrath, and infinite despair?
> Which way I fly is Hell; myself am Hell;
> And in the lowest deep a lower deep
> Still threat'ning to devour me opens wide,
> To which the Hell I suffer seems a Heav'n.[6]

Satan, of course, is not of human origin, although his vision refracts that of man.[7] The main theme of *Paradise Lost* is "the fall of man," with all its attendant implications.[8]

Borges, however, is less interested in Milton's elaboration of a biblical theme than in the philosophical reverberations of Satan's situation. The fall denotes the fundamental weakness of man,[9] a weakness that cannot be transcended. Even admitting that Satan's fall represents not only his "fierceness" but his "glory" as well,[10] it is obvious that he cannot overcome the limitations of the condition to which he has reduced himself.

Thus "which way I fly is Hell" accurately sums up his situation. Hell may be Satan's voluntary self-exile from his creator, as Crosman puts it,[11] but once accomplished it becomes an irreversible fact. Asks Borges, what is Hell (I, 176)? The answer enlarges the scope of philosophical consideration.

Hell is a place of punishment, Borges states, a *"lugar de castigo eterno para los malos"* (I, 176). Satan is a volume, volume is space, therefore Satan is a physical presence in time.[12] Satan is trapped in his situation. Only God can probe beyond created space, only God has the inclusive vision of past, present, and future.[13] Satan cannot move from sight to foresight.[14] Milton, like Borges, intimated metaphorically the eternity of Hell. The "ever-burning sulphur" unmistakably suggests eternity.[15] Satan knows that he cannot escape.[16] Wilding calls our attention to Milton's use of the word "alone," both as an adjective and as an adverb.[f17] Satan is not envious of Adam's and Eve's lesser predicament, but of their togetherness.

The solitude of the Borgesian protagonist is a matter of critical record. As we have emphasized elsewhere, Borges' protagonist is solitary but not necessarily lonely. Milton's Satan is both solitary and lonely, while Adam and Eve are only solitary. It is not by accident that in Milton's poem Adam's and Eve's plight is viewed as a single act viewed through different perspectives.[18] Borges' "La otra muerte" exemplifies this sort of perspectivism, but most of Borges' protagonists are individuals surprised in a single, self-redeeming act. This is Borges' *modus operandi*, and his understanding of literature as a myth. In literary myth, George quotes Cassirer, reality is presented as a structure, not as a process.[19] Cassirer tells us that mythical perception always carries an emotive charge, and that "the real substratum of myth is not a substratum of thought but of feeling."[20] In theory and in practice, Borges partakes of this proposition.

If Milton allows Satan to express his particular vision, Quevedo allows Christ a similar prerogative. The very essence of Christianity is condensed in the verses that Quevedo attributes to Christ:

Con los doce cené; yo fui la cena:
mi cuerpo les di en pan, mi sangre en vino;
previne mi partida de amor llena,
y Viático queda a su camino.
Que me quede en manjar amor ordena,
cuando a la Cruz me lleva amor divino;
encarné, por venir, y, al despedirme,
en el Pan me escondí por no partirme.[21]

While Quevedo's celebrated literary virtuosity is amply in evidence here, what engages our attention is the signal importance of the content. The composition, "Poema heroico a Cristo resucitado," accredits both the humanity and the divinity of Christ, the indissolubility of God's love, the passion and the resurrection, hope.

An author's work, Borges insists, does not have to be sentimental, but it must exact emotion (II, 164). This is brought to the fore when Borges discusses the issue of eternity. First, Borges formulates a rationale. There is an eternity of heaven and an eternity of hell, for free will can only be posited in these terms. If we do not have the latitude to exert our free will, then the I is an illusion (I, 178). As Borges will never surrender the I, he distances himself from syllogistic reasoning: "La virtud de ese razonamiento no es lógica, es mucho más: es enteramente dramática" (I, 178). In other words, the issue and its considerations are perceived as valid only within the realm of the I. The argument imposes itself: "Tu destino es cosa de veras, nos dice, condenación eterna y salvación eterna están en tu minuto; esa responsabilidad es tu honor" (I, 178–79).

Just as Borges brings Schopenhauer into the thematic elaboration of God's pronouncement, "Soy El Que Soy," we bring Borges into the thematic possibilities of Milton's "Which way I fly is Hell" and Quevedo's "Con los doce cené; yo fui la cena." Borges deals with the notion in "Nueva refutación del tiempo." After giving it proper consideration, he finds the logical, abstract refutation of time unconvincing: "And yet, and yet . . . " (II, 300). He prefers instead an explanation not devoid of the presence of the I. We quote *in extenso*:

Nuestro destino (a diferencia del infierno de Swedenborg y del infierno de la mitología tibetana) no es espantoso por irreal; es espantoso porque es irreversible y de hierro. El tiempo es la sustancia de que estoy hecho. El tiempo es un río que me arrebata, pero yo soy el río; es un tigre que me destroza, pero yo soy el tigre; es un fuego que me consume, pero yo soy el fuego. El mundo, desgraciadamente, es real; yo, desgraciadamente, soy Borges.

II, 300

Quevedo is redemption, and redemption is Quevedo; Milton is hell and Swedenborg is hell, and hell is Milton and Swedenborg; Borges is time, and time is Borges. Water, fire, the raw vitality of the tiger, are the elemental components of Borges' reality and of his consciousness of it. The tiger in "La escritura del Dios" is time. The old man in "Las ruinas circulares," the man destroyed and regenerated by fire, is time. And Borges is time.

It is not the promise of immortality that Borges seeks in the endless cycle man-river-river-man, man-tiger-tiger-man, man-fire-fire-man, a promise of unseen certainty, but the salutary consolation that it can bring to the present:

En tiempos de auge la conjetura de que la existencia del hombre es una cantidad constante, invariable, puede entristecer o irritar: en tiempos que declinan (como éstos), es la promesa que ningún oprobio, ninguna calamidad, ningún dictador podrá empobrecernos.

I, 369

Notes

[1] Virtually all publications on Borges have elaborated, to various extents, on his fascination with the mystery of time and space. For the most recent bibliography on Borges see David W. Foster, *Jorge Luis Borges: An Annotated Primary and Secondary Bibliography* (New York: Garland, 1984).

[2] Patrick Gardiner, *Schopenhauer* (Baltimore: Penguin Books, 1963), p. 97.

[3] For a detailed analysis of this matter, see Ion T. Agheana, *The Prose of Jorge Luis Borges*, pp. 211–19.

[4] *The Poems of Sextus Propertius*, ed. and transl. by J. P. McCulloch (Los Angeles, Boston: University of California Press, 1972).

[5] Francisco de Quevedo, *Obras completas*, ed. by José Manual Blecua (Madrid: Editorial Castalia, 1969), I, p. 657.

⁶ John Milton, *Paradise Lost*, ed. by Merrit Y. Hughes (New York: Odyssey Press, 1962), IV, p. 86.

⁷ Isabel G. Maccaffrey, "The Theme *Paradise Lost*," in *New Essays on Paradise Lost*, ed. by Thomas Kranidas (Berkeley, Los Angeles, and London: University of California Press, 1971), p. 81.

⁸ A. G. George, *Milton and the Nature of Man* (Bombay, New York: Asia Publishing House, 1974), p. 75.

⁹ Ibid., pp. 84–85.

¹⁰ Jackson I. Cope *The Metaphoric Structure of Paradise Lost* (Baltimore: The Johns Hopkins University Press, 1962), p. 93.

¹¹ Robert Crosman, *Reading Paradise Lost* (London: Indiana University Press, 1980), p. 32.

¹² Cope, p. 52. Also, Stanley Eugene Fish, "Discovery as Form in *Paradise Lost*," in *New Essays on Paradise Lost*, pp. 1–15.

¹³ Cope, p. 62.

¹⁴ Maccaffrey, p. 62.

¹⁵ Cope, p. 93.

¹⁶ Michael Wilding, *Milton's Paradise Lost* (Sydney: Sydney University Press, 1969), p. 40.

¹⁷ Ibid., p. 28.

¹⁸ E. L. Marilla, *Milton and Modern Man* (Alabama: University of Alabama Press, 1968), p. 40.

¹⁹ George, p. 91.

²⁰ Ibid., p. 92.

²¹ Francisco de Quevedo, *Obra poética*, I, p. 364.

Language and Dialect

In the prolog to *Elogio a la sombra* Borges confesses to have dedicated his long life "a las letras, a la cátedra, al ocio, a las tranquilas aventuras del diálogo, a la filología, que ignoro" (II, 351). His interest in linguistic matters is not a personal idiosyncrasy. "De Echevarría en adelante," writes Ana María Barrenechea, "las cuestiones idiomáticas han apasionado a la Argentina."[1] Borges' fondness of philology is self avowedly instinctive rather than acquired, a matter of preference not of discipline. Although philology and linguistics are inextricably related, philology—the cultural study of language and literature—interests Borges more than linguistics—the study of formal aspects of the language. He likes etymology, and delights in tracing the evolution of certain words but is ultimately aware that knowing the original meaning of *calculus* (pebble), *hypocrite* (actor), and *classis* (fleet), does not improve one's understanding of algebra, ethics, or literature. Borges does not espouse any particular esthetic doctrine ("no soy poseedor de una estética" (II, 351). His literature, to paraphrase one of Borges' own statements on existence (I, 155), is a series of esthetic adaptations, not the expression of an unified system. Borges is not, in any readily identifiable form, a committed author, an *écrivain engagé* (II, 369). He praises modernism not for any prescriptive ideas, but for the freedom that it allows—"esa gran libertad" (II, 439).

Borges, as everybody knows, is fascinated by language. In Saussurean terms, he is interested both in *langue* and *parole*, in the general system, and in its individual manifestations. Without speech (*parole*), language (*langue*) would be only an abstract and empty system. Language, in any tongue, is self-sufficient. All languages are self-sufficient:

> Así, mi desconocimiento de las letras malayas o húngaras es total, pero estoy seguro que si el tiempo me deparara la ocasión de su estudio, encontraría en ellas todos los alimentos que requiere el espíritu.
>
> II, 302–03

There is no essential need to consider another language, because, "dadas las repercursiones incalculables de lo verbal," everything is possible within the same literature (I, 181).

What is, then, language for Borges? In his last prose volume Borges tells us that language is a system of quotations (II, 514). This severe statement, however, must be analyzed in contextual terms. The story, "Utopía de un hombre que está cansado," deals with a world which has exhausted man's capacity for hope, a world in which neither life nor death hold any special significance, a world in which people have ceased to matter to each other. Only when communication has no real purpose, when there is no affective or esthetic emotion left (II, 449), does language become a system of quotations (II, 514). When Borges is reflective, outside of the internal needs of a story, his pronouncement on language is objective: "Un idioma es una tradición, un modo de sentir la realidad, no un arbitrario repertorio de símbolos" (II, 440). A lexigraphic definition may vary in formulation but not in substance.

Borges makes a clear distinction between the spoken and the written word, and attempts to educe from it the birth of literature. "Del culto de los libros" begins with two propositions: a) that of the *Odyssey*, where we read that the Gods weave misfortunes in the destinies of men so that future generations would have something to sing about, and b) that of Mallarmé, "tout aboutit a un livre" ("*El mundo existe para illegar a un libro*," II, 229). The two approaches, which Borges calls "theologies," indicating that such postulates are more a matter of faith than of scientific rigor, have different emphases. The Greek proposition belongs to the time of oral literature, the second, to that of the written word. Borges lists the *kenningar—*

the creation of Icelandic scalds—as the first deliberate enjoyment of instinctive literature (I, 335). Here, as in "Historia del guerrero y de la cautiva" (II, 39), factual accuracy is unimportant. The *kenningar* are not metaphorical interpretations of reality but "equivalences" of reality (I, 337). Their possible symbolism, Borges believes, is only a palliative to intelligence (I, 337). Again, Borges formulates one of his challenging hypotheses: "La metáfora no habrá sido pues lo fundamental sino, como la comparación anterior, un descubrimiento tardío de las literaturas" (I, 350). To be sure, true metaphors are justified by emotion (I, 351). The metaphor is, then, not an equivalent of reality but an esthetic reconstruction of it. Borges' *Averroes* underscores the transitional process:

> Además, los frutos y los pájaros pertenecen al mundo natural, pero la escritura es un arte. Pasar de hojas a pájaros es más fácil que de rosas a letras.
>
> II, 72

The transition from rose to letter, to literature, would be impossible without the metaphor.

There remains the spiritual aspect of language. Up to a certain moment in the past, Borges considers written literature to have been the equivalent of oral literature. He draws an example from G. B. Shaw. Someone, in Shaw's dramas, is afraid that if the library of Alexandria were to burn, the memory of mankind would perish, to which Caesar replies: "Déjala arder. Es una memoria de infamias" (II, 229). The historical Julius Caesar, Borges suggests, would have approved or disapproved of such a statement, but would not have considered it to be sacrilegious joke: "La razón es clara: para los antiguos la palabra escrita no era otra cosa que un sucedáneo de la palabra oral" (II, 229).

When does the written word cease to be an equivalent of the spoken one? Who is responsible for such a signal moment in the history of Western culture? Borges' example is as moving as it is beautiful. He credits St. Augustine with having recorded the event; its originator was St. Ambrose.

> Cuando Ambrosio leía, pasaba la vista sobre las páginas penetrando su alma, en el sentido, sin proferir una palabra ni mover la lengua. Muchas veces—pues a nadie se le prohibía entrar, ni había la costumbre de avisarle quién venía—, lo vimos leer calladamente y nunca de otro modo, y al cabo de un tiempo nos íbamos, conjeturando que aquel breve intervalo que se le concedía para preparar su espíritu, libre del tumulto de los negocios ajenos, no quería que se le ocupasen en otra cosa, tal vez receloso de que un oyente, atento a las dificultades del texto, le pidiera la explicación de un pasaje oscuro o quisiera discutirlo con él, con lo que no pudiera leer tantos volúmenes como deseaba. Yo entiendo que leía de ese modo por conservar su voz, que se le tomaba con facilidad. En todo caso, cualquiera que fuese el propósito de tal hombre, ciertamente era bueno.
>
> II, 230–31

This is Borges. St. Augustine, with moving simplicity, ignores the true significance of St. Ambrose's habit. Reading alone. A pivotal spiritual awareness was born and took hold in literature:

> Aquel hombre pasaba directamente del signo de escritura a la intuición, omitiendo el signo sonoro; el extraño arte que iniciaba, el arte de leer en voz baja, conduciría a consecuencias maravillosas. Conduciría, cumplidos muchos años, al concepto del libro como fin, no como instrumento de un fin.
>
> II, 231

Plato's virtues passed to mysticism, and from mysticism to profane literature, thus making a Flaubert, a Mallarmé, a Henry James or a James Joyce possible (II, 230).

Did St. Ambrose's practice of silent reading indeed mark the detachment of language from strict functionality? Borges expresses himself with the force of conviction:

> A fines del siglo IV se inició el proceso mental que, a la vuelta de muchas generaciones, culminaría en el predominio de la palabra escrita sobre la hablada, de la pluma sobre la voz.
>
> II, 230

Language and literature come of age. Esthetic enjoyment and spirituality add to the meaning of language. Man has found the means to renew himself. Is Borges' theory reliable? Like Borges' story "Historia del guerrero y de la cautiva," the essay "Del culto de los libros" is not a scientific work (II, 39). Borges admits that many conjectures can be applied to Droctulft, the hero of the story, and that his is only one. We extend to the essay under consideration one of Borges' own remarks: "si no es verdadera como hecho, lo será como símbolo" (II, 40).

If Borges speaks about language with almost mystical reverence, he reserves endless irony for the term "dialect." The reader should be warned that for Borges a dialect is not a deviation from a linguistic standard, but a marked departure from intelligibility, from reason, common sense, usage. In other words, for Borges a dialect is not a linguistic category but an aberration of sorts, with literary, philosophical, and political implications. Malmstrom writes: "A *dialect* is a variety of language spoken by a group of people united by geographic, social, ethnic, historical, psychological, religious, or other factors. A dialect varies in pronunciation, vocabulary, and grammar from other varieties of the same language."[2] Banded together, idiolects—particularities of expression—form a speech community.[3] In "El congreso," a story published in one of Borges' last prose volumes, we read: "Todas las agrupaciones tienden a crear su dialecto y sus ritos" (II, 472). Ironically, the Congress, which intends to unify the world, fails to produce an universal language, disintegrating through dialectal fragmentation. In ordinary conversation, Malmstrom writes, the term often designates "a corrupted language."[4]

A translation, for instance, an arbitrary translation, is a dialectal product. In "Las versiones homéricas" Borges considers rather extensively the issue of translations, with the attendant problems of faithfulness to the letter or the spirit of the text. A translation that accommodates both the exigencies of the letter and of the spirit, like Butler's, comes close to Borges' ideal. By contrast, he finds Alexander Pope's version extraordinary: "Su lujoso dialecto (como el de Góngora) se deja definir por el empleo desconsiderado y mecánico de los superlativos" (I, 186). The word "dialect" places Pope's translation outside the spirit and the text of the *Iliad*: the solitary black sheep becomes a squadron; reality is forced to simplify itself into a show, the movement is oratorical rather than lyrical (I, 186). Pope's *Iliad* is a deformation, not a legitimate rendition of the text.

"El acercamiento a Almotásim" confirms Borges' predilection for the term "dialect" as an aberration. A Cecil Roberts, we learn, accuses Mir Bahhadur Ali, author of *The Approach to Al-Mu'tasim*, of having produced a work which is an incongruous combination of elements from Wilkie Collins and from a 12th century Persian writer, Ferid Eddin Attar, a combination rendered into a choleric dialect—"un dialecto colérico" (I, 393). The work is almost intractable:

> Hay una vertiginosa pululación de *dramatis personae*-para no hablar de una biografía que parece agotar los movimientos del espíritu humano (desde la infamia hasta la especulación matemática) y de una peregrinación que comprende la vasta geografía del Indostán.
>
> I, 395

Bahhadur, we are told, diffuses the individuality of the protagonist, sacrificing it to oratorical effects: "el inaudito y no mirado Almotásim debería dejarnos la impresión de un carácter real, no de un desorden de superlativos" (I, 396).

Flaubert broke new ground when he set out to create the first purely esthetic prose work (I, 213). Assuming that the possibilities of expression in prose had yet to be exhausted, Flaubert refused to follow a model. He was utterly convinced that something could only be expressed in a certain way, and that it was a writer's duty to find that elusive way. Disregarding period classifications like Classicism and Romanticism, Flaubert asserted that failure might differ but that perfection was always the same, that a good verse was equally good in Boileau or in Hugo. He believed in the preestablished harmony between the euphonic and the precise (I, 214). Having set up the issue and its background, Borges intervenes with critical authority:

Esta superstición del lenguaje habría hecho tramar a otro escritor un pequeño dialecto de malas costumbres sintácticas y prosódicas; no así en Flaubert, cuya decencia fundamental lo salvó de los riesgos de su doctrina. Con larga probidad persiguió el *mot juste*, que por cierto no excluye el lugar común y que degeneraría, después, en el vanidoso *mot rare* de los cenáculos simbolistas.

I, 214

Carried away by the possibilities of his theory, Flaubert would have transformed his language into a dialect of bad literary habits. What saved him, Borges points out, was his fundamental decency. We thus know that for Borges a dialect, ultimately, marks a departure from fundamental decency. Borges, of course, could have limited the issue to a purely literary context. Flaubert's dialect, in such a case, as in that of the symbolists, would have merely indicated a linguistic deviation, a transition, say, from the "mot juste" to the "mot rare." By using the expression "fundamental decency," Borges focuses not on specialized aspects of human activity but on the very essence of individualized humanity. To speak of literary decorum is one thing, to speak of fundamental decency is quite another.

The peculiar use of the word 'dialect" is, therefore, not confined to literature alone. Among the books reviewed by Borges, there is one by H. G. Wells, *Guide to the New World. A Handbook of Constructive World Revolution*. More than an encyclopedia of insults, Borges assures the reader, Wells' book is a manifesto of quintessential decency. With freedom of conscience, he inveighs against Hitler, against Goering, against Stalin, even against Eden. Well's invectives, Borges justly points out, have no particular literary merit. Wells, we read, denounces "A José Stalin, que en un dialecto irreal sigue vindicando la dictadura del proletariado" (II, 242). Now Wells' own words, "aunque nadie sabe qué es el proletariado, ni cómo y dónde dicta" (II, 242). By unreal Borges simply means that such a dialect is unintelligible to *homo sapiens*, not that it does not exist. Borges transfers the characteristics of dialect to an irrational context. Appropriateness, not correctness, is the key to intelligent language usage.[5] As Borges construes the matter,

Stalin's pronouncements may be grammatically correct but utterly inappropriate to rational man, and they are irrelevant precisely because they are inappropriate. Exponents of nationalism, even when they wish to vindicate democracy, even when they consider themselves to be quite different from Goebbels, "instan a sus lectores, en el dialecto mismo del enemigo, a escuchar los latidos de un corazón que recoge los mandatos de la sangre ye de la tierra" (II, 243). Borges could not be more explicit. He detests the "isms" which corrupt the fundamental decency of man, the dialects which mesmerize man. During the Spanish Civil War Republicans, Nationalists, and Marxists, all proclaimed their righteousness: "todos, en un léxico de *Gauleiter*, hablaban de la Raza y del Pueblo. Hasta los hombres de la hoz y del martillo resultaban racistas . . . " (II, 243). It is not casually that Borges speaks of Wells:

> Wells nos exhorta a recordar nuestra humanidad esencial y a refrenar nuestros miserables rasgos diferenciales, por patéticos o pintorescos que sean. En verdad, esa represión no es exorbitante: se limita a exigir de los estados, para su mejor convivencia, lo que una cortesía elemental exige de los individuos. "Nadie en su recto juicio—declara Wells—piensa que los hombres de Gran Bretaña son un pueblo elegido, una más noble especie de nazis, que disputan la hegemonía del mundo a los alemanes. Son el frente de batalla de la humanidad. Si non son ese frente, no son nada. Ese deber es un privilegio."
>
> II, 244

Stalin's or Goebbels' dialects are not only strident linguistic deviations, they are an affront to our "essential humanity," to "elemental courtesy," to reason.

We are quite far from Pope's "dialectal" version of Homer's *Iliad*, from Góngora's luxurious "dialect," from Bahhadurs' unchecked verbosity. Yet the diversification of the term "dialect" is useful in ascertaining Borges' range of intention. A dialect, for him, is a misleading compendium of meaningless superlatives, it is an oratory that feeds upon itself and alienates man from himself and from his purpose—an aberration. Language and dialect encompass the best and the worst of man. What is a dialect for Borges? In "Utopía de un hombre que está cansado" Borges says that, when it depletes itself of emotion, language becomes a system of quotations ("La lengua es un sistema de citas," II, 514). Building upon Borges' reasoning, one can state that dialect, within a Borgesian context, is language which has degenerated into a system of quotations.

Notes

[1] "Borges y el lenguaje," in *El escritor y la crítica*, p. 217.

[2] Jean Malmstrom, *Language in Society*, 2nd ed. (Rochelle Park: Hayden Book Co., 1973), p. 52.

[3] Ibid., p. 52.

[4] Ibid., p. 53.

[5] Ibid., p. 115.

Part III

Chromatic Experience

The Point of View

There is a conspicuous visual quality to Borges' work: the dynamic interplay between light and dark, the explicit and implicit presence of colors, chromatic symbolism. The fact that progressive blindness had affected both Borges' depth of field and range of chromatic perception justifies only peripherally his use of colors. Like Hladik, one of his protagonists, Borges knows that reality is not as rich as man's imagination (I, 511). The significant fact is that Borges ennobles and enriches esthetically the world which is gradually and inexorably disappearing for him.

> Todo esto debería atemorizarme,
> pero es una dulzura, un regreso.
> De las generaciones de los textos que hay en la tierra
> sólo habré leído unos pocos,
> los que sigo leyendo en la memoria,
> leyendo y transformando.
>
> *(Obras*, 1017)

The very title of the poem, "Elogio a la sombra," establishes Borges' positive attitude about his condition and underscores the regenerative power of literature. It is also a statement of exemplary intellectual honesty.

Luminosity and darkness, more than light and dark, are the primary visual characteristics of Borges' writings, with shadows altering the perceptual balance. There is emphasis on noon, the hour without shadows. The passage of time, with its attendant philosophical and metaphysical implications, is at the center of this Borgesian awareness. "Funes el memorioso" is an accomplished illustration in this sense. Day and night, in

199

their cyclical manifestation, frame the presence of man both circumstantially and philosophically. A grey man emerges from the "unanimous night" in "Las ruinas circulares." It is not by accident that a significant number of Borges' short stories take place at night.

When actual colors are mentioned, white, black, and grey, are among the most prevalent. They are almost invariably charged with symbolism, whether in Borges' own short stories or in his essays about other authors. Thus in "El tintorero enmascarado Hákim de Merv" Borges weaves into the fabric of the story the complex issue of chromatic symbolism, while in "El arte narrativo y la magia" he discusses the meaning of the color white in Poe's *Narrative of A. Gordon Pym*, Melville's *Moby Dick*, and Mallarmé's poetry. Borges analyzes critically and elaborates esthetically black and white as absolutes.

Through chromatic awareness Borges explores not only the realm of philosophy, but that of literary creation as well, the mystery of what he felicitously calls the "esthetic fact." The last vital act in the life of the Italian poet Giambattista Marino, in "Una rosa amarilla," is an esthetic one, the ephemeral glimpse of a Platonic rose. It is an extraordinary statement—literary creativity as an esthetic redemption of life. The esthetic fact retrieves the last moment of Marino's existence from its biological insignificance. The yellow rose that he sees in a vase is not the rose about which he recites a few verses or the ineffable one which he lastly beholds. The actual rose constitutes the impulse for an esthetic fact, which in turn leads to the supreme esthetic fact, the revelation. The color yellow, one of the primary colors of nature, is for Borges a seminal source of meaningful human creativity, of regenerative hope. This is the essence of "Utopía de un hombre que está cansado," one of Borges' last short stories.

There is deliberate chromatic reticence in Borges' works. Colors, of course, are frequently mentioned—a yellow window, a black cat, etc.—but there are numerous instances in which colors are implied, with the deductive role left to the reader, to the depth of his experience. When Borges writes that a certain dawn has the color of a leopard's gums, he eschews definition, thus establishing a dynamic relationship between the reader and the text. For Borges this is not only an efficacious literary device but also a matter of honesty, of unwillingness to falsify the esthetic act of the reader. The reader thus becomes an esthetic participant. In order to complete the story, he has to draw from his own imagination and experience.

Borges' preoccupation with chromatic awareness and its dimension is comprehensive. It recommends a man of letters who wished to explore yet another possibility of being a man.

Painting—The Medium

The theoretical framework of Borges' thinking on painting is to be found in "El duelo," one of the Argentine's last short stories. Two ladies of uneasy friendship and cordiality, Marta Pizarro and Clara Glencairn, enact an allegorical duel between figurative and non-figurative painting. They belong, Borges pointedly writes, to the sect of painters. While the term eventually acquires esthetic significance, it initially suggests a religious context. A sect is a religious anomaly, a deviation from orthodoxy or an exacerbation of it. While "sect" may be extended to any association of persons pursuing jealously a narrow range of specialized interest, its first acception is that of a religious or philosophical splinter group. Thus when Borges speaks of the *secta de pintores*, he projects the esthetic issue against a wider and more profound background. Borges, who uses the occasion to deride his country's notorious trendiness, writes: "La secta de pintores, hoy tan injustamente olvidada, que se llamó concreta o abstracta, como para indicar su desdén de la lógica y del lenguaje, es uno de los tantos ejemplos" (II, 407). First, concrete and abstract painting are not defined esthetically but in terms of logic and language. Borges thus points out a seminal error of interpretation.

Borges attributes the potentiality of erroneous interpretation to painting's lack of autonomy. In "La muralla y los libros," where Borges tentatively discusses esthetics, we read: "Pater, en 1877, afirmó que todas las artes aspiran a la condición de la música, que no es otra cosa que forma" (II, 133). The autonomy of music should legitimize the other arts' claim to esthetic individuality. Painting is a case in point: " . . . de igual modo que a la música le está permitido crear un orbe propio de sonidos, la pintura, su hermana, podría ensayar colores y formas que no reprodujeran los de las cosas que nuestros ojos ven" (II, 407–08).

Behind this esthetic ideal, by way of a tradition that can be turned to our advantage, Borges subtly places the biblical injunction, shared by Islam, against the creation of idols of living beings by human hand (II, 408). Borges' Lee Kaplan, whose abstract canvases scandalize the bourgeoisie, does more than explore the limits of visual recognition; he restores the true spirit of the Bible (II, 408). "Los iconoclastas, argüía, estaban restaurando la genuina tradición del arte pictórico, falseada por herejes como Durero o como Rembrandt" (II, 408). Thus Borges imparts a religious-moral dimension to the statement that esthetic revolutions tempt the public into irresponsibility (II, 408). Rising to the challenge, Clara Glencairn, one of the protagonists, opts for abstract painting: "se dispuso a enriquecer el arte concreto con sus esplendores indefinidos" (II, 408). Having set the stage, Borges engages the reader in an interesting argument.

The official publication of the sect, with more zeal than critical rigor, attacks Clara Glencairn. The essence of her modernism remains misunderstood. Her paintings, Borges tellingly writes, "sugerían el tumulto de un ocaso, de una selva o del mar y no se resignaban a ser austeros redondeles y rayas" (II, 408). Clara's critics fail to notice that her paintings are abstractions of an existing creation, of common realities, not pure flights of fancy. "Hay una hora en la tarde," Borges writes in "El fin," "en que la llanura está por decir algo" (I, 523). "Ciertos crepúsculos y ciertos lugares," says Borges elsewhere, "quieren decirnos algo" (II, 133). There is a previous materiality in Clara's idealism. This is the kind of abstractions that her paintings project, not the kind totally generated or contrived by imagination. Her paintings are "esthetic facts," rather than arbitrary projections of the imagination.

Marta Pizarro, Clara Glencairn's cordial adversary, is, instead, a traditional, representational painter. She paints portraits of local notables and old houses in Buenos Aires, houses "cuyos modestos patios delineó con modestos colores" (II, 407). It is an incisive critique. Marta's art does not transcend recognizable reality, it's modesty masking an inability to capture a dynamic essence. There are no *esplendores indefinidos* in her work, as in that of Clara, no attempts at trying out forms and colors that go beyond ordinary visual recognition. Marta has no vision of her own. Clara, instead, like Jules Verne, deals in probabilities (II, 209). She does not invent, in the sense in which Verne accuses H. G. Wells. Reacting to Wells' adventures—a man who returns from the future with a flower in hand, a person who comes back from another world with the heart on the right side—Verne is supposed to have exclaimed, scandalized: "Il invente!" (II, 210). Clara does not invent, in the proper sense of the word; she interprets, synthesizes, enriches. When Borges speaks of the *esplendores indefinidos* projected by Clara's paintings, we are led to an important realization: the indefinite, such as Borges postulates it here, is not the equivalent of invisible. Acevedo-Borges, in "Utopía de un hombre que está cansado," does not see anything specific on the yellow canvas that he is shown, not because there is not anything on it, but because his eyes are old (II, 515). Clara, however misunderstood, is essentially an artist. Marta, technically adept but without a vision, is not. She deals neither in probability nor in possibility, but in a modest, timidly polite rendition of reality.

While Borges claims not to espouse any particular esthetics (II, 351), the judgements expressed in "El duelo" form a rather complete and consistent esthetic entity—complete in theory and consistent in practice. The presence of color is unmistakable in Borges' work. But it is chromatic symbolism, educed from the culture and knowledge of man, not circumstantial description or fantastic invention, that engages Borges. He diversifies the possibilities of human expression. Literature, which often traps itself in *vanidad palabrera*, is not always the best exponent of thought and passion (II, 407). Borges himself does not claim any artistic virtues for the story, stating that the subject matter is not literary and that relating the occurrence is a rather modest enterprise. He warns the reader that the episodes are less important than the situation they integrate, and the characters. Thus Borges, the man of letters, and the craft that he epitomizes, discreetly recede into the background, allowing *la pintura* the center of the stage. There is little doubt that the matter is projected beyond the affective rivalry between two painters. The discussion about Clara Glencairn's modernism or lack of it is inconsequential. The irony is inescapable. A jury, against its own esthetic preference but afraid of being judged unsophisticated, votes for Clara (II, 409). The medium, however, is of interest. "Ajena a este espisodio" writes Borges, "la pintura seguía su camino" (II, 408). Life needs a passion (II, 410), and passion, in whatever form, strives for expression. Borges examines both, through the use of color.

Chromatic Perception

Burgin was one of the first critics to observe and comment upon the visual quality of Borges' work.[1] It is a valuable observation, for its suggests another facet of the experience that is to be found in the Argentine author's work. Since colors are both mentioned and suggested, perhaps chromatic conditions are a closer approximation than pictorial quality. The moon is yellow (I, 502), the waters of the Río de la Plata estuary have the color of the desert (I, 495). In one image the color is defined, in the other, suggested. The latter occurs almost as frequently as the former. The presence of both defined and suggested colors is significant and has significant implications. An object defined by form and by color is pictorially static, while one defined by a form whose color is only suggested is dynamic. This is the peculiarity of Borges' work. Of course, Borges' medium is literature, which makes the reader's esthetic perception different from that of a viewer of a representational painting. Paul Frankle states: "Art is the particular interrelationship of form and meaning, in which form becomes the *symbol* of meaning."[2] What is the role of color in this interplay between form and meaning? Does color belong to both? As usual, Borges prefers to suggest rather than define. There is no explicit discussion of esthetics. Instead, he dwells upon the experience of the reader, whom he draws into esthetic participation.

Further elaboration of pictorial concepts is necessary. There are always two esthetic acts, that of the artist creating a work of art, and that of the viewer experiencing it. Even when the artist and the viewer are one and the same person, the two acts are not simultaneous. Matisse is supposed to have said: "When a painting is finished, it is like a new-born child. The artist himself must have time to understand it."[3] "I paint what I see, I paint what I paint, I paint what I think," says Diego Rivera in an E. B. White poem.[4] Even in impressionism, which requires of the artist as direct a contact as possible with the subject matter, the two acts are distinguishable.[5] This directness affects the sensitivity of the viewer, who perceives the painter's choice of subject, of form, of colors, and is guided by them. Impressionists did away with shadows by treating them as colors and as light. This, of course, gives the viewer novel possibilities of interpretation, but leaves his primary sensorial experience out. In a representational painting, or in any painting, for that matter, the color sets the mood of perception. Great art, Cecil Allen tells us, is not descriptive.[6] To be sure, there is a narrative line in painting, but such a line is secondary. What matters is the perception, the esthetic experience of the work of art, the esthetic art. Color and form, in the words of Kandinsky, are active entities. They are not interchangeable, however. Kandinsky's thinking on form:

> Form, in the narrow sense, is the boundary between one surface and another: that is external meaning. But it has also an internal significance, of varying intensity; and properly speaking, *form is the external expression of an inner meaning.*[7]

Form can stand alone, color cannot.[8] Does color contribute to the external expression of an inner meaning or to the meaning itself? Are colors, from a philosophical point of view, "secondary qualities," as Sartre believes?[9] Green, yellow, or red, do not affect the "appleness" of an apple, so to speak, or to use Borges' own words, the "tableness" of a table (I, 320). An apple drawn in black ink is still the representation of an apple. Colors add verisimilitude and symbolism to form.[10] The degree of verisimilitude and of symbolic charge depend on the sensorial and intellectual experience of the viewer. This is where Borges reduces the jurisdiction of the artist, and augments the autonomy of the viewer, in the case of his craft, of the reader. Borges, whom Modernism has taught the privilege of freedom, gives his reader considerable esthetic latitude. When Borges writes that the waters of the Río de la Plata are of the color of the desert, the reader is left to his own devices.

As a man of letters, Borges educes the distinction between the dynamic and static aspects of the word from the Hebrew, Greek, and Scandinavian cultures. Quoting Coleridge, Borges states that men are born either Platonic or Aristotelian, that is to say, predisposed to accept or negate the reality of abstractions (II, 236). This proposition affects language as well. To it, we add Hebrew and Nordic understanding of the matter. A brief consideration of the term "word" and its meanings will bring forth cultural differentiations.

Logos, the Greek term for word, implies order. It is an intellectual product; it seeks meaning, "the ordered and reasonable content."[11] Word is thus viewed as an abstraction of reality, a conceptually defined entity, a symbol. In Hebrew, the term is *dabhar,* and it signifies word, deed, and concrete object, all in one.[12] In the primitive Scandinavian culture, the *kenningar* was a verbal object, an equivalent of reality (I, 335–50). While for the Greeks *logos* meant not only being but non-being as well, for the Hebrews it comprised only being. A lie, then, is something different in Greek and Hebrew cultures, non-agreement with the truth in the former, a destroyed reality in the other. As "word" is something static in one culture and something dynamic in the other, the effect of a non-truth has different consequences. In "Parábola de palacio," in which an emperor commissions a poet to write a composition, Borges' intention is clear: "Lo cierto, lo increíble, es que en el poema estaba entero y minucioso el palacio enorme" (II, 340). A hush came over the emperor's retinue: "Todos callaron, pero el Emperador exclamó: ¡*Me has arrebatado el palacio!*" (II, 340). The poet is beheaded on the spot. Coleridge's poem "Kubla Khan" is a verbal reconstruction of a palace built by Kubla Khan according to a dream in the 13th century (II, 144). "Historia de los dos que soñaron" carries a similar intention.

The Greeks admired the beauty of nature, in both its configuration and colors. Their favorite color was blue, for the heavens, the sea, and the far mountains are blue.[13] The Old Testament, in contrast, has no word for blue.[14] The Hebrews favored the colors white and red, vivid colors. What they really appreciated, however, was not color but light and luminosity. In Boman's words:

> If white and red were most preferred, this is connected with the fact that they came closest to light and fire and therefore illuminate the most. In sunlight and firelight, white, golden, and red pass over one another and appear thus as colors that stand very close to one another.[15]

This was the Israelites' ideal of beauty. We are told in the Psalms (104.2) that God shrouded himself not in color but in light. In "Paradiso, XXXI, 108" Borges speaks of the irretrievable face of Jesus:

> Pablo la vio como una luz que lo derribó; Juan como el sol cuando resplandece en su fuerza; Teresa de Jesús, muchas veces, bañada en luz tranquila, y no pudo jamás precisar el color de los ojos.
>
> II, 337

As opposed to the Greeks, for whom beauty was harmonious form, the Hebrew found beauty in something amorphous but dynamic: "They found beauty in the formless, dreadful fire and in the lifegiving light."[16] To the Greeks, light was only an esthetic category, beauty.

In Borges, sun and fire are sources of light as well as of colors. "Los teólogos," "La escritura del dios," "El tintorero emascarado Hákim de Merv," and "Las ruinas circulares" are centered on the symbolic meaning of light and fire. Neither light nor fire are admired as forms of beauty. We recall the noon sun in "Los teólogos" and "La escritura del dios," the hour without shadow, as a symbol of moral rectitude or divine impartiality, rightly or wrongly claimed. We remember the noon hour in "El tintorero emascarado Hákim de Merv," in whose blinding whiteness Hákim roots his symbolism. The fire which envelops the purposeful dreamer of "Las ruinas circu-

lares" is neither beautiful nor utilitarian in the common accep-
tation of the term. Rather, it is the God of life and death, of the
endless cycle of affirmation and negation. We are in the realm
of the Hebrew thinking of the Old Testament. There is another
Hebrew peculiarity. In man's lucid dream the divinity reveals
itself as Fire. It is not the God of fire, but Fire itself. This is
consistent with the Hebrew *dabhar*, the word as an act, deed or
thing, something in the making, rather than with the Greek
logos, a concept, a static abstraction.[17] Heraclitus, whose dialectic skill Borges admires (II, 290), conceives of a world which
is engendered and devoured cyclically by fire (I, 367), but such
a dynamic interpretation is an exception to Greek thinking.
Heraclitus' statement, "No bajarás dos veces al río," quoted by
Plato in *Cratylus* is, from a philosophical point of view un-
Greek, for it goes counter to the Eleatic thinking, which denies
the reality of motion and change, or Plato, who considers the
matter geometrically, with time a finite—if moving—entity.[18]

To say God of Fire rather than Fire is to imply a duality,
possible in Greek thinking but inadmissible in the Hebrew one
unless considered an un-truth. Borges subtly enlarges the
scope of his intention by adducing Icelandic mythology. In the
prolog to *El oro de los tigres* (1972), Borges, as we have mentioned elsewhere, speaks of Thor: "Thor no era el dios del
trueno; era el trueno y dios" (II, 439). The prolog, tellingly,
begins with a reference to the biblical David. It should be
pointed out that the Nordic *kenningar*—linguistic equivalents of
reality, verbal objects, as Borges calls them—are closer in
meaning and intent to the Hebrew *dabhar* than to the Greek
logos.

There is yet another distinction between Hebrew and Greek
thinking that surfaces in Borges' work, that of time defined by
light rather than by motion. In Aristotle's *Physics* (iv, 14), for
instance, time is almost physical, manifested by motion. The
Greeks measured time by the movements of the planets, which
they called heavenly bodies.[19] The Greeks called the sun and
the moon "lamps of light," thus emphasizing function rather
than form.[20] The Greek use of space as thought-form, even in

referring to time, intrigues Borges, who considers it in the extreme form of Zeno's paradoxes. Light as time is less conspicuous among his preoccupations, but nevertheless present. Tzinacán, in "La escritura del dios," knows that it is noon because this is the time that light penetrates through the shaft above; John of Pannonia chooses the noon light for its purity; in "El tintorero enmascarado Hákim de Merv" the intensity of the heat indicates the noon time.

An illustration. Funes, the memorious, experiences reality without mediation, with an almost intolerable precision. Yet it is a changing reality:

> Una circunferencia en un pizarrón, un triángulo rectángulo, un rombo, son formas que podemos intuir plenamente; lo mismo le pasaba a Irineo con las aborrascadas crines de un potro, con una punta de ganado en una cuchilla, con el fuego cambiante y con la innumerable ceniza, con las muchas caras de un muerto en un largo velorio.
>
> I, 481–82

The changing fire and the mysterious changing expression on a dead man's face during a long wake unambiguously point to a perception of time based on light rather than movement. Funes has difficulties with conventions arbitrarily grafted on reality: "le molestaba que el perro de las tres y catorce (visto de perfil) tuviera el mismo nombre que el perro de las tres y cuarto (visto de frente)" (I, 483). Why shouldn't the dog's name, Funes asks, register the mutations induced by the changing light and angle? Is there really a change? Does the changing light mark it? We read in "El fin": "La llanura, bajo el último sol, era casi abstracta, como vista en un sueño" (I, 522). When chromatic conditions change, our perception of reality changes as well, as any reader of Borges' description of his touch with eternity can attest (I, 331). "Waking up" from his "dream" Dahlmann faces a chromatically changing present: "Ya el blanco sol intolerable de las doce del día era el sol amarillo que precede al anochecer y no tardaría en ser rojo" (I, 532). Borges appreciates the chromatic ambiguity of William Morris, in *The Life and Death of Jason*:

for they were near now
To see the gusty wind of evening blow
Long locks of hair across those bodies white
With golden spray hiding some dear delight.

I, 165

"El último pormenor: *el rocío de oro*—¿de sus violentos rizos, del mar, de ambos o de cualquiera?—*ocultando alguna querida delicia,* tiene otro fin, también: el de significar su atracción" (I, 165). Borges dramatizes the issue of light as time in "La doctrina de los ciclos," a Greek doctrine that he, in this context, rejects:

La luz se va perdiendo en calor; el universo minuto por minuto, se hace invisible. Se hace más liviano también. Alguna vez, ya no será más que calor: calor equilibrado, inmóvil, igual. Entonces habrá muerto.

I, 363

We will have died, too. The premise, if not the conclusion, is recognizably Hebrew. While there is light, not the artificial, continuous light of "La biblioteca de Babel," but the dynamic light of the sun—the transcendant light that holds the mystery—there is life. While there are shadows, the light of declining intensity which marks the passing of time, there is life. Borges dedicates to the shadow an entire volume of poetry and prose, *Elogio a la sombra* (1969). He states in the poem "Elogio a la sombra": "Vivo entre formas luminosas y vagas /que no son aún la tiniebla" (*Obras*, 1017). While the poetic statement undoubtedly marks a place in the progression of Borges' blindness, it also underscores the metaphysical interplay between light and dark, of life and death. The memory of the dying Hacedor searches the past for momentous experiences, the *sabor preciso* of such experiences, a manly stand, the first promise of love, privileged moments of literature. Borges' final phrase: "Sabemos estas cosas, pero no las que sintió al descender a la última sombra" (II, 311).

Borges' chromatic awareness and the esthetic and philosophical ways in which he diversifies it is a significant Borgesian dimension. Whether such a preoccupation is engendered in his own experience or educed from erudition is of little importance. What matters is that Borges tries to project natural or learned sensorial perceptions into a possible extension of man, experientially, esthetically, philosophically. Borges' visual infirmity permits him to see most things in white and gray, for instance, but this would not justify his interest in Poe's, Melville's and Mallarmé's obsession with white. Borges' father taught him early on that the color of an orange is orange, and that an orange tastes like an orange.[21] In other words, both the color of an orange and its taste are culturally inherited entities, not knowledge yielded by unmediated individual experience. It is, so to speak, everybody's reality. But in literature—as in life—experience perceptually individualizes reality, in a dynamic interplay between the general and the particular. Novels, Borges states, in which abstractions are personified, contain an allegorical element, while allegories (*fábula de abstracciones*) contain novelistic elements (II, 270). In the case of chromatic perceptions Borges, not infrequently, shifts the attention of the reader from a paradigmatic context to a syntagmatic one, which allows the individualization of experience. The reader thus completes, with his particular experience, the syntagmatic process.

Notes

[1] Richard Burgin, *Conversations with Borges* (Chicago, San Francisco: Holt, Rinehart and Winston, 1968), p. 99.

[2] Cf. Hans Hesse, *How Pictures Mean* (New York: Pantheon Books, 1974), p. 9.

[3] Cf. John Dewey, in *Practical Cogitator*, p. 479.

[4] Ibid., pp. 504–05.

[5] Bernard Innstad, *Painting Methods of the Impressionists* (London: Pitman Publishing, 1976), p. 42.

[6] Cecil Allen, *The Mirror of the Passing World* (New York: W. W. Norton & Co., Inc., 1928), p. 54.

[7] Wassily Kandinsky, *Concerning the Spiritual Art* (New York: George Wittenbon, Inc., 1947), p. 47.

[8] Ibid., p. 46.

[9] Jean Paul Sartre, "Herman Melville's *Moby Dick*," *Twentieth Century*

Interpretations of Moby Dick, ed. Michael E. Gilmore (Englewood Cliffs, N.J.: Prentice Hall, 1977), p. 94.

[10] Kandinsky, p. 46.

[11] Thorlief Boman, *Hebrew Thought Compared with Greek.* (Philadelphia: The Westminster Press, 1960), p. 67.

[12] Ibid., p. 56.

[13] Ibid., p. 115.

[14] Ibid., p. 115.

[15] Ibid., p. 88.

[16] Ibid., p. 89.

[17] Ibid., p. 60.

[18] Ibid., p. 51.

[19] Ibid., p. 131.

[20] Ibid., p. 131.

[21] *Borges at Eighty*, p. 157.

Black and White

Black and white appear less circumstantially than symbolically and emblematically in Borges' prose. When they appear circumstantially, in a merely descriptive capacity, we have, as Borges puts it, a shared representation ("representación compartida," I, 38). When they appear in a distinct cultural context, we are in the realm of symbology. In order to be able to share the representation, the reader needs guidance, cultural orientation. Burton, one of the translators of *Thousand Nights and One Night*, explains, in the many notes accompanying the text, the emblematic colors of death in the Arab world (I, 381). The casual reader of Borges' "El tintorero enmascarado Hákim de Merv," for instance, cannot possibly understand the story without the chromatic symbolism of black and white in Islam. Reading that "el día era infinito de puro blanco" (*Obras*, 64) in Borges' poetry without understanding the meaning of white in painting or literary symbolism would diminish the range of our esthetic enjoyment. The homes that Funes, the memorious, imagines are "negras, compactas, hechas de tiniebla homogénea" (I, 483). Everything, during Borges' celebrated nocturnal stroll in Buenos Aries, seemed made of "la misma sustancia infinita de la noche" (I, 331). The polarization white-black is pregnant with significance.

"El tintorero emascardo Hákim de Merv" deals with a certain Hákim, a dyer by trade, born, we read, in the year 120 of the *hegira* (AD 736), who wished to impose himself as *The Prophet*. The subsequent events constitute the story. As usual, Borges provides a quasi-historical background, factually plausible if chronologically unreliable. To be sure, there was a real Hákim,

217

a Fatimid caliph (996–1021), whom an eleventh-century leader, Darazi, and his followers, the Druzes, considered to be the manifestation of God in His unity. The claim was anathema, for Islam does not admit any divine plurality or human divinity. To the orthodox Muslims, "There is no God but God, and Mohammed is His Messenger." The historical Hákim, then, whom the dissidents called "Our Lord," was an impostor on two counts.[1] Such as it stands, the matter is interesting but not esthetically meaningful.

Let us see how Borges frames the historical fact literarily. The chronological discrepancy is unessential. The Borgesian Hákim was born in the old, desolate city of Merv, "cuyos viñedos y prados miran tristemente el desierto" (I, 284). The colors black and white, which foreshadow the impending symbolism, make their appearance: "El mediodía es blanco y deslumbrador, cuando no lo oscurecen nubes de polvo que ahogan a los hombres y dejan una lámina blancuzca en los negros racimos" (I, 284). If, for instance, in "Dos teólogos," Borges speaks only of noon and its light, here he is chromatically precise: noon is white, the bunches of grapes are black, occasionally whitish under the blowing dust. The entire symbolic structure is before us: the diffusing whiteness, the black of the grapes, the cosmetic gray produced by the dust settling on the grapes. The gray is not substantial, only a thin film cosmetically altering the blackness of the grapes. Its artificiality stems from its utterly static quality, for, technically speaking, grey is composed of black and white, two inactive noncolors.[2] We read, in "El inmortal," that Cartaphilus, the antiquarian, was a man" de rasgos singularmente vagos" (II, 9). Such a statement is carefully prepared by two descriptive elements that precede it: a man "de ojos grises y barba gris, de rasgos singularmente vagos" (II, 9). The conclusion is a logical extension of the inexpressiveness of grey.

We are now ready to meet Hákim. The text reads: "Sabemos que un hermano de su padre lo adiestró en el oficio de tintorero: arte de impíos, de falsarios y de inconstantes que inspiró los primeros anatemas de su carrera pródiga" (I, 284).

Hákim's impending heresy is prefigured by his profession, the art of changing the color of objects, of tampering chromatically with nature, of falsifying. The very choice of the term "art" rather than "craft" to designate Hákim's profession is significant in itself, for it enlarges the scope of our awareness. Like the people of his trade, the text reads, Hákim is fickle. This qualification further underscores the subjectivity of his (and any artist's) enterprise. Later, he confesses:

> *Mi cara es de oro* (declara en una página famosa de la *Aniquilación*) *pero he macerado la púrpura y he sumergido en la segunda noche la lana sin cardar y he saturado en la tercera noche la lana preparada, y los emperadores de las islas aún se disputan esa ropa sangrienta. Así pequé en los años de juventud y trastorné los verdaderos colores de las criaturas. El Angel me decía que los carneros no eran del color de los tigres, el Satán me decía que el Poderoso quería que lo fueran y se valía de mi astucia y mi púrpura.*
>
> I, 284

The artificial red simulates blood, thus creating the impression of vital legitimacy. This explains the seriousness with which each of the emperors in question dispute the character of the clothing items manufactured by Hákim. In retrospect, Hákim sees it as a sin. The deception should have been obvious. Muttons simply are not of the color of tigers.

But the sin of altering the color of objects and animals pales in comparison to that of falsifying faith. Black and white now symbolically frame the process. Usurping the authority of Mohammed, he presents himself as the real prophet. Mohammed was a messenger, a medium rendered important by God's wish, not by his own merit. Unlike Christ, "the Word was not made flesh" in him. Aside from the mystery of The Revelation, Mohammed was thought to be quite ordinary.[3] Not so Hákim, who could induce a miracle—not the miracle of sight, like Jesus, but that of blindness. When Hákim came across a motley group of faithful awaiting the Ramadan and told them that he was the prophet, they greeted his claim with cries of *impostor* and *brujo* (I, 285). At this moment, a leopard which belonged to someone got loose, and everyone but

Hákim fled in panic. When they returned, the animal was blind. The miracle brings about a conversion: "Ante los ojos luminosos y muertos, los hombres adoraron a Hákim y confesaron su virtud sobrenatural" (I, 286). Borges writes, not without irony: "un harem de 114 mujeres ciegas trataba de aplacar las necesidades de su cuerpo divino" (I, 286). Ever so subtly, Borges introduces an element of encompassing interest. Hákim wishes to eliminate color perception rather than enhance it, to dispense with an accepted reality, to do away with the established visual symbolism that stands in the way of his purpose:

> Hákim, ya entonces, descartó su efigie brutal por un cuádruple velo de seda blanca recamado de piedras. El color emblemático de los Banú Abbás era el negro; Hákim eligió el color blanco—el más contradictorio—para el Velo Resguardador, los pendones y los turbantes.
>
> I, 286

Black and white. Black, of course, is the emblematic color of religious respect in Islam. Mohammed's soul departed for heaven from the black stone of Kaaba, Islam's holiest shrine, in Mecca. Ancient Arabic illuminations depict the holy black meteorite covered in black brocade.[4] Mohammed was clad in white when he received a revelation from God through the archangel Gabriel.[5] Inevitably, the emblematic color of the Umayyad dynasty (AD 661-750) that succeeded the first caliphs was white. That of the Abbasid dynasty, which ruled in Baghdad from AD 750 onward, was black. The emblematic color of the dissident Fatimid caliphs, who ruled in Egypt from AD 969 to 1171, was green.[6]

The color white adopted by Hákim is contradictory because it is a blasphemous claim to a purity given through revelation only to Mohammed. It also stands in absolute chromatic opposition to black, the emblematic color of the orthodox Umayyads, the heirs to Mohammed's legacy. For Hákim, any other emblematic color would have been a compromise, a departure from the Prophet's consecrated color. Only white, the opposite of black, would have served his purpose, only the new symbolism of white could replace the old symbolism of black, perversely suggesting a return to the original religious order. This is Hákim's unforgivable sin. Borges manipulates the matter masterfully, with habitual irony. The necessity of white as a new symbol was dictated by the existence of a previous symbol, black. In other words, white did not have a predetermined symbolic value for Hákim. It acquired it by antithesis.

There remains the issue of leprosy. It is difficult—and not particularly useful—to ascertain whether Hákim contracted leprosy in his younger years, or later when, already acclaimed a prophet, he embraces and kisses the lepers he encounters. Hákim's hopes of elevating his tainted, impure whiteness to the purity of perfection, transforming it and himself into a symbol, are dashed. He is unable to transcend his individuality and the orthodoxy of Islam. When two of his captains rip the veil off Hákim's face, the hideous, imperfect whiteness fails to be recognized as a symbol. He is put to the sword: "La prometida cara del Apóstol, la cara que había estado en los cielos, era en efecto blanca, pero con la blancura peculiar de la lepra manchada" (I, 288). The man who changed the true color of objects, who tried to falsify the color of symbols, was unable to alter his own reality. This is Borgesian irony at its best.

In "Formas de una leyenda" the future of a man destined to become Buddha was symbolically prefigured by a white elephant in his mother's dream. The night of the child's conception, the mother dreamed that an elephant, "de color de la nieve y con seis colmillos" (II, 263), penetrated her right side. The elephant, symbol of gentleness, its six tusks, symbols of God's universal divinity, the color white, symbol of purity, induce the court soothsayers to predict Siddhartha's preeminence. Whiteness, also, holds a meaning for Siddhartha as well. His first inkling of the transitoriness of life comes to him upon contemplating, for the first time, an old man "cuyo pelo no es como el de los otros" (II, 263). As in Borges' poetry, whiteness here designates a fading of individuality into nothingness. It marks the passage of Siddhartha into a new consciousness.

In the third room that the ill-advised usurper of a small Andalusian kingdom opens, in the forbidden wing of a castle, there are two books: "uno era negro y enseñaba las virtudes de los metales de los talismanes y de los días, así como la preparación de veneos y de contravenenos; otro era blanco y no se pudo descifrar su enseñanza, aunque la escritura era clara" (I, 299). Such is the mystery of "La cámara de las estatuas," a short narrative in *Historia universal de la infamia*. The story is reminiscent of Hladik's dream in "El milagro secreto." Twenty-four monarchs had successively sealed the door which led to the secret chambers. During the reign of twenty-four kings, the chambers had not been accessible to the curiosity of man. The twenty-fifth monarch, an impostor, failed to heed the ancestral wisdom, and was defeated by the magic that he could not understand. He deciphered the black book of magic, of man-made magic, so to speak, but was unable to understand the mystery of the white one, the key to the supernatural.

It was to be a fatal misunderstanding. Black and white, here, are not simply colors describing the covers of two books. Rather, they are symbols of human and divine jurisdictions. The restoration of such a distinction implies the demise of the disruptive agent. The imposter is put to death. The two Semitic chess players in "El milagro secreto," one Jewish, the other Arabic, play the game without the benefit of rules, which are locked in a tower. The mystery of the game is not revealed in the dream. The partial revelation of the mystery in our story is sufficient to destroy the imposter. The king, we are told, was not of royal blood. He was an impostor and an apostate as well, the victim of his hubris.

The symbolism of white and black is not confined to exotic Eastern motifs, as might be deduced from the preceding examples. There is an active literary domain permeated by it. One of the works that Borges discusses in "El arte narrativo y la magia," is Poe's *Narrative of A. Gordon Pym*. Why precisely Poe and this narrative by him? Given Borges' notorious economy of expression and selectivity, the question is legitimate. What attracts Borges is Poe's obsession with the color white in the story in question, the centrifugal possibilities of such an obsession, the symbolic projection. "El secreto argumento de esa novela", Borges elucidates, "es el temor y la vilificación de lo blanco" (I, 167). We read:

> Poe finge unas tribus que viven en la vecindad del Círculo Antárctico, junto a la patria inagotable de ese color, y que de generaciones atrás han padecido la terrible visitación de los hombre y de las tempestades de la blancura.
>
> I, 167

There is a further clarification: "Los argumentos de ese libro son dos: uno inmediato, de vicisitudes marítimas; otro infalible, sigiloso y creciente, que sólo se revela al final" (I, 167). Is not white the impersonal color preferred by Mallarmé, asks Borges (I, 167)?

According to Borges, Poe explored the same symbolic possibilities of the color white as Melville: "Creo que Poe prefirió ese color, por intuiciones o razones idénticas a las declaradas luego por Melville, en el capítulo *The Whiteness of the Whale* de su también espléndida alucinación de *Moby Dick*" (I, 167). The reference to Melville's novel is helpful not only in enlarging the background of Poe's obsessive preoccupation with white, but also in tracing Borges' own thematic indebtedness. Melville, as we know, dedicates an entire chapter to whiteness, first to that of the whale, then to the spectral quality of whiteness, to what he considers to be an intrinsic wickedness. While most cultures, from that of the Indians of America to that of old Persia, have invested the color white with spiritual or esthetic purity, the truth, in Melville's view, is that we fear it more than we understand it:

> Yet for all these accumulated associations, with whatever is sweet, and honorable, and sublime, there yet lurks an elusive something in the innermost idea of this hue, which strikes more of panic to the soul than the redness which affrights in blood.[7]

Why do we fear whiteness? We fear it because, Melville suggests, its indefiniteness invokes the immensity of the universe.[8] We fear whiteness because, beyond the ennobling attributes that we have attached to it, beyond the euphemisms with which we court it, we sense it to be evil. This mysterious whiteness, Melville asserts, stabs us from behind.[9] It is insidious because, to use Melville's own words, it is "not actually inherent in substances, but only laid on from without."[10] Such a light can ultimately render everything white: "the palsied universe lies before us a leper."[11] Borges, we recall, describes the leperous whiteness of Hákim's face as corrupt, impure. Whiteness, "the most meaningful symbol of spiritual things, nay, the very veil of the Christian's Deity," "stabs us from behind with the thought of annihilation."[12] As in Mallarmé, whiteness symbolizes an impersonal infinity that is oblivious of individuality. In order to understand it, to put in perspective and determine his place within this perspective, man must infuse it with some concreteness, with recognizable individuality. The cycle is white-whiteness-white. Psychologically, archetypes need to be translated into archetypal images through a process of personalization or incarnation.[13] Hence the whale in Melville, the snow and water in Poe, Hákim's face, etc., in Borges. In playing with the symbolic possibilities of white-whiteness-white, was Borges inspired by Melville's imagery? The only certainty that we have is that Borges mentions expressly Melville's pivotal chapter in *Moby Dick*, "The Whiteness of the Whale."

In "El arte narrativo y la magia," Borges ponders Poe's esthetic resolution of magic, of the delicate interaction between the relative and the absolute. The aspect that Borges singles out is that of the chromatic quality of the rivers of an island: "determinar que su agua era colorada o azul, hubiera sido recusar toda posibilidad de blancura" (I, 168). Its whiteness is not accredited by the presence of the color white, but by the absence of any definite color.[14] This is, to clinch the argument in Borges' own terms, "La primitiva claridad de la magia" (I, 168). White as the absence of color is a notion common to both

Poe and Melville, and the source of their avowed fear of it. In Melville, Brodtkorb felicitously writes, whiteness is frightening because it suggests "not a perceivable order but a perceivable chaos: darkness visible rather than light: atheism, not the presence of God."[15] For Poe, as for Melville, whiteness is illusory, for it constantly breaks down in a profusion of chromatic nuances, "como los tonos de una seda cambiante," as Borges puts in his translation of Poe (I, 168).

At this point, Borges' interest in white is clearly recognizable. As in the two authors mentioned, in Borges there is a double consideration of the issue, that of white, and that of whiteness, the perceived color and its symbolism. The color white is ultimately an optical illusion, a *trompe-l'oeil*. Sartre treats it as such in his essay on Melville.[16] Certainly Hákim deemed his first profession, that of dyer, to be one of chromatically induced deceit, visually and spiritually. If we proceed from the particular to the general, then the issue of white leads to the issue of whiteness. Ahab's fear is engendered by the color white but is inexorably aggravated by whiteness, an undefinable entity. For Poe, the fear of whiteness is the fear of the absolute, not as a remote, uncountenanced possibility, but as an immediate, contiguous presence. "Stevenson," writes Borges, "refiere que en los sueños de la niñez lo perseguía un matiz abominable del color pardo" (II, 252). By banking on the suggestive potential of the color white, Hákim hoped to impose on his followers the awe of whiteness. Had he been successful, it would have instituted a new order, and would have saved his life. While aspiring to live a white, pure life, he dies a "black death," the most ignominious in Islam, violent, dreadful, without forgiveness of sins.[17] The color black symbolically triumphs. Beyond the particularity of this story, Borges treats the color black rather conventionally. Darkness is a primordial medium from which things evolve, the raw matter of creation, an affirmative presence, a beginning rather than an end. In Borges' celebrated hallucinatory night in Buenos Aires the tangible reality appears born out of darkness, made of it: "los portoncitos—más altos que las líneas estiradas de las paredes—parecían obrados de la

misma sustancia infinita de la noche" (I, 331). Funes imagines
the unknown house in a block yet to be completed, the same
way: "Funes las imaginaba negras, compactas, hechas de
tiniebla homogénea" (I, 483).

Borges broaches the subject of whiteness as achromatic
infinity in "Utopía de un hombre que está cansado." Borges-
Acevedo, the protagonist magically projected into the future,
finds himself in a world of dehumanized uniformity: all the
objects in the kitchen are made of metal, all homes are similar,
all the inhabitants—men and women—are disconcertingly
alike, all the paintings have the same color, and so on. "He
construido esta casa," confesses the man from the future, "que
es igual a todas las otras" (II, 514). A man and a woman enter
the room: "Diríase que eran hermanos o que los había igualado
el tiempo" (II, 515). Outside, everything was white: "Afuera, la
llanura estaba blanca de silenciosa nieve y de luna" (II, 514).
The white becomes whiteness, uniformity. The will to exist is
broken. The inhabitants of the place, with predictable uniformity, do not simply die, which would be allowing life to follow
its normal course, but commit suicide—the ultimate indifference. The only remark that a woman makes, before Borges-
Acevedo's host enters the lethal chamber, is, "La nieve
seguirá" (II, 516). Everything has dissolved into a whiteness of
indifference. If there is regenerative hope, in Borges' chromatic
symbolism, it is not in the color white or in whiteness, but in
the color yellow.

Notes

¹ Edward Mortimer, *Faith and Power. The Politics of Islam* (New York: Vintage
Books, 1982), p. 49.

² Kandinsky, p. 61.

³ Mortimer, p. 31.

⁴ Desmond Stewart, *Early Islam* (New York: Time Inc., 1967), pp. 21–22.

⁵ Ibid., p. 23.

⁶ Richard Burton, *Thousand Nights and One Night* (Printed by the Burton
Club for Private Subscribers Only, 1885), vol. V., p. 86.

⁷ Herman Melville, *Moby Dick* (Boston: Houghton Mifflin Co., 1956), p. 158.

⁸ Ibid., p. 163.

[9] Ibid., p. 163.

[10] Ibid., p. 163.

[11] Ibid., p. 163.

[12] Ibid., p. 163.

[13] Edward F. Nekyia, *Melville's Moby Dick* (New York: New Directions Publishing Co., 1978), p. 82.

[14] Kandinsky, p. 60.

[15] Paul Brodtkorb, Jr., *Ishmael's White World* (New Haven and London: Yale University Press, 1965), p. 119.

[16] Jean-Paul Sartre, "Herman Melville's Moby Dick," in *Twentieth Century Interpretations of Moby Dick*, p. 94.

[17] Burton, p. 250.

The Yellow Rose

In "Una rosa amarilla" (*El hacedor*, 1960) Giambattista Marino, the Italian poet to whom Borges dedicates the essay, has a revelation which gives him a glimpse of esthetic eternity: he sees a rose, a perfect rose, an ineffable Platonic rose. Like his own fame, unaffected by the passage of time, Marino's rose is above actuality or factuality. The choice of the rose—the poetic quintessence of natural beauty—would not have surprised Marino, a poets' poet in his day. The color of the rose, however, would most likely have raised a question, for yellow here is Borges' preference, not Marino's:

> Nada cuesta imaginar a unos pasos un sereno balcón que mira al poniente y, más abajo, mármoles y laureles y un jardín que duplica sus graderías en un agua rectángular. Una mujer ha puesto en una copa una rosa amarilla; el hombre murmura los versos inevitables que a él mismo, para hablar con sinceridad, ya lo hastían un poco: Púrpura del jardín, pompa del prado, gema de primavera, ojo de abril . . .
>
> II, 329,

Borges, ever so subtly, points out that the esthetic revelation that the dying Marino experiences is only tenuously connected with reality. Marino does not see the garden that Borges imagines beyond the peaceful balcony, not even its reflection in the water of the pond. He may vaguely perceive the rose in the vase, even its color, but this is not the flower of his creation. The rose of his poem is not yellow, but purple—*púrpura del jardín*. Neither the real garden nor the "unreal" garden reflected in the water are the primary impulses of Marino's revelation, but an esthetic creation, his own purple rose. What occurs in the silent, motionless, last moments of Marino's life is not a vital act, but a literary one. The two, of course, are simultaneous, but the obvious emphasis falls on the esthetic fact: ". . . el hecho inmóvil y silencioso que entonces ocurrió fue en verdad el último de su vida" (II, 329). The reader is being prepared for a momentous statement. In this very same volume, *El hacedor*, in "Parábola de Cervantes y de Quijote," Borges asserts with conviction: "Porque en el principio de la literatura está el mito, y asimismo en el fin" (II, 336). Marino's death is hereof a symbolic illustration. Marino returns to myth via an esthetic act which becomes a revelation. The actual yellow rose in his room is only an object, like the many gold lined books in his chamber, incapable of transcending itself (II, 329-30). It is only under the spell of his vanity that Borges' Marino dreams of mirroring the world in his books (like the garden in the pond?). In the shadow of death the esthetic revelation is illuminating. He is seeing the light, the rose. We are not told what was the color of the rose that he saw:

> Entonces ocurrió la revelación. Marino *vio* la rosa, como Adán pudo verla en el Paraíso, y sintió que ella estaba en su eternidad y no en sus palabras y que podemos mencionar o aludir pero no expresar y que los altos y soberbios volúmenes que formaban en un ángulo de la sala una penumbra de oro no eran (como su vanidad soñó) un espejo del mundo, sino una cosa más agregada al mundo.
>
> II, 329-30

Like Santa Teresa de Jesús, who saw Jesus' face bathed in light but could not tell the color of his eyes (II, 337), Marino cannot tell us the color of the *Rose*.

Why, the question needs to be asked, has Borges chosen specifically the color yellow? The answer rests with both Borges the man and Borges the writer. Yellow, simply, is the most pervasive and clearest of colors which his progressive blindness allows him. To his younger *alter ego*, whom he "meets" one winter morning in "El otro," Borges states:

> Cuando alcances mi edad habrás perdido casi por completo la vista. Verás el color amarillo y sombras y luces. No te preocupes. La ceguera gradual no es trágica. Es como un lento atardecer de verano.
>
> II, 463

This is much more than a declaration of stoic resignation. From its very phrasing we perceive that Borges ennobles esthetically his visual infirmity. Instead of accepting the limitations of his condition, instead of deploring the chromatic particularity of his meager vision, Borges produces a yellow rose. Rather than decrying the monotony of the yellow, Borges infuses it with metaphysical possibilities. The field is wide open. "Nadie", declares Borges in "La noche de los dones," "recuerda la primera vez que vio el amarillo o el negro o la primera vez que le tomó el gusto a una fruta" (II, 496). In his last prose works, Borges weaves the color yellow into a theory of continuity, of a plausible eternity, of hope.

There is, then, much more to the presence of yellow in Borges' work than the peculiarity of a visual infirmity or circumstantial use.[1] Yellow is a primary color, a fundamental color that can be combined with all the other colors.[2] As opposed to yellow, white, an artificial color, does not exist in nature. Maurice Boigey, in *La science des couleurs*, asserts that at any rate the human eye is better adapted to perceive colors derived from orange-yellow than from any other color.[3] Wheelock, one of Borges' critics, is certainly right in noting the color yellow in Borges' writings and in underscoring its universal or primordial symbolism.[4] For Kandinsky yellow is the typical earthly color.[5] Yellow keeps us rooted in nature, in a reality that we, however imperfectly, recognize. Its symbolism is visceral. Kandinsky again: "White has the appeal of the nothingness that is before birth, of the world in the ice age."[6] It is, both in terms of its synthetic nature and Kandinsky's intention, an unreality. Borges, contrary to some critical opinions, is not interested in a regression conspicuous by the absence of life, of man.[7] He does not fit Appolinaire's judgment that "artists are men who want to become non-human."[8] Rather the contrary is true, and the choice of the color yellow must be construed as evidence, as in Paul Klee's case, of man's interaction with nature. We owe the discerning of an affinity between Borges and Klee to Hans Hess.[9] For Klee yellow becomes a "pictorial metaphor." In the many landscapes of Klee, particularly in "Mild Tropical Landscape," yellow gradually becomes the foreground color, thus bringing the untamed vitality of the landscape, the fundamental yellow, to the viewer's esthetic attention and participation. Klee opts for yellow, for life-giving yellow (the setting sun is gradually yellow, orange, red, etc.),[10] not for white or black, two silent, motionless, inactive colors.[11] As in Klee's case, yellow is a metaphor for Borges.

If in "El otro" Borges meets the past, in "Utopía de un hombre que está cansado" he encounters the future. Somewhere on the endless plains of the Southwest Borges crosses paths with a man from the future. The tenuous continuity that unites them is Latin. Borges, rather transparently, introduces himself as Eudoro Acevedo, born in 1897 in Buenos Aries, professor of English and American letters, and writer of fantastic stories. From the future that is his present, Borges' host declares himself to be the inhabitant of a world in which the authority of facts has been usurped by doubt and the art of forgetting. Ignoring facts, which are considered mere "puntos de partida para la invención y el razonamiento," that is to say, ignoring the workings of reason and imagination, the exotic host describes a present without a future, a world without surprises and expectations: "Nunca pudimos evadirnos de aquí y de un ahora" (II, 514). Imagination has ceased to promise and redeem. Man faces nothing but his own solitude. There is discussion of a gradual, collective suicide. Love and friendship are discarded. Language is but a system of quotations. There are no museums or libraries. Individuality is atrophied by uniformity and confirmity. All the houses are identical, all the kitchens and the utensils are of metal, men and women look alike, as if levelled by time (II, 515). Everything appears homogenous, definitive, doomed. Outside, white snow is falling relentlessly; "la llanura estaba blanca de silenciosa nieve y de luna" (II, 514).

Borges, predictably, does not leave matters here. There is hope. He can, of course, return from this future before it becomes his own present. He can discover, rediscover, or invent hope. He even discerns it in the oxymoronic utopia in which he finds himself. Yellow will provide the attendant symbolism. First, however, a basic reality must be taken into account. The man of the hypothetical future is no longer a social animal, has given up the fruits of sociality, and, with them the possibility of fulfilling his humanity. Life is measured by the existence of a few biological functions and a few activities. The exception, surprisingly, is painting. Borges, here, confers redeeming, regenerative virtues to painting, to art. Mallarmé may well say that "tout aboutit a un livre," but a book, in Marino's revelation, is not a mirror of the world but another object added to it. The library of Babel is dead. Borges is interested in painting, even though his interest is peculiar. Neither the visual definition of painting nor the technically finished product interest him. What appeals to him are the seemingly endless esthetic possibilities of painting. Of a peculiar kind of painting, that is. *Everybody* still paints in "Utopía de un hombre que está cansado." Nils, one of the persons mentioned, continues to devote himself to painting, hopefully with better results than his father (II, 515). And, curiously, all the paintings represent the same thing, an almost blank yellow canvas, in a multitude of hues and nuances: "En las paredes había telas rectangulares en las que predominaban los tonos del color amarillo. No parecían proceder de la misma mano" (II, 515). Borges-Acevedo continues: "Examiné las telas y me detuve ante la más pequeña, que figuraba o sugería una puesta de sol y que encerraba algo infinito" (II, 515).

As white is a synthetic color, if all the canvases were white then the infinity that Borges contemplates would be a man-made infinity, an artificial infinity in which man has trapped himself, a labyrinth like the desert in "Los dos reyes y los dos laberintos." The infinity suggested by the yellow canvases is, by contrast, a natural attribute of a world of which man is part. The primordial color has witnessed the cyclical changes of nature and man. Sunset is followed by sunrise, it is an end and a beginning. The color cannot be white because, to quote Kandinsky, white "is a symbol of a world from which all colors as material attributes have disappeared."[12] When Borges "returns" to the present he brings with him one of the yellow canvases, an implicit form of hope: "En mi escritorio de la calle México guardo la tela que alguien pintará, dentro de miles de años, con materiales hoy dispersos en el planeta" (II, 516). In the color yellow, to borrow one of Valéry's expressions, Borges finds a vital and esthetic infinity.

Does the future exist? Why is Borges making himself part of it? Within the world of the story the future does indeed exist, for we have not only the author's literary account of it but tangible evidence as well, the yellow canvas that Acevedo brings from the future. The presence of the yellow painting makes the future not only a potential present but a plausible one as well. Since the painting is both finished and unfinished—finished, because it is painted with colors, which Acevedo is unable to discern; unfinished, because future generations can add to it. It suggests continuity of human experience, esthetically and otherwise. The future exists but it has not been experienced yet, like the term "eternity" in Borges' nocturnal occurrence in Buenos Aires, "palabra ya antedicha por mí, pero no vivida hasta entonces con entera dedicación de mi yo" (I, 330). Interestingly, yellow is the color that Acevedo perceives, although the painting has many other colors. There is, therefore, human continuity in the painting, however tenuous it may be. The yellow painting is to Borges what the flower of the future is to Coleridge in one of his writings (II, 139), evidence of a future and its connection with the present. Wells, in *The Time Machine*, offers a similar proposition: "Más increíble que una flor celestial o que la flor de un sueño es la flor futura, la contradictoria flor cuyos átomos ahora ocupan otros lugares y que no se combinaron aún" (II, 139). Borges builds upon illustrious examples: "Basta que un libro sea posible para que exista" (I, 461). And so it is with the future symbolized by the color yellow.

Literature and the color yellow are the objects of esthetic and philosophical considerations in yet another Borgesian short story, "Parábola de palacio," published together with "Utopía de un hombre que está cansado." Two protagonists animate the story, the Yellow Emperor, and a poet, both possessors of different kinds of infinity. Huang-ti, like all ancient Chinese, took for granted that the Yellow River region was the center of his infinite empire. Huang-ti, one of the three cultural heroes of ancient China, introduced writing and literature to his empire.[13] The antithesis is set. The Yellow Emperor takes the poet for a vast and protracted visit of his seemingly infinite empire, marked every hundred paces by a yellow tower. The towers present a chromatic peculiarity: "para los ojos el color era idéntico, pero la primera era amarilla y la última escarlata, tan delicades eran las gradaciones y tan larga la serie" (II, 340). This is, of course, the spectrum of light diffusion of the setting sun.[14] The circular labyrinth in which the two travel suggests infinity (II, 339). The poet, oblivious to this specious infinity, creates his own infinity, a poem consisting of one word, the embodiment of the universe. The event has momentous consequences: "Todos callaron, pero el emperador exclamó: ¡*Me has arrebatado el palacio*! y la espada de hierro del verdugo segó la vida del poeta" (II, 340). Such "literary" evidence, however, is not reliable: "El texto se ha perdido" (II, 340). An echoed, vaguely remembered, virtually lost infinity. "Las luces del crepúsculo"—the shades of yellow, the cyclical continuity of nature—will continue to shine, while the spoken and written word which encapsulated the universe has disappeared.

The essential unreliability of the word, perhaps most dramatically expressed in "El idioma de los argentinos," is underscored anew. Speaking of the hapless poet, Borges states: "su composición cayó en el olvido porque merecía el olvido y sus descendientes buscan aún, y no encontrarán, la palabra del universo" (II, 340). The word remains an imperfect mnemonic tool, the spurious carrier of a precarious continuity. Chinese emperors, both in the works of Borges and in history, have indulged in massive destructions of books in order to initiate new "eternities," renewed promises of immortality.[15] That the descendants of the poet will not encounter the word of the universe is not surprising. Borges tells us elsewhere that the esthetic fact is the imminence of a revelation that does not, but almost, takes place (II, 133). Yet it is both man's privilege and curse to keep trying (II, 224). It is his nobility.

Notes

[1] The color yellow, explicit or implied, is not infrequently found in Borges' work. There are yellow, diamond shaped windows in "La muerte y la brújula," a yellow opal as a symbol of misfortune (II, 241), a moon of the color of the sand (II, 10), a lion of the color of the sun (II, 92), etc.

[2] See Maurice Boigey, *La science des couleurs* (Paris: Librairie Félix Alcan, 1923), p. 39; M.E. Chevreuil, *The Principles of Harmony and Contrast of Colors*, 3d. ed. (London: George Bell & Sons, 1890), p. 71.

[3] Boigey, p. 10.

[4] Wheelock, *The Mythmaker*, p. 82.

[5] Kandinsky, p. 58.

[6] Ibid., p. 58.

[7] See present work, chapter 1.

[8] Cf. Hesse, *How Pictures Mean*, p. 34.

[9] Ibid., p. 115.

[10] Boigey, p. 53.

[11] Kandinsky, p. 61.

[12] Ibid., p. 60.

[13] See Charles O. Hucker, *China's Imperial Past* (Stanford: Stanford Univ. Press, 1975), p. 22.

[14] Boigey, p. 53.

[15] J.L. Borges, "La muralla y los libros," II, 131–33; Hucker, pp. 43, 48, 96, 197, 275, 300, 361, 393–94, 406.

Chromatic Reticence

Whether Borges' fondness for colors was educed from Chesterton rather than from unmediated experience, as he intimated to Burgin,[1] whether it was generated by literature rather than by nature, is open to debate. What matters here, however, is Borges' marked pictorial disposition, his demonstrable susceptibility to color and its expressive possibilities. In Borges' fiction, along with chromatically defined images, there are pictorial conditions, chromatic intimations, *ambience*. While his fiction exudes polychromism, colors as such are rather infrequently mentioned. Instead, there is the insistent, dynamic presence of light and dark, of shadows and angles, which allows the reader to form his own chromatic composition and create his own esthetic mood. The reader is free to participate, to summon his own experience to the esthetic fact, or to draw from his imagination. Moreover, this is not done with the idiosyncratic freedom with which one fills in a coloring book. The luminosity of natural light in Borges' works is forever changing; there is dawn light, morning light, noon light, afternoon light, moon light. The changing luminosity, of course, affects not only the chromatic qualities of objects, but also the symbolism that we attach to such qualities. The only uniform light—Borges calls it incessant—is the artificial, eerie light of "La biblioteca de Babel." Borges creates the pictorial mood, the reader—each reader—adds the chromatic touches. The reader transforms a spectacle into a representation.[2]

The elements for a schematic justification for Borges' chromatic reticence are to be found in the short story already dealt with, "El tintorero enmascardo Hákim de Merv" (*Historia*

universal de la infamia, 1935). Hákim de Merv, later known as
The Veiled One, was a dyer by trade; a trade of counterfeiters,
we are told (I, 284). Some of the information that we have about
him, Borges writes, comes from an Arabic codex, *La aniquilación
de la rosa*, in which he is quoted.

> Mi cara es de oro pero he macerado la púrpura y he sumergido en la
> segunda noche la lana sin cardar y he saturado en la tercera noche la
> lana preparada, y los emperadores de la isla se disputan esa ropa
> sangrienta. Así pequé en los años de juventud y trastorné los verda-
> deros colores de las criaturas. El Angel me decía que los carneros no
> eran del color de los tigres, el Satán me decía que el Poderoso quería
> que lo fueran y se valía de mi astucia y mi púrpura. Ahora yo sé que el
> Angel y el Satán erraban la verdad y que todo color es aborrecible.
>
> I, 284

Hákim is speaking of a color symbolism that he invented, a
symbolism that perverts the true colors of beings. He eventually realizes that color symbolism polarized along dogmatic
lines is deceiving, that it separates man from the truth. Falsifying the color of beings and objects is not merely an idiosyncratic act but a grievous transgression perpetrated against a
higher order, that of the Almighty. Gabriel and Satan tug at the
strings of his conscience. By way of a freeing from error—of a
desengaño—he concludes that any color, that is to say any
chromatic definition, is detestable, for it can only be an approximation to God's true creation. The statement, framed in a
vague Mazdean dualism, is clear.[3] While the particulars refer to
this story, the general idea—the speciousness of color symbolism—has a considerably larger resonance. When man makes
colors transcend visual perception, he is on speculative
grounds.

Borges gives expression to this approach in this very story.
Next to colors expressly mentioned—scarlet, white, black—
there are chromatic intimations which elicit the reader's esthetic participation without altering the contextual experience
of the story. A multitude of slaves await the moon of *ramadan*:
"Miraban el ocaso, y el ocaso era del color de la arena" (I, 285).
Thus the chromatic perception becomes the reader's, rather

than the author's, interpretation. Borges is present here in an invisible way, like Flaubert in his works (I, 214). "Bogle vagó hasta que una luna del color de la miel se duplicó en el agua rectangular de las fuentes públicas" (I, 257). The mysterious man in "Las ruinas circulares" crawls to a circular plaza "que corona un tigre o caballo de piedra, que tuvo alguna vez el color del fuego y ahora el de la ceniza" (I, 435). There are no expressed chromatic preferences, no color definition imposed from without, only interpretative hints. What is the sunset that the faithful are contemplating like? What is really the color of the sand in the light of the dying sun? Any specific answer rests with the experience of the individual reader and the implicit perception of the protagonists. The reader must complete the canvas. Yet the dynamic process does not alter in any way the perception of the people who experience the sunset, the inhabitants of the story. Marco Flaminio Rufo, Roman legion-naire, protagonist of "El inmortal," describes the beginning of his adventure in the following terms: "Me levanté poco antes del alba; mis esclavos dormían, la luna tenía el mismo color de la infinita arena" (II, 10). This is not only a felicitous literary device, vaguely reminiscent of Oriental expression, but an honest, deliberate attempt at not tampering with the organicity of experience. We know that, in "El congreso," the color of both Alejandro Glencoe's and his guest's hair is imprecisely red. Borges refines it: "su violento color sugería el fuego y el de la barba del señor Glencoe, las hojas del otoño" (II, 472). Siddharta, the man who would become Buddha, sees an old man "cuyo pelo no es como el de los otros" (II, 263). The night Siddharta was conceived, his mother dreamed of an elephant, "del color de la nieve" (II, 263). An Eskimo, who distinguishes better than eight nuances of whiteness, would find such a description rather imprecise. In imagining the color of the elephant, he would have to make a choice based on his personal experience. This deliberate linguistic peculiarity is present in Borges' poetry as well: "las tapias tenían el color de las tardes" (*Obras*, 82).

It is good literature, literature that wishes to forget that it is literature. Shaw, whom Borges admires with undimmed enthusiasm, states with his habitual aphoristic wisdom that inexperienced writers strive to acquire a literary language, while adept ones struggle to get rid of it.[4] What shade of yellow is the moon? What is the color of the infinite sand? Again, the reader's imagination is called into play. This, of course, does not mean that the use of colors is altogether avoided. Later on, Marco Flaminio Rufo is specific: "Fatigamos otros desiertos, donde es negra la arena" (II, 11). In this context, Borges does not say that the moon has the color of the sand, for such a moon, to use Borges' own words about the scope and limitations of the craft of literature, could not be sincerely imagined. In "Abencaján el Bojarí," Borges describes a lion and a man: "la fiera del color del sol y el hombre del color de la noche" (II, 92). The two chromatic suggestions engage our imagination contextually and frame the story symbolically. In "El zahir," Borges mentions a book by Julius Barlach, *Urkunden zur Geschichte der Zahirsage*, and Meadows Taylor's work, *Confessions of a Thug*. Taylor is fascinated by a tiger which can, like the *zahir*, induce madness or sanctity. The mural painting of this tiger is in a prison cell:

> Años después, Taylor visitó las cárceles de ese reino; en las de Nithur el gobernador le mostró una celda, en cuyo piso, en cuyos muros, y en cuya bóveda un faquir musulmán había diseñado (en bárbaros colores que el tiempo, antes de borrar, afinaba) una especie de tigre infinito. Ese tigre estaba hecho de muchos tigres, de vertiginosa manera; lo atravesaban tigres, estaba rayado de tigres, incluía mares e Himalayas y ejércitos que parecían otros tigres.
>
> II, 83

We perceive both the crude colors of the tiger and the "tigerness" of the animal, so to speak, the essence suggested by the seemingly infinite superimposition of tigers. It is an infinity. We read in "El acercamiento a Almotásim": "Una chusma de perros color de luna (a lean and evil mob of mooncoloured hounds) emerge de los rosales negros" (I, 394). Again, we have one color defined, the black of the rose bushes, one suggested, that of the hounds, moon-colored hounds. It would be impossible to determine with any degree of chromatic certainty the color of the hounds. Are they really yellowish in color, or is the color artificially perceived in the moon light? Borges sometimes surprised Herbert Ashe, one of the protagonists in "Tlön, Uqbar, Orbis Tertius," "mirando a veces los colores irrecuperables del cielo" (I, 412). We can possibly imagine the colors that Ashe contemplated, only by drawing from our own experience. Here is how Yu Tsun, the ill-fated protagonist of "El jardín de los senderos que se bifurcan," describes the lantern with which Stephen Albert meets him at the gate: "un farol de papel, que tenía la forma de los tambores y el color de la luna" (I, 467). Borges writes in "Funes el memorioso": "una enorme tormenta color pizarra había escondido el cielo" (I, 478). The first crime in "La muerte y la brújula" occurs in the Hotel du Nord, "ese alto prisma que domina el estuario cuyas aguas tienen el color del desierto" (I, 495).

Such imagery, very effective in its evoking power, appears with more than casual frequency, which indicates the presence of a conceptual framework, for literature is a directed, deliberate dream. As usual, Borges himself offers a point of departure. Human language is a tradition, a way of feeling reality, Borges tells us, not an arbitrary system of symbols (II, 440). Such an opinion, formulated in later years, has been long in the making. Among other things, it suggests a question mark. That language is not an arbitrary system of symbols vindicates the authenticity of man's endeavors, of his earnestness, of his consciousness, of his sincerity with himself, as it were, not with the surrounding world. Positing the latter possibility is troublesome. Borges examines a Platonic variation by DeQuincey:

Hasta los sonidos irracionales del globo deben ser otras tantas álgebras y lenguaje que de algún modo tienen sus llaves correspondientes, su severa gramática y sintaxis, y así las mínimas cosas del universo pueden ser espejos secretos de las mayores.

II, 238-39

Novalis and Machen also consider the external world to be a
language, a language that we have forgotten or barely remember (II, 238). Let us retrieve the issue from the realm of
metaphysics, of God and truth, and focus on the notion that
the external world is a language of rigorous grammar and
syntaxis, a structure. Words are the elements that integrate
such a structure. Are words, as the Icelandic *kenningar* pretended to be, equivalents of reality? We are now at the heart of
Borges' chromatic reticence. Were Borges to say that the moon
is yellow, how far would he be from reality, that is to say, from
the outer reality? The moon is nature's reality, the color yellow
is Borges'. The moon is an object, colors are symbols. When
Borges says that a beast was of the color of the sun, and the
man of the color of night, he does not define the color of the
lion and of the man, which imply certainty, but suggests it,
which is an approximation. Of course, all reality is reality
perceived by someone, so the subjective presence cannot be
eliminated, but Borges refrains from creating a symbol that
might be arbitrary. The lion and the sun, the man and the
night, have colors undefined by Borges. In every such example
previously mentioned, one can detect the same reticence.
Borges, of course, is an experimenter, and he enjoys experi-
menting rather than finding definitive forms of expression. Nor
is Borges a conceptual innovator in this sense. In "La metáfora," for instance, he quotes Malherbe who, in the 16th
century, wrote about the defunct daughter of a friend: *"Et, rose,
elle a vécu ce que vivent les roses"* (I, 353). This poetic expression
eschews any definition. Malherbe, simply, avoids falsifying
reality, and frames his reticence poetically. So does Borges. The
Mexican Juan Rulfo often avoids experiential definition. In "Es
que somos muy pobres," for example, instead of formulating a
comparison and therefore bringing in an element extraneous to
the experience, he writes about a cow's sighing: "suspirando,
como se oye suspirar a las vacas cuando duermen."

How are we to understand Borges' reticence? Are there any
clues? In "La busca de Averroes," there is an explanatory
possibility that must be taken into account. When Farach, one

of the interlocutors, speaks of a special variety of roses, sung by Ibn Qutaiba, whose petal disposition "writes" the Islamic prayer, "There is no God like the God, and Mohammed is His Prophet," Averroes intervenes: "me cuesta menos admitir un error en el docto Ibn Qutaiba, en los copistas, que admitir que la tierra da rosas con la profesión de la fe" (II, 71). In other words, if there is an error, it is a human one, either that of the poet or of the scribes, not a natural one. Abdalmálik, the poet, offers a counterpoint: "Algún viajero habla de un árbol cuyo fruto son verdaderos pájaros. Menos me duele creer en él que en rosas con letras" (II, 72). Averroes elucidates the point:

> El color de los pájaros parece facilitar el portento. Además, los frutos y los pájaros pertenencen al mundo natural, pero la escritura es un arte. Pasar de hojas a pájaros es más fácil que de rosas a letras.
>
> II, 72

Because of their colors, birds look like fruit. The delineation is clear: birds and fruits belong to the natural world, writing is an artifact. Birds have colors, of course, and color is part of their reality if not essential to their "birdness." The colors that we would ascribe to them, through language, can only be symbols. Figuratively speaking, in the instances that are discussed here, Borges is reluctant to go from roses to letters. It is like Berkeley's idealism applied to language. Says Borges about Berkeley's negation of the existence of matter:

> Ello no significa, entiéndase bien, que negó los colores, los olores, los sabores, los sonidos y los contactos; lo que negó fue que, además de esas percepciones, que componen el mundo externo, hubiera dolores que nadie siente, colores que nadie ve, formas que nadie toca.
>
> II, 294

Without approving or refuting Berkeley's theory that the world is an illusory creation of the senses, we retain the notion that color is a perceptual matter. To go any further would be to take arms against or in favor of Berkeley's idealism. Hume recognizes the object but not the subject, the spirit which can interpret it (II, 296). Borges eschews any unifying theory, preferring to consider the part rather than the whole: "yo rechazo el todo para exaltar cada una de las partes" (II, 299). Borges does not negate the existence of color, with or without material reality. He does not discuss "colorness," so to speak. What concerns him is a specific color, its possible chromatic qualities and modes of interpretation. It is not that a person affected by Daltonism does not see colors, but that the colors that he sees are not those of ordinary color perception. This is the realm of Borges's intellectual curiosity and its literary expression. For Borges, the cerebral Borges, does not separate himself from perception: "El tiempo es un río que me arrebata, pero yo soy el río" (II, 300). He does not separate himself from colors, even if his progressive blindness prevents him from unmediated chromatic experience. What concerns him is the changing nature of the perception, not perception itself or its object. Paraphrasing Berkeley, one can say that Averroes—and Borges, within the scope here circumscribed—set the conventions produced by art apart from the realities created by nature. Borges accepts the existence of both, but doubts that art, literary language included, can "match" reality. He deals subtly with Berkeley's point of view. Whether sensorial in origin or not, Borges ascribes to objects continuous existence, since, if man does not perceive them, God does (II, 287). Debatable idealism, that of Berkeley. In Hume we seek an example, not supporting evidence. "Para Hume", Borges asserts, "no es lícito hablar de la forma de la luna o de su color; la forma y el color *son* la luna" (II, 288). It may be so in nature but not in literature. It may have been so before the advent of literature. In the prolog to *El oro de los tigres* (1972), we read:

> En el principio de los tiempos, tan dócil a la vaga especulación y a las inapelables cosmogonías, no habrá habido cosas poéticas o prosaicas. Todo sería un poco mágico. Thor no sería el dios del trueno; era el trueno y dios.
>
> II, 439

This is, essentially, Hume's thought cast into Borgesian mold. DeQuincey, we recall, considers the universe to be a rigorous grammar, an entity governed by a structure of meanings. To graft on it a false symbol, even a minimal one—a color—is to pervert its true nature. By saying that the moon had the same color as the infinite sand, while not discounting the individual visual experience, Borges avoids deforming the natural order. In the practice of his craft, Borges, of course, avails himself of poetic license, which, among other things, allows him to define reality chromatically, but he does not extend such license to ethics. The matter is movingly and unambiguously put forth in a short piece, significantly called "Una oración," in *Elogio de la sombra* (1969). We quote *in extenso*:

> Es evidente, en primer término, que me está vedado pedir. Pedir que no anochezcan mis ojos sería una locura; sé de millares de personas que ven y que no son particularmente felices, justas o sabias. El proceso del tiempo es una trama de efecto y causas, de suerte que pedir cualquier merced, por ínfima que sea, es pedir que se rompa un eslabón de esa trama de hierro, es pedir que ya se haya roto. Nadie merece tal milagro.
>
> ....
>
> Desconocemos los designios del universo, pero sabemos que razonar con lucidez y obrar con justicia es ayudar a esos designios, que no nos serán revelados.
>
> II, 362

We now have the two sides of the coin. In the directed dream that literature is, poetic license is excusable: "puedo dar o soñar que doy" (II, 362). At the level of action, however, the giving must be real, lest it invalidate the honesty with which we try to justify our place in the universe. Borges does not only think that he is Borges, he unfortunately is Borges (II, 300). To ask for a favor is an enormity, is to request, wittingly or unwittingly, a restructuring of the mysterious mechanism of time. Nobody, Borges assures us, is worthy of such a favor.

Notes

[1] Burgin, p. 99.

[2] Foucault, p. 20.

[3] Ahura Mazda and Ahriman are the good and evil creative spirits of Zoroastrianism, the religion which florished in Persia during the first mille-

nium B. C. The former expressed itself in light and life, the latter in darkness and death. Both forces have man at the center of their attention. The Zoroastrian man is born with a free will, thus he can do service to both good and evil. Blindness and ignorance can easily lead man astray. See "Zoroaster," in *Dictionary of Philosophy and Religion*.

[4] Pearson, p. 111.

Bibliography

Adkins, Arthur W. H. *Merit and Responsibility. A Study in Greek Values,* Oxford: Clarendon Press, 1960.

Agheana, Ion T. *The Prose of Jorge Luis Borges: Existentialism and the Dynamics of Surprise.* New York, Berne, Frankfort on the Main, Nancy: Peter Lang, 1984.

―――. "Borges, 'Creator' of Cervantes; Cervantes Precursor of Borges." *Revista de estudios hispánicos.* 9(1982): 17–22.

Alazraki, Jaime. *La prosa narrativa de Jorge Luis Borges.* Madrid: Gredos, 1974.

Allen, Cecil. *The Mirror of the Passing World.* New York: W. W. Norton & Co. Inc., 1928.

Allen, G. W. and Clark, H. H., eds. *Literary Criticism.* Detroit: Wayne State University Press, 1962.

Allen, John. *Don Quijote: Hero or Fool?.* Gainsville: University of Florida Press, 1969.

Alonso, Amado. "Borges, narrador." *El escritor y la crítica.* Edited by Jaime Alazraki. Madrid: Taurus, 1976.

Anderson-Imbert, Enrique. *Teoría y práctica del cuento.* Buenos Aires: Ediciones Marymar, 1979.

Aristotle. *Ethics.* Baltimore: Penguin Books, 1953.

Armstrong, Edward A. *Shakespeare's Imagination.* Lincoln: University of Nebraska Press, 1963.

Arvin, Newton. *Hawthorne.* Boston: Little, Brown, Co., 1929.

―――. *Whitman.* New York: The Macmillan Co., 1938.

Barnstone, Willis., ed. *Borges at Eighty.* Bloomington: Indiana University Press, 1982.

Barrenechea, Ana María. *Borges. The Labyrinth Maker.* New York: New York University Press, 1965.

―――. "Borges y el lenguaje." In *El escritor y la crítica.* Edited by Jaime Alazraki. Madrid: Taurus, 1976.

Barth, John. "Literatura del agotamiento." In *El escritor y la crítica.* Edited by Jaime Alazraki. Madrid: Taurus, 1976.

Bégun, Albert. *Pascal.* Bourges: Editions du Seuil, 1967.

Bell-Villada, Gene. *Borges and his Fiction.* Chapel Hill: The University of North Carolina Press, 1981.

Bergson, Henri. "Duration and Intuition." In *Problems of Space and Time.* Edited by J. J. C. Smart. New York: The Macmillan Co., 1964.

―――. "The Object of Art." In *Literary Criticism.* Edited by G. W. Allen and H. H. Clark. Detroit: Wayne State University Press, 1962.

Bjornson, Richard, ed. *Approaches to Teaching Cervantes.* New York: MLAA, 1984.

Blanco Aguinaga, Carlos. "Cervantes and the Picaresque Mode: Notes on Two Kinds of Realism." In *Cervantes.* Edited by Lowry Nelson, Jr. Englewood Cliffs, N. J.: Prentice Hall, 1969.

Boigey, Maurice. *La science des couleurs.* Paris: Librairie Félix Alcan, 1923.

247

Boman, Thorlief. *Hebrew Thought Compared with Greek*. Philadelphia: The Westminster Press, 1960.

Borges, Jorge Luis. *Obras completas*. Buenos Aires: Emecé, 1974.

———. *Prosa completa*. 2 vols. Barcelona: Bruguera, 1980.

Brodin, Pierre. *Les écrivains francais de l'entre-deux-guerres*. Montreal: Editions Bernard Valiquette, 1942.

Brodtkorb, Paul Jr. *Ishmael's White World*. New Haven and London: Yale University Press, 1965.

Burgin, Richard. *Conversations with Borges*. Chicago, San Francisco: Holt, Rinehart and Winston, 1968.

Burton, Richard. *Thousand Nights and One Night*. Printed by the Burton Club for Private Subscribers Only, 1885.

Campbell, Joseph. *The Masks of God: Occidental Mythology*. New York: The Viking Press, 1962.

———. *The Masks of God: Oriental Mythology*. New York: The Viking Press, 1962.

Chesterton, G. K. *Varied Types*. New York: Dodd, Mead and Company, 1903.

Chevreuil, M. E. *The Principles of Harmony and Contrast of Colors*. London: George Bell & Sons, 1890.

Christ, Ronald J. *The Narrow Act. Borges' Art of Illusion*. New York: New York University Press, 1969.

———. "Borges Justified: Notes and Texts toward Stations of a Theme." In *Prose for Borges*. Edited by Mary Kinzie. Evanston: Northwestern University Press, 1972.

Cioran, Emile M. *The Fall into Time*. Chicago: Quadrangle Books, 1970.

———. *Valéry face a ses idoles*. Paris: Editiones de L'Herne, 1970.

Cope, Jackson I. *The Metaphoric Structure of Paradise Lost*. Baltimore: The Johns Hopkins University Press, 1962.

Crosby, James O. *En torno a la poesía de Quevedo*. Madrid: Castalia, 1967.

———. "Quevedo, la antología griega y Horacio." In *Francisco de Quevedo*. Edited by Gonzalo Sobejano. Madrid: Taurus, 1978.

Crosman, Robert. *Reading Paradise Lost*. London: Indiana University Press, 1980.

Curtis, Charles P. Jr., and Greenslet, Ferris. ed., *The Practical Cogitator*. Boston: Houghton Mifflin Co., 1962.

di Giovanni, Norman Thomas, Halpern, Daniel, and Shane, Frank. eds. *Borges on Writing*. New York: E. D. Sutton & Co., 1973.

Durán, Manuel. *Quevedo*. Madrid: Edaf, 1978.

El Saffar, Ruth S. *Novel to Romance*. Baltimore and London: The Johns Hopkins University Press, 1974.

Fish, Stanley Eugene. "Discovery as Form in *Paradise Lost*." In *New Essays on Paradise Lost*. Edited by Thomas Kranidas. Berkeley, Los Angeles, and London: University of California Press, 1971.

Flores, Angel, and Benardete, M. J. eds. *Cervantes Across the Centuries*. New York: The Dryden Press, 1947.

Foster, David W. *Jorge Luis Borges: An Annotated Primary and Secondary Bibliography*. New York: Garland, 1984.

Foucault, Michel. *Les mots et les choses*. Paris: Gallimard, 1966.

Fromm, Erich. *The Art of Loving*. New York: Harper and Brothers Publishers, 1956.

Gardiner, Patrick. *Schopenhauer*. Baltimore: Penguin Books, 1963.

George, A. G. *Milton and the Nature of Man*. Bombay, New York: Asia Publishing House, 1974.

Gibbs, A. M. *The Art and Mind of Shaw*. New York: St. Martin's Press, 1983.

Gilman, Stephen. "The Apocryphal Quijote." In *Cervantes Across the Centuries*. Edited by Angel Flores and M. J. Benardete. New York: The Dryden Press, 1947.

Gilmore, Michael E., ed. *Twentieth Century Interpretations of Moby Dick*. Englewood Cliffs, N. J.: Prentice Hall, 1977.

Gómez de la Serna, Ramón. "El fervor de Buenos Aires." *El escritor y la crítica*. Edited by Jaime Alazraki. Madrid: Taurus, 1976.

Hauser, Arnold. *Dialéctica de lo estético*. Madrid: Ediciones Guadarrama, 1977.

Hesse, Hans. *How Pictures Mean*. New York: Pantheon Books, 1974.

Hollis, Christopher. *The Mind of Chesterton*. Coral Gables: University of Miami Press, 1970.

Hucker, Charles O. *China's Imperial Past*. Stanford: Stanford Univ. Press, 1975.

Innstad, Bernard. *Painting Methods of the Impressionists*. London: Pitman Publishing, 1976.

Kandinsky, Wassily. *Concerning the Spiritual Art*. New York: George Wittenbon, Inc., 1947.

Kant, Immanuel. "Transcendental Reality of Space and Time." In *Problems of Space and Time*. Edited by J. J. C. Smart. New York: The Macmillan Co., 1964.

———. "Mirror Images." In *Problems of Space and Time*. Edited by J. J. C. Smart. New York: The Macmillan Co., 1964.

Kinzie, Mary, ed. *Prose for Borges*. Evanston: Northwestern University Press, 1972.

Knox, Bernard M. W. *The Heroic Temper*. Berkeley and Los Angeles: University of California Press, 1966.

Kranidas, Thomas, ed. *New Essays on Paradise Lost*. Berkeley, Los Angeles, and London: University of California Press, 1971.

Lawrence, D. H. "Whitman." In *A Century of Whitman Criticism*. Edited by Edwin Haviland Miller. Bloomington, London: Indiana University Press, 1969.

Levin, Harry. "*Don Quijote* and *Moby Dick*." In *Cervantes Across the Centuries*.

250

Edited by Angel Flores and M. J. Benardete. New York: The Dryden Press, 1947.

Lukács, Georg. *The Theory of the Novel*. Cambridge: The M.I.T. Press, 1971.

Maccaffrey, Isabel G. "The Theme *Paradise Lost*." In *New Essays on Paradise Lost*. Edited by Thomas Kranidas. Berkeley, Los Angeles, and London: University of California Press, 1971.

Malmstrom, Jean. *Language in Society*. Rochelle Park: Hayden Book Co., 1973.

Marilla, E. L. *Milton and Modern Man*. Alabama: University of Alabama Press, 1968.

Marín, Luis Astrana. *Ideario de Don Francisco de Quevedo*. Madrid: Almagro, 1940.

May, Rollo. *Love and Will*. New York: W. W. Norton & Co. Inc., 1969.

McCulloch, J. P., ed. and transl. *The Poems of Sextus Propertius*. Los Angeles, Boston: University of California Press, 1972.

McKay, Agnes. *The Universal Self. A Study of Paul Valéry*. Toronto: The University of Toronto Press, 1961.

Mead, George Herbert. *The Philosophy of the Present*. Chicago, London: Open Court Publishing Co., 1932.

Melville, Herman. *Moby Dick*. Boston: Houghton Mifflin Co., 1956.

Menéndez-Pidal, Ramón. "The Genesis of *Don Quijote*." In *Cervantes Across the Centuries*. Edited by Angel Flores and N. J. Benardete. New York: The Dryden Press, 1947.

Miller, Edwin Haviland, ed. *A Century of Whitman Criticism*. Bloomington, London: Indiana University Press, 1969.

Milton, John. *Paradise Lost*. New York: Odyssey Press, 1962.

Molloy, Sylvia. *Las letras de Borges*. Buenos Aires: Editorial Sudamericana, 1979.

Mortimer, Edward. *Faith and Power. The Politics of Islam*. New York: Vintage Books, 1982.

Mounier, Emmanuel. *Introduction aux existentialismes*. Paris: Gallimard, 1962.

Naumann, Walter. "Polvo enamorado: Muerte y Amor en Propercio, Quevedo y Goethe." In *Francisco de Quevedo*. Edited by Gonzalo Sobejano. Madrid: Taurus, 1978.

Nekyia, Edward F. *Melville's Moby Dick*. New York: New Directions Publishing Co., 1978.

Nelson, Lowry Jr., ed. *Cervantes*. Englewood Cliffs: Prentice Hall, Inc., 1969.

Nietzsche, Friedrich. *The Birth of Tragedy and the Genealogy of Morals*. Garden City: Doubleday Anchor, 1956.

Ortega y Gasset, José. *Meditaciones del Quijote*. Buenos Aires: Espasa Calpe, S. A., 1942.

Pater, Walter H. "Studies in the History of Renaissance." In *Literary Criticism*. Edited by G. W. Allen and H. H. Clark. Detroit: Wayne State University Press, 1962.

Pearson, Hesketh. *G.B.S. A Full Length Portrait*. New York and London: Harper and Brothers, 1942.

Pérez, Alberto C. *Realidad y suprarrealidad en los cuentos fantásticos de J. L. Borges*. Miami: Ediciones Universal, 1971.

Pietra, Régine. *Valéry: directions spatiales et parcours verbal*. Paris: Minard, 1981.

Prabhavananda, Swami. *The Spiritual Heritage of India*. New York: Doubleday and Co. Inc., 1964.

Predmore, Richard L. *The World of Don Quijote*. Cambridge: Harvard University Press, 1967.

Quevedo, Francisco de. *Obras completas*. Madrid: Editorial Castalia, 1969.

Reese, W. L. *Dictionary of Philosophy and Religion*. Atlantic Highland: Humanities Press Inc., 1980.

Robert, Marthe. *The Old and the New*. Berkeley, Los Angeles, London: University of California Press, 1977.

Rodríguez Monegal, Emir. "Borges: the Reader as Writer." In *Prose for Borges*. Edited by Mary Kinzie. Evanston: Northwestern University Press, 1972.

Running, Thorpe. *Borges' Ultraista Movement and its Poets*. Lathrup Village: International Book Publishers, 1981.

Sartre, Jean-Paul. *L'existentialisme*. Paris: Nigel, 1958.

———. "Herman Melville's *Moby Dick*." In *Twentieth Century Interpretations of Moby Dick*. Edited by Michael E. Gilmore. Englewood Cliffs, N. J.: Prentice Hall, 1977.

Serrano-Plaja, Arturo. *"Magic" Realism in Cervantes*. Berkeley and Los Angeles: University of California Press, 1970.

Shaw, George Bernard. *Man and Superman*. Baltimore: Penguin Books, 1952.

Smart, J. J. C., ed. *Problems of Space and Time*. New York: The Macmillan Co., 1969.

Sobejano, Gonzalo, ed. *Francisco de Quevedo*. Madrid: Taurus, 1978.

Spencer, Theodore. *Shakespeare and the Nature of Man*. New York: The Macmillan Co., 1942.

Spinoza, Baruch. Chapter I of *Tractatus Politicus*. In *The Practical Cogitator*. Edited by Charles P. Curtis, Jr. and Ferris Greenslet. Boston: Houghton Mifflin Co., 1962.

Stevenson, Robert L. "The Gospel According to Walt Whitman." In *A Century of Whitman Criticism*. Edited by Edwin Haviland Miller. Bloomington, London: Indiana University Press, 1969.

Stewart, Desmond. *Early Islam*. New York: Time Inc., 1967.

Stoll, Elmer Edgard. *Art and Artifice in Shakespeare*. New York: Barnes and Noble, 1951.

Terry, Arthur. "Quevedo y el concepto metafísico." In *Francisco de Quevedo*. Edited by Gonzalo Sobejano. Madrid: Taurus, 1978.

Tilguer, Adrian. *Moralitá*. Roma: Libreria di Scienze e Lettere, 1938.

252

Traversi, Derek A. *An Approach to Shakespeare*. Garden City: Doubleday and Co., 1956.

————. *Shakespeare: The Roman Plays*. Stanford: Stanford University Press, 1963.

Turco, Alfred. *Shaw's Moral Vision*. Ithaca and London: Cornell University Press, 1976.

von Gothe, Johann Wolfgang. "Conversations with Ekerman." In *Literary Criticism*. Edited by G. W. Allen and H. H. Clark. Detroit: Wayne State University Press, 1962.

Wheelock, Carter. *The Mythmaker*. Austin and London: University of Texas Press, 1969.

Whitman, Cedric H. *Homer and the Heroic Tradition*. New York: W. W. Norton and Co., 1965.

Wicks, Ulrich. "Metafiction in *Don Quijote*." In *Approaches to Teaching Cervantes*. Edited by Richard Bjornson. New York: MLA, 1984.

Wilding, Michael. *Milton's Paradise Lost*. Sydney: Sydney University Press, 1969.

Zambrano, María. *El hombre y lo divino*. México: Fondo de cultura económica, 1955.

Ziomek, Henry K. *Reflexiones del Quijote*. Madrid: Gráficas Molina, 1969.

Index

Act, existential, 7, 61–64 *passim*
Adkin, A. W. H., 14
Aguinaga, Carlos B., 102
Aleph, El, phenomenon, 78f, 80, 115, 125f
Allegory, 5
Allen, Cecil, 208
Alter ego, 15, 19, 31f, 169, 230
Alonso, Amado, 83
Ambrose, Saint, 190f
Anachronicity, 51, 55, 140
Anaxagoras, 160
Aristotelianism, 18, 23, 89, 148, 209. *See* Platonism
Aristotle, 13, 19, 22, 90, 92
Armstrong, Edward E., 118
Art, 5f, 14, 49, 110, 208
Arvin, Newton, 158
Astrana Marín, Luis, 137
Augustine, Saint, 19, 23, 69, 189f
Averroes, 18, 243
Azar, 105, 111

Balzac, Honoré de, 115
Barth, John, 99
Barrenechea, Ana María, 187
Beckett, Samuel, 65
Bell-Villada, Gene, 9
Bergson, Henri, 13, 20, 38
Berkeley, George, 16, 243f
Bioy Casares, Adolfo, 118f
Bloy, Léon, 132
Boethius, 19, 70

Boigey, Maurice, 231
Boman, Thorlief, 210
Bradley, Francis H., 19, 23, 44f
Brahms, Johannes, 115
Brodin, Pierre, 169
Brodtkorb, Paul, 225
Browning, Robert, 131f
Bruno, Giordano, 115
Burgin, Richard, 237
Burton, Richard, 217

Calvin, Jean, 98, 132
Cansinos-Asséns, Rafael, 49
Cantor, Georg, 49
Carlyle, Thomas, 53, 124, 171
Cassirer, Ernst, 165, 183
Castro, Américo, 106
Causality, 45, 51, 66f, 110
Cervantes, Miguel de, 16, 36, 99, 101–112 *passim*
Chaide, Malón de, 19
Chesterton, Gilbert K., 42, 171, 237
Christ, Ronald, 83
Cioran, Emile, 88, 170, 175
Coleridge, Samuel, 148, 209, 234
Conrad, Joesph, 36
Croce, Benedetto, 103
Crosby, James O., 131
Crosman, Robert, 182

Dante, 125, 127

De Quincey, Thomas, 49, 241
Destiny, 23f, 79
Dialect, 191–195 *passim*
Donne, John, 117
Dostoevsky, Fyodor, 30, 32
Drama, 21f, 115, 184
Dream, 43, 56, 106f, 124f
Dunsany, Lord, 132

Epictetus, 117
Erigena, John Scotus, 19, 147, 178
Eros, 83
Esthetics, 53f, 57f, 160, 187f, 210
Eternal Return, 49f
Eternity, 20, 69ff
Ethics, 89f, 152
Event, 19, 41
Experience, 11, 13, 17f, 25, 46, 106

Faulkner, William, 53
Fervor, 84f
Flaubert, Gustave, 14f, 43, 171, 192f
Foucault, Michel, 9f

Gabriel, 238
George, A. G., 183
George, Stefan, 162
Gibbon, Edward, 103
Gilman, Stephen, 109
God, 3, 8, 64, 70, 119, 123f, 159, 162, 178, 184, 221
Goethe, Johann Wolfgang, 14
Gómez de la Serna, Ramón, 83
Góngora y Argote, Luis de, 127, 131

Harris, Frank, 147
Hauser, Arnold, 49

Hawthorne, Nathaniel, 36, 44, 117, 168
Hazlitt, William, 34, 115
Hegel, Georg, 18, 92, 102, 121
Heidegger, Martin, 145
Hell, 68, 182f
Heraclitus, 31, 162, 211
Hernández, José, 147
Hesiod, 84
Hess, Hans, 231
History, 111, 121; universal, 22
Hobbes, Thomas, 13, 18
Homer, 37, 42, 106, 127
Houseman, Alfred E., 53
Hugo, Victor, 53, 115, 155, 192
Hume, David, 23, 244

Identity, personal, 6f, 9, 19, 33f, 102, 123, 125, 213
Individual, 4, 29
Individuality, 5, 18, 25, 35, 37f, 48, 88, 144, 150f, 168
Irenaeus, 19, 69

James, William, 18
Jaspers, Karl, 145
Jesus, 23, 52, 81, 117, 183f
Johnson, Samuel, 59
Justice, 91ff; private, 11; divine, 76

Kafka, Franz, 127, 132
Kandinsky, Wassily, 208, 231, 233
Kant, Immanuel, 16, 20, 25, 133
Kenningar, 21, 37, 84, 135, 189, 242
Kierkegaard, Søren, 8, 132
Klee, Paul, 231f
Knowledge, self, 7f

Language, 10, 172, 187–195 *passim*
Laotse, 171

Lawrence, D. H., 163
Lawrence, Thomas E., 52
Leibniz, Gottfried Wilhelm, 18, 46
Levin, Harry, 113
Literature, 23, 139f, 148, 150, 177–185 *passim*, 243
Locke, John, 23
Logos, 209–212 *passim*
Lucretius, 127
Lugones, Leopoldo, 127
Lukács, Georg, 87
Lull, Raymond, 139

Malmstrom, Jean, 191
Manichaeism, 81
Mallarmé, Stephane, 127, 131, 162, 188, 200, 214, 233
Marcus Aurelius, 26
Maravilloso, lo, 108–112 *passim*
Marino, Gianbattista, 200, 229–236 *passim*, 233
Matisse, Henri, 208
Mead, George H., 18, 26, 41f, 46f
Melville, Herman, 127, 200, 214, 223–225 *passim*
Memory, 19, 58f
Menéndez-Pidal, Ramón, 109
Metaphor, 3f, 57, 128, 189, 242
Mill, John Stuart, 13, 139
Milton, John, 182, 185
Mirror, 20, 87, 119
Molina, Tirso de, 75
Moment, the, 6f, 44, 61–71 *passim*, 102, 105, 157, 170
Morris, William, 212f
Movement, *ultraista*, 155
Mystery, 51f, 68, 107f, 124
Myth, 9, 108, 172f

Naumann, Walter, 127, 130
Nietzsche, Friedrich, 9, 39, 47ff, 141, 145

Nominalism, 5. *See* Aristotelianism, Platonism
Novel, 5

Ortega y Gasset, José, 7, 65

Painting, 203ff
Paradox, 13f
Parmenides, 13, 23
Pascal, Blaise, 115, 169
Passion, 83ff, 145, 181
Pater, Walter H., 49, 203
Pearson, Hesketh, 146
Philosophy, 14f, 18, 24, 152, 174
Plato, 5, 18, 22, 190, 211, 229
Platonism, 23, 74, 81, 148, 209, 241. *See* Aristotelianism
Plotinus, 19, 22
Plutarch, 120, 122
Poe, Edgar Allen, 172, 200, 214, 222–225 *passim*
Polarities, 74, 81, 107, 173, 199
Predmore, Richard, 106
Propertius, 135, 180f

Quevedo, Francisco de, 99, 127–137 *passim*, 180, 182

Realism, 5, 17, 106f, 118, 173
Reality, 16f, 44, 47, 51, 101, 123, 173
Redemption, 71, 81; self, 64, 79
Religion, 45; Buddhist, 81, 123; Hindu, 18, 24, 45, 148
Reticence, chromatic, 237–245 *passim*
Robert, Marthe, 108
Royce, Josiah, 160
Rulfo, Juan, 242
Russell, Bertrand, 13f, 51, 165

Sartre, Jean-Paul, 208, 225
Satan, 182ff, 238
Schopenhauer, Arthur, 19, 26, 80, 84, 116f, 123, 133f, 180
Scotus, Duns, 16
Seneca, 19
Sentir, 20f, 33, 159
Shakespeare, William, 6, 34, 99, 112, 115–125 *passim*, 141, 151
Shaw, George B., 49, 89, 99, 139–152 *passim*, 182, 189–201 *passim*
Socrates, 79
Sophocles, 127
Space, 25, 116, 133f, 165, 169, 178, 183, 211
Species, 4f
Spencer, Herbert, 133f
Spengler, Oswald, 121
Spinoza, Baruch, 88, 178
Stoll, Elmer, 118
Suicide, 9
Superman, 9, 145f, 162
Swedenborg, Emanuel, 19, 185
Swift, Jonathan, 103, 127, 179
Swiss Festspiele, 120
Symbolism: noon, 75–81 *passim*, 165f; chromatic, 199–201 *passim*, 207–214 *passim*, 217–226 *passim*

Tacitus, 47, 52
Taylor, Jeremiah, 19
Terry, Arthur, 129

Tilguer, Adrian, 88
Time, 13, 17, 19, 21, 25f, 41f, 43–49 *passim*, 54, 59, 63, 69, 71, 226
Translations, 191
Traversi, Derek, 118
Trinity, 22, 69f
Truth, 18, 111

Valéry, Paul, 99, 115f, 141, 165–175 *passim*
Valmiki, 112
Verisimilitude, 36, 110f
Vico, Giovanni Batista, 121
Vindication, 14, 106
Virgil, 115
Voltaire, 103

Wells, Herbert G., 32, 61, 193, 234
Wheelock, Carter, 9, 75
White, E. B., 208
Whitman, C. H., 144
Whitman, Walt, 15, 31, 53, 99, 115, 127, 149, 155–164 *passim*, 165f, 174
Wicks, Ulrich, 109
Wilding, Michael, 183

Zambrano, María, 7f
Zeno, 13, 132, 212
Zoroastrianism, 81
Zwingly, Huldreich, 19

Cheselka, Paul

THE POETRY AND POETICS OF JORGE LUIS BORGES

American University Studies: Series 2 (Romance Languages and Literature). Vol. 44

ISBN 0-8204-0318-0   197 pp.   hardback US $ 34.00/sFr. 51.00

Recommended prices – alterations reserved

This study traces Borges' career as a poet from his earliest poetic endeavors before the 1923 publication of *Fervor de Buenos Aires* through the middle of the 1960's. Paul Cheselka considers Borges' better-known poetry collections, such as *Fervor de Buenos Aires, Luna de enfrente*, and *Cuaderno San Martin*; and he shows the often-neglected 1930-1960 period to be an important phase in the evolution of Borges' poetry. The poems are studied chronologically with particular emphasis on the relation of their themes to the poet's life and ideas. Cheselka's contribution is that of providing a clearer delineation of borgesian poetics; the poems themselves are shown to be the evidence and very substance of the poet's definitions.

Contents: Borges' life and ideas as they relate to his career as a poet – Discussion of borgesian poetic theory – Analyses of the poems.

PETER LANG PUBLISHING, INC.
62 West 45th Street
USA – New York, NY 10036

Chiles, Frances

OCTAVIO PAZ
The Mythic Dimension

American University Studies: Series 2 (Romance Languages and Literature). Vol. 6
ISBN 0-8204-0079-3 224 pp. hardback approx. US $ 33.50/sFr. 56.00

Recommended prices – alterations reserved

Octavio Paz: The Mythic Dimension is a study of myth and mythmaking in the eminent Mexican writer's poetry based on an archetypal analysis of the central theme of the dialectic of solitude and communion. The author also attempts to illustrate Paz's mission to redeem the positive values of biblical, classical, pre-Columbian, and oriental mythologies by re-creating and enriching them in new forms and meanings more appropriate to a contemporary world view. Poems are selected from both early and recent collections to illustrate the continuity of Paz's works; quoted passages are in the original Spanish with English translations. In addition to mythological sources, significant contributions of certain literary sources to Paz's thought and poetry are also discussed to demonstrate his place in the modern literary tradition.

Contents: *The Wasteland* and *The Garden* deal with the poet's vision of contemporary reality as the demonic world. *Love and the Beloved* and *The Poetic Revelation* explore eroticism and poetry as communion experiences. *The End of the Cir-* cuitous *Journey* is a synthesis and epilogue.
Dr. Chiles has done a superlative job of exposing the indebtedness to myth and the mythopoetic contri- bution *of a man whom consensus now considers the world's greatest poetic talent.*
Eugen E. Reed, The University of Idaho)

PETER LANG PUBLISHING, INC.
62 West 45th Street
USA – New York, NY 10036